Exam Ref MS-100
Microsoft 365 Identity
and Services

Orin Thomas

Exam Ref MS-100 Microsoft 365 Identity and Services

Published with the authorization of Microsoft Corporation by:
Pearson Education, Inc.

ISBN-13: 978-0-13-746905-5
ISBN-10: 0-13-746905-5

Library of Congress Control Number: 2021948676

1 2021

TRADEMARKS

Microsoft and the trademarks listed at http://www.microsoft.com on the "Trademarks" webpage are trademarks of the Microsoft group of companies. All other marks are property of their respective owners.

WARNING AND DISCLAIMER

Every effort has been made to make this book as complete and as accurate as possible, but no warranty or fitness is implied. The information provided is on an "as is" basis. The author, the publisher, and Microsoft Corporation shall have neither liability nor responsibility to any person or entity with respect to any loss or damages arising from the information contained in this book or from the use of the programs accompanying it.

SPECIAL SALES

For information about buying this title in bulk quantities, or for special sales opportunities (which may include electronic versions; custom cover designs; and content particular to your business, training goals, marketing focus, or branding interests), please contact our corporate sales department at corpsales@pearsoned.com or (800) 382-3419.

For government sales inquiries, please contact governmentsales@pearsoned.com.

For questions about sales outside the U.S., please contact intlcs@pearson.com.

CREDITS

EDITOR-IN-CHIEF
Brett Bartow

EXECUTIVE EDITOR
Loretta Yates

SPONSORING EDITOR
Charvi Arora

DEVELOPMENT EDITOR
Kate Shoup

MANAGING EDITOR
Sandra Schroeder

SENIOR PROJECT EDITOR
Tracey Croom

COPY EDITOR
Liz Welch

INDEXER
Timothy Wright

PROOFREADER
Abigail Manheim

TECHNICAL EDITOR
Boyd Nolan

EDITORIAL ASSISTANT
Cindy Teeters

COVER DESIGNER
Twist Creative, Seattle

COMPOSITOR
codeMantra

Pearson's Commitment to Diversity, Equity, and Inclusion

Pearson is dedicated to creating bias-free content that reflects the diversity of all learners. We embrace the many dimensions of diversity, including but not limited to race, ethnicity, gender, socioeconomic status, ability, age, sexual orientation, and religious or political beliefs.

Education is a powerful force for equity and change in our world. It has the potential to deliver opportunities that improve lives and enable economic mobility. As we work with authors to create content for every product and service, we acknowledge our responsibility to demonstrate inclusivity and incorporate diverse scholarship so that everyone can achieve their potential through learning. As the world's leading learning company, we have a duty to help drive change and live up to our purpose to help more people create a better life for themselves and to create a better world.

Our ambition is to purposefully contribute to a world where:

- Everyone has an equitable and lifelong opportunity to succeed through learning.
- Our educational products and services are inclusive and represent the rich diversity of learners.
- Our educational content accurately reflects the histories and experiences of the learners we serve.
- Our educational content prompts deeper discussions with learners and motivates them to expand their own learning (and worldview).

While we work hard to present unbiased content, we want to hear from you about any concerns or needs with this Pearson product so that we can investigate and address them.

- Please contact us with concerns about any potential bias at https://www.pearson.com/report-bias.html.

Contents at a glance

Contents

Chapter 2   Manage user identity and roles   93

Chapter 3   Manage access and authentication   **159**

About the Author

ORIN THOMAS is a Principal Cloud Advocate at Microsoft. He has written more than three dozen books for Microsoft Press on such topics as Windows Server, Windows Client, Azure, Office 365, System Center, Exchange Server, security, and SQL Server. He has authored Azure Architecture courses at Pluralsight and has authored multiple Microsoft Official Curriculum and EdX courses on a variety of IT Pro topics. You can follow him on Twitter at http://twitter.com/orinthomas.

Introduction

The MS-100 exam deals with advanced topics that require candidates to have an excellent working knowledge of Microsoft 365 identity and services functionality. Some of the exam relates to topics that even experienced Microsoft 365 administrators may rarely encounter unless they are consultants who deploy new Microsoft 365 tenancies on a regular basis. To successfully pass this exam, candidates not only need to understand how to manage Microsoft 365 identity and services, they also need to understand how to integrate Microsoft 365 with an on-premises Active Directory environment. And they must keep up to date with new developments with Microsoft 365, including new features and changes to the interface.

Candidates for this exam are information technology (IT) professionals who want to validate their advanced Microsoft 365 identity and services management skills, configuration skills, and knowledge. To pass this exam, candidates require a strong understanding of how to design and implement Microsoft 365 services, manage user identity and roles, manage access and authentication, and understand the steps involved in planning Office 365 workloads and applications. To pass, candidates require a thorough theoretical understanding as well as meaningful practical experience implementing the technologies involved.

This edition of this book covers Microsoft 365 and the MS-100 exam objectives in mid-2021. As the Microsoft 365 suite evolves, so do the Microsoft 365 exam objectives, so you should check carefully if any changes have occurred since this edition of the book was authored and study accordingly.

This book covers every major topic area found on the exam, but it does not cover every exam question. Only the Microsoft exam team has access to the exam questions, and Microsoft regularly adds new questions to the exam, making it impossible to cover specific questions. You should consider this book a supplement to your relevant real-world experience and other study materials. If you encounter a topic in this book that you do not feel completely comfortable with, use the "Need more review?" links found in the text to locate more information and take the time to research and study the topic. Great information is available on MSDN and TechNet and in blogs and forums.

Organization of this book

This book is organized by the "Skills measured" list published for the exam. The "Skills measured" list is available for this exam on the Microsoft Learn website at *https://aka.ms/ms-100*. Each chapter in this book corresponds to a major topic area in the list, and the technical tasks in each topic area determine a chapter's organization. If an exam covers six major topic areas, for example, the book will contain six chapters.

Microsoft certifications

Microsoft certifications distinguish you by proving your command of a broad set of skills and experience with current Microsoft products and technologies. The exams and corresponding certifications are developed to validate your mastery of critical competencies as you design and develop, or implement and support, solutions with Microsoft products and technologies both on-premises and in the cloud. Certification brings a variety of benefits to the individual and to employers and organizations.

> ***MORE INFO*** **ALL MICROSOFT CERTIFICATIONS**
>
> For information about Microsoft certifications, including a full list of available certifications, go to *http://www.microsoft.com/learn*.

Check back often to see what is new!

Quick access to online references

Throughout this book are addresses to webpages that the author has recommended you visit for more information. Some of these addresses (also known as URLs) can be painstaking to type into a web browser, so we've compiled all of them into a single list that readers of the print edition can refer to while they read.

Download the list at *MicrosoftPressStore.com/ExamRefMS1002e/downloads*.

The URLs are organized by chapter and heading. Every time you come across a URL in the book, find the hyperlink in the list to go directly to the webpage.

Errata, updates, & book support

We've made every effort to ensure the accuracy of this book and its companion content. You can access updates to this book—in the form of a list of submitted errata and their related corrections—at:

MicrosoftPressStore.com/ExamRefMS1002e/errata

If you discover an error that is not already listed, please submit it to us at the same page.

For additional book support and information, please visit *MicrosoftPressStore.com/Support*.

Please note that product support for Microsoft software and hardware is not offered through the previous addresses. For help with Microsoft software or hardware, go to *http://support.microsoft.com*.

Stay in touch

Let's keep the conversation going! We're on Twitter: *http://twitter.com/MicrosoftPress*.

CHAPTER 1

Design and implement Microsoft 365 services

Although it is possible to simply start deploying Microsoft 365 after your organization has made the decision to adopt the technology, you will get more out of the Microsoft 365 deployment if you do some planning and design work before configuring any Microsoft 365 services. In this chapter you will learn about planning a Microsoft 365 architecture, deploying a Microsoft 365 tenant, and configuring that tenancy and subscription, and you will learn the steps you will need to take to plan the migration of users and data from a traditional on-premises environment to a Microsoft 365 environment.

Skills in this chapter:

- Skill 1.1: Plan architecture
- Skill 1.2: Deploy a Microsoft 365 tenant
- Skill 1.3: Manage Microsoft 365 subscription and tenant health
- Skill 1.4: Plan the migration of users and data

Skill 1.1: Plan architecture

This section deals with planning your Microsoft 365 architecture. To master this skill, you will need to understand how to plan the integration of your existing on-premises environment with Microsoft 365, identify your deployment workloads team, determine which identity and authentication solution you want to use, and plan the modernization of your enterprise application.

This section covers the following topics:

- Plan integration of Microsoft 365 and on-premises environments
- Identify deployment workloads team
- Plan an identity and authentication solution
- Plan enterprise application modernization

Plan integration of Microsoft 365 and on-premises environments

When planning a migration to Microsoft 365, or starting from scratch, greenfield, or a brand-new deployment, you will have to make sure certain on-premises infrastructure prerequisites have been met. These on-premises infrastructure requirements relate to networking configuration, identity dependencies, client operating systems, and the deployment of Microsoft 365 Apps for enterprise. You must also make choices pertaining to strategy for mobile device management and information protection.

Networking

Traditional networks provide users with access to data and applications hosted on data centers owned and operated by the organization and protected by strong perimeter defenses such as firewalls. In this traditional model, users access resources primarily from protected internal networks, over WAN links from branch locations, or remotely via VPN connections.

The Microsoft 365 and Office 365 models shift some (if not all) applications and data from locations on protected internal networks to locations hosted beyond the network perimeter in the public cloud. When moving from an environment in which all resources are hosted on-premises to one where a substantial amount of infrastructure is hosted in the cloud, you must ensure that the on-premises networking environment is configured such that Microsoft 365 can function effectively and efficiently. Unless steps are taken to optimize the flow of traffic between users and Microsoft 365 or Office 365 services, this traffic will be subject to increased latency caused by packet inspection, network hairpins, and possible inadvertent connections to geographically distant Microsoft 365 and Office 365 service endpoints.

Understanding the networking requirements for Microsoft 365 also enables you to assess whether Microsoft 365 is appropriate for a particular organization. For example, it would be challenging to deploy Microsoft 365 at a scientific base in Antarctica where there is limited low-bandwidth connectivity to the internet.

INTERNET CONNECTIVITY FOR CLIENTS

To use Microsoft 365 software and services, clients must establish unauthenticated connections over port 80 and port 443 to the Microsoft 365 and Office 365 internet servers. On some networks, especially those configured for small businesses, you may run into the following network connectivity problems:

- **Clients configured with APIPA addresses**   If clients are configured with IP addresses in the Automatic Private IP Addressing (APIPA) range (169.254.0.0 /16), they most likely cannot connect to the internet and therefore cannot interact with Microsoft 365 and Office 365 resources. Clients configured with an APIPA address should be configured with IP addresses in the private range with an appropriate default gateway set to connect either directly or indirectly to the internet.

- **No default gateway** Clients must be configured with the default gateway address of a device that can route traffic to the internet. The default gateway device does not need to be directly connected to the internet, but it does need to be able to route traffic to a device that is. Clients without a default gateway configured will not be able to connect to Microsoft 365 or Office 365 resources.

- **Firewall configuration** Clients require access to certain endpoints used by Microsoft 365 and Office 365. Details about these endpoints are covered later in this chapter.

- **Proxy server authentication** Microsoft 365 and Office 365 will not function if an intervening proxy server requires authentication for connections. You will have to configure an authentication bypass for Microsoft 365 and Office 365 endpoints or disable proxy server authentication to Microsoft 365 and Office 365 endpoints on the internet.

MANAGE OFFICE 365 ENDPOINTS

A Microsoft 365 or Office 365 endpoint is a URL or IP address that hosts a specific Microsoft 365 or Office 365 service. Examples include the addresses used when connecting an Outlook client to Exchange Online or a mobile device to an enrollment point. Organizations that have one or more office locations must ensure that their network is configured to allow access to these endpoints.

Microsoft recommends that organizations optimize traffic for Microsoft 365 and Office 365 endpoints by routing all traffic directly through the perimeter firewall and exempting that traffic from packet-level inspection and processing. Doing so will reduce latency when connecting to Microsoft 365 and Office 365 resource endpoints. It will also reduce the impact on those perimeter devices, which will ignore traffic to known trusted locations.

Microsoft places each Microsoft 365 and Office 365 endpoint in one of three categories. These categories help you determine how to deal with traffic to Microsoft 365 and Office 365 endpoints in the most appropriate manner. The category endpoints are as follows:

- **Optimize** Endpoints with this classification are required for connectivity for every Microsoft 365 and Office 365 service. Endpoints in this category account for approximately 75% of bandwidth, volume of data, and individual connections. These endpoints cause the most problems when disruptions to network performance, latency, or availability occur.

- **Allow** Endpoints with this classification are also required for connectivity for every Microsoft 365 and Office 365 service, but they are less problematic than endpoints in the optimize category when disruptions to network performance, latency, or availability occur.

- **Default** Endpoints with this classification don't require any specific optimization and can be treated the same as other traffic bound for locations on the internet.

Microsoft provides recommendations for how to configure traffic flow to endpoints. These recommendations are listed in Table 1-1.

TABLE 1-1 Endpoint optimization methods

Endpoint Type	Recommendation
Optimize Allow	Bypass or whitelist endpoints on network devices and services that perform Transport Layer Security (TLS) decryption, traffic interception, content filtering, and deep packet inspection.
Optimize	Bypass on-premises and cloud-based proxy devices or services used for general internet browsing.
Optimize Allow	Treat these endpoints as fully trusted by network infrastructure and perimeter systems.
Optimize Allow	Reduce or eliminate WAN backhauling. Facilitate direct distributed internet egress for endpoints from branch office locations.
Optimize	Configure split tunneling for VPN users to allow direct connectivity to these endpoints.
Optimize Allow	Configure prioritization for endpoints when configuring software-defined wide area networking (SD-WAN) to minimize latency and routing.
Optimize Allow	Ensure Domain Name System (DNS) name resolution matches routing egress path for endpoints.

NOTE In the past, Microsoft defined different endpoint categories from the ones listed here: *required* and *optional*. Some documentation still refers to these earlier endpoint categories.

MORE INFO **ENDPOINT CATEGORIES**

You can learn more about Microsoft 365 and Office 365 endpoint categories at *https://docs. microsoft.com/microsoft-365/enterprise/urls-and-ip-address-ranges?view=o365-worldwide*.

OUTBOUND FIREWALL PORTS

Clients such as computers running Windows 10 must be able to connect to Microsoft 365 and Office 365 endpoints on the internet using specific protocols and ports. If certain ports and protocols are blocked by a perimeter network firewall, clients will be unable to use specific Microsoft 365 and Office 365 services. Table 1-2 lists the protocols and ports that must be open for clients on an internal network to connect to hosts on the internet.

TABLE 1-2 Microsoft 365 outbound port requirements

Protocol	Port	Used by
TCP	443	Microsoft 365 Admin Portal Outlook Outlook Web App SharePoint Online Skype for Business client Active Directory Federation Services (AD FS) AD FS Proxy
TCP	25	Mail routing
TCP	587	SMTP relay
TCP	143/993	IMAP Simple Migration Tool
TCP	80/443	Microsoft Azure Active Directory Connect Tool Exchange Management Console Exchange Management Shell
TCP	995	POP3 secure
PSOM/TLS	443	Skype for Business Online outbound data sharing
STUN/TCP	443	Skype for Business Online outbound audio, video, and application-sharing sessions
STUN/UDP	3478	Skype for Business Online outbound audio and video sessions
UDP	3478–3481	Teams
TCP	5223	Skype for Business mobile client push notifications
UDP	20000–45000	Skype for Business Online outbound phone
RTC/UDP	50000–59000	Skype for Business Online outbound audio and video sessions

The number of IP addresses and URLs that you must configure for exclusion is substantial, and a complete list is beyond the scope of this book. The URLs and IP address ranges associated with Microsoft and Office 365 are always changing. You can subscribe to a REST-based web service that provides a list of endpoints, including the current version of the list and changes made to the list for use in configuring network perimeter devices, including firewalls and proxy servers.

> **MORE INFO** **MANAGING MICROSOFT 365 ENDPOINTS**
>
> You can learn more about Microsoft 365 URLS and IP addresses at *https://docs.microsoft.com/ microsoft-365/enterprise/urls-and-ip-address-ranges*.

EGRESS NETWORK CONNECTIONS LOCALLY

One way to reduce connection latency is to configure branch office networks for local DNS and internet egress rather than forcing all DNS and internet egress traffic to be routed over a WAN link to a head office before being routed to the internet. Routing internet-bound branch-office traffic across a WAN before allowing it to egress is called *WAN backhauling*. It is especially important to avoid doing this with Microsoft 365 and Office 365 traffic in the optimize category.

Microsoft 365 and Office 365 services run on the Microsoft global network. This network is configured with servers around the world. So, there is most likely a front-end server near each branch office location. Routing traffic across a WAN rather than letting it egress directly from the branch office will introduce unnecessary latency.

DNS traffic to Microsoft 365 and Office 365 endpoints should also egress at the branch office. This will ensure that DNS servers respond with the closest local frond-end server. If DNS queries are relayed across WAN links and only egress through a single head-office location, clients will be directed to front-end servers closest to the head office location rather than the branch office where the DNS query originated.

AVOID NETWORK HAIRPINS

Network hairpins occur when VPN or WAN traffic destined for a specific endpoint must first pass through an intermediate location, such as a security appliance, cloud-based web gateway, or cloud access broker, which may introduce a redirection to a geographically distant location. For example, suppose a company called Tailwind Traders has an Australian branch office but all traffic to Microsoft 365 and Office 365 endpoints must go through a cloud-based security device located in a data center in Canada. This configuration will most likely introduce unnecessary latencies. Even if branch office traffic is egressed locally, there will be a deleterious impact on performance if it is routed through a geographically distant intermediate location.

Ways to minimize the chances of network hairpins include the following:

- Ensuring that the ISP that provides internet egress for the branch office has a direct peering relationship with the Microsoft global network near that location
- Configuring egress routing to send trusted Microsoft 365 and Office 365 traffic directly to Microsoft 365 and Office 365 endpoints rather than having them processed by intermediate services or devices

DEPLOY SD-WAN DEVICES

Software-defined wide area network (SD-WAN) devices are networking devices that can be configured automatically so that traffic is most efficiently routed to Microsoft 365 and Office 365 endpoints in the optimize and allow categories. When configured, other network traffic—including traffic to on-premises workloads, general internet traffic, and traffic to Microsoft 365 and Office 365 default endpoints—can be forwarded to appropriate locations, including network security devices. Microsoft has a partner program for SD-WAN providers to enable the automatic configuration of devices.

RECOMMENDED BANDWIDTH

Many factors influence the amount of bandwidth an organization will require to successfully use Microsoft 365. These factors include the following:

- The specific Microsoft 365 services to which the organization has subscribed
- The number of client devices connecting to Microsoft 365 from a site at any point in time
- The type of interaction the client is having with Microsoft 365
- The performance of the internet browser software on each client computer
- The capacity of the network connection available to each client computer
- Your organization's network topology

EXPRESSROUTE

ExpressRoute for Office 365 provides high-speed private connectivity between an organization's on-premises network and Microsoft's data centers. Clients using an organization's on-premises network on which ExpressRoute for Office365 is present will automatically have their Microsoft 365 traffic routed across the ExpressRoute circuit rather than having that traffic pass across the internet. If an organization already has an Azure ExpressRoute circuit, it can enable access to Office 365 by configuring route filters to ensure that Microsoft 365 services are available.

Windows 10 Enterprise edition

A Microsoft 365 Enterprise license includes a license for the Windows 10 Enterprise edition operating system. Part of the process of adopting Microsoft 365 will involve ensuring that all Windows client computers are running this edition of the Windows 10 operating system.

Organizations that have an existing Windows client deployment should perform an in-place upgrade using Configuration Manager (formerly System Center Configuration Manager) or Microsoft Deployment Toolkit. System Center Configuration Manager (current branch) provides organizations with the most automated method of upgrading and migrating existing computers from previous versions of the Windows client operating system to Windows 10.

Organizations that are deploying new computers that have Windows 10 Enterprise edition version 1703 or later can use Windows Autopilot to trigger the deployment and configuration process by signing in using their school or work credentials. Organizations running the Pro edition can also use Windows Autopilot to automatically update those computers to the Enterprise edition.

> **MORE INFO**   **MICROSOFT 365 AND WINDOWS 10 ENTERPRISE**
>
> You can learn more about the relationship between Microsoft 365 and Windows 10 Enterprise edition at *https://docs.microsoft.com/windows/deployment/deploy-m365*.

Information protection

When planning your organization's Microsoft 365 information protection strategy, the first and perhaps most important step is to liaise with the organization's legal and compliance teams to determine which compliance standards the organization is subject to—for example, the General Data Protection Regulation (GDPR) or the Health Insurance Portability and Accountability Act (HIPAA). After you have identified the specific compliance standards or regulations to which your organization must adhere, you must answer the following questions:

- What are the appropriate security and information protection levels for our organization?
- What is an appropriate document classification schema for our organization?
- What steps must be taken to ensure the appropriate security level is configured within Microsoft 365 and Office 365?
- Is it necessary to configure privileged access management for Microsoft 365 and Office 365?

SECURITY AND INFORMATION PROTECTION LEVELS

Microsoft 365 enables organizations to develop their own security and protection levels. Although it is possible to create a bewildering number of information protection security levels, doing so increases complexity for end users attempting to understand which level is appropriate and for compliance staff who must determine whether the appropriate level has been selected.

Microsoft recommends that organizations plan to use at least three separate information protection security levels. As information protection security levels increase, data becomes more protected, but it also becomes more cumbersome for users to interact with that data. Only accessing the most sensitive data should require a user to go through a multifactor authentication (MFA) process each time they open a document. Microsoft suggests the following levels:

- **Baseline**   A minimum standard for the protection of data, identities, and the devices used to interact with organization data.

- **Sensitive**   An intermediate standard appropriate for data that is considered sensitive but for which the most stringent security controls are not needed.

- **Highly regulated**   Requires the most stringent security controls. This standard is likely appropriate only for a small amount of an organization's data. For example, you might require that data only be accessed from a managed device for a limited amount of time after a user has performed MFA.

CLASSIFICATION SCHEMAS

Classification schemas enable you to assign an information protection level to specific information such as a document or email message. Microsoft 365 includes the following classification schemas:

- **Sensitive information types for Office 365**   Office 365 automatically recognizes specific information types, such as credit card or passport numbers. You can leverage Office 365 sensitive information types to automatically apply data loss–prevention rules and policies so that this data has the appropriate level of protection.

- **Office 365 retention labels**   Office 365 retention labels enable you to determine how long specific data should be stored in Exchange, SharePoint Online, and OneDrive. Office 365 retention labels can use the security and information protection levels outlined earlier: baseline, sensitive, highly regulated. They can also use custom information protection levels set by the organization.

- **Azure Information Protection (AIP) labels and protection**   AIP provides another set of options for the classification and protection of documents and email messages. An advantage of AIP is that it can be used with documents stored beyond Office 365 locations such as Exchange Online, SharePoint Online, and OneDrive. AIP labels and protection can be applied automatically based on rules and conditions defined by an administrator, manually by users, or in conjunction with automatic recommendations displayed to users.

IMPROVING SECURITY LEVELS

When planning your Microsoft 365 information protection strategy, you will need to go beyond information classification, retention policies, and information protection. You will also need to enable additional Microsoft 365 security technologies. These technologies include the following:

- **Threat-management policies**   You can configure threat-management policies in the Security & Compliance Center. Policies include Advanced Threat Protection (ATP) antiphishing, anti-malware, ATP Safe Attachments, ATP Safe Links, anti-spam (mail filtering), and email authentication.

- **Exchange Online tenant-wide settings**   You can improve security by implementing the appropriate mail flow (also known as transport rules) and enabling modern authentication, which enables you to use MFA.

- **SharePoint tenant-wide settings**   You can strengthen security by configuring external sharing settings. Options include limiting sharing to authenticated external users, allowing anonymous access links, configuring anonymous access link expirations, and default link types.

- **Azure Active Directory settings**   You can enhance security by configuring named locations, which is part of conditional access, and blocking apps that don't support modern authentication.

- **Cloud App Security**   Cloud App Security enables organizations to improve their security posture by evaluating risk, issuing alerts for suspicious activity, and automatically performing remediation actions. Cloud App Security requires a Microsoft 365, Office 365, or Enterprise Mobility + Security (EMS) E5 plan.

PRIVILEGED ACCESS MANAGEMENT

The effectiveness of an information protection strategy depends on how secure the administrative accounts used to manage that strategy are. If accounts that can be used to configure and manage an information protection strategy are not properly secured, then the information protection strategy itself can be easily compromised.

Privileged access management enables you to configure policies that apply just-in-time administrative principles to sensitive administrative roles. For example, if someone needs temporary access to configure an information protection policy, that person would need to go through an approval process to obtain the necessary set of rights instead of having an Azure Active Directory (Azure AD) account with those rights permanently assigned.

> ***MORE INFO***   **INFORMATION PROTECTION INFRASTRUCTURE**
>
> You can learn more about the Microsoft 365 information protection infrastructure at *https:// docs.microsoft.com/microsoft-365/compliance/information-protection*.

Identify deployment workloads team

Assembling a deployment workloads team requires you to assess which members of your staff should be responsible for deployment tasks and to ensure that they have the required training and are given the appropriate permissions to perform these tasks. You should identify which staff members will be responsible for specific areas of your organization's Microsoft 365 deployment before you begin rollout.

You should identify personnel to assume leadership and responsibility for the following areas for deployment:

- **Identity infrastructure**   Responsible for determining the characteristics of Microsoft 365 identity, including hybrid requirements and authentication configuration.

- **Networking**   Responsible for ensuring that the on-premises network is configured to support Microsoft 365 services.
- **Client software and Windows 10**   Responsible for the deployment and management of client software including Microsoft 365 Apps. Also responsible for configuring the client operating system.
- **Exchange**   Responsible for the deployment and configuration of Exchange Online.
- **SharePoint**   Responsible for the deployment and configuration of SharePoint Online.
- **Skype for Business or Microsoft Teams**   Responsible for the deployment and configuration of Skype for Business and/or Microsoft Teams.
- **Security and compliance**   Responsible for configuring Microsoft 365 so that all compliance requirements are met before deployment.

You should also ensure that your deployment workloads team has the necessary training and knowledge. You might also opt to have the team perform a pilot deployment using a trial subscription before attempting the production deployment. Doing so will enable them to identify and remediate potential blocking issues before they affect users in an actual rollout.

MORE INFO   **TRANSITION TO MICROSOFT 365**

You can learn more about transitioning your organization to Microsoft 365 at *https://docs. microsoft.com/microsoft-365/enterprise/microsoft-365-overview*.

Plan an identity and authentication solution

Identity providers are the primary source of authority, and they host user and group accounts. When you select a primary source of identity, that location is where authoritative changes to an account or group are made. For example, if you perform a password change, the password change isn't understood to apply unless it applies at the primary source of identity.

NOTE   In a hybrid scenario, it is possible to change the password of an account that is replicated from an on-premises directory to a cloud-based Azure Active Directory on the cloud. However, that change might be overwritten the next time the replicated account is synchronized with the primary identity source.

Microsoft 365 and Office 365 use Azure AD as the user and group identity and authentication service. Azure AD stores user, group, and device account objects and is also responsible for performing Microsoft 365 and Office 365 authentication.

When deploying Microsoft 365 and Office 365, you can choose whether identity management is cloud only or if a relationship exists between an on-premises identity provider such as Active Directory Domain Services (AD DS) and Azure AD.

Cloud authentication

When you opt for cloud authentication, authentication occurs against Azure AD. How you implement cloud authentication depends on whether your organization has an existing on-premises AD DS deployment and what your plans are for that deployment in the future.

CLOUD-ONLY

The cloud-only authentication model addresses the management of user and group accounts that exist only from within Microsoft 365. You can create and manage users in the Microsoft 365 Admin Center (shown in Figure 1-1), in the Azure AD portal or blade, or by using the appropriate PowerShell cmdlets.

FIGURE 1-1 Create and manage Microsoft 365 users

A cloud-only identity and authentication solution is appropriate if:

- Your organization has not deployed an on-premises AD DS environment.
- Your organization has a very complex on-premises directory solution and wants to avoid attempting to integrate it.
- Your organization has an on-premises AD DS environment but wants to run a pilot or trial of Microsoft 365 and will worry about integrating with the existing environment only if the pilot or trial proves successful.

PASSWORD HASH SYNC WITH SINGLE SIGN-ON

When planning an identity and authentication solution using password hash synchronization, your organization will synchronize on-premises AD DS user accounts with the Azure AD service used by Microsoft 365 and Office 365. When you adopt this strategy, cryptographic hashes of on-premises user passwords are synchronized to Azure AD.

The cryptographic hashing operation is one way. This means it is not possible to run a reverse cryptographic operation on the hash to derive the password from which it was generated, although there are techniques that iterate possible passwords to see if they match a cryptographic hash should one manage to be captured.

The use of cryptographic hashes means that user passwords aren't stored in Azure AD. When authentication occurs, the password entered by the user has the same cryptographic operation performed on it, and the hash of that password is then compared to the one stored in Azure AD. If the hashes match, the user is authenticated. If the hashes do not match, the user is not authenticated. If a password is changed in the on-premises account database, a new password hash is calculated, and the new cryptographic hash is synchronized with and stored in Azure AD.

Choose this method if you want to have on-premises AD DS remain the authoritative source for user accounts and if the regulations that your organization is subject to allow for the storage of cryptographic password hashes in the cloud. This solution requires Azure AD Connect, which you will learn about in Chapter 2, "Manage user identity and roles."

PASS-THROUGH AUTHENTICATION WITH SINGLE SIGN-ON

When you implement pass-through authentication with single sign-on (SSO), you install a software agent on one or more on-premises AD DS domain controllers. When a user authenticates against Azure AD, the request is passed through to the on-premises AD instance through the agent to determine whether the authentication request is valid.

This solution is appropriate when your organization is constrained from allowing any form of password synchronization with the cloud. This may include being restricted from allowing cryptographic password hashes to be stored in the cloud. In this scenario, pass-through authentication with SSO would be an appropriate solution. It is also appropriate where on-premises account states, password policies, and logon hours must be enforced. You will learn more about configuring pass-through authentication with SSO in Chapter 2.

Federated authentication

Federated authentication is an alternative to cloud authentication, although it is often substantially more complicated to configure and maintain. Most organizations use Azure AD Connect to synchronize identity information between on-premises AD DS and Azure AD. Organizations that want to allow additional authentication options, such as smart card–based authentication, or third-party multifactor authentication such as an RSA token device, should implement federated authentication.

FEDERATED IDENTITY WITH ACTIVE DIRECTORY FEDERATION SERVICES

When you use federated identity with Active Directory Federation Services (AD FS), you deploy servers hosting the AD FS role on your organization's on-premises network and perimeter network. You then need to configure federation between your on-premises AD FS instance and Azure AD. When you implement this identity and authentication technology, users employ the same authentication options to access Microsoft 365 and Office 365 resources as they do on-premises resources. This authentication method is generally chosen by organizations that have authentication requirements that are not natively supported by Azure AD.

THIRD-PARTY AUTHENTICATION AND IDENTITY PROVIDERS

Organizations that use a non–Active Directory on-premises identity provider can integrate that identity provider with Azure AD through federation as long as that third-party identity provider's federation solution is compatible with Azure AD. When this solution is implemented, users can access Microsoft 365 and Office 365 resources using their on-premises identity provider user name and password.

> **MORE INFO**   **UNDERSTANDING MICROSOFT 365 AND OFFICE 365 IDENTITY**
>
> You can learn more about identity at *https://docs.microsoft.com/microsoft-365/enterprise/about-microsoft-365-identity*.

EXAM TIP

Remember the difference between password hash sync with single sign-on and pass-through authentication with single sign-on.

Plan enterprise application modernization

Application modernization can enable organizations to reduce their on-premises data-center footprint. An organization that has migrated all its Exchange and SharePoint workloads to Microsoft 365 is likely to also want to shift as many of its on-premises line-of-business (LOB) applications to the cloud as well.

Enterprise application modernization is a broad label for updating enterprise LOB apps so that they run on modern platforms. A challenge for many organizations is that they have enterprise LOB apps that are dependent on older versions of software that may not be compatible with newer technologies. For example:

- Web applications that may have used Flash, which is no longer supported by current browsers
- Applications or plug-ins that were written for older versions of Microsoft Office, but are incompatible with Microsoft 365 Apps for enterprise
- Applications that use an older version of SQL Server, such as SQL Server 2005, which are only compatible with unsupported versions of Windows Server

Organizations can use a variety of methods to modernize its enterprise applications. These can include, but are not limited to, the following:

- Rewriting the application to work with supported software. An example might be updating a web application so that it uses modern web standards and runs on a supported browser.
- Migrating an existing application so that it runs in a container rather than on a server dedicated to hosting that application. Containerizing an existing application also simplifies the process of migrating that application to the cloud.

- Rewriting or updating an application or plug-in written for a previous version of Microsoft Office so that it is compatible with Microsoft 365 Apps for enterprise.
- Rewriting the application so that it can be hosted on an appropriate Azure platform-as-a-service (PaaS) offering, such as Web App, Azure Functions, Azure SQL, or a serverless offering rather than hosting it in an on-premises data center on an operating system managed by your organization.

> **MORE INFO**   **CONTAINERIZE ENTERPRISE APPLICATIONS**
>
> You can learn more about containerizing enterprise applications at *https://docs.microsoft. com/dotnet/architecture/microservices/architect-microservice-container-applications/ containerize-monolithic-applications*.

Skill 1.2: Deploy a Microsoft 365 tenant

This section deals with the steps you must take to deploy and configure a Microsoft 365 tenant. To master this skill, you will need to understand how to manage Microsoft 365 domains, be familiar with organization settings, know how to add a Microsoft partner or work with FastTrack, and learn how to configure tenant-wide workload settings.

> **This section covers the following topics:**
> - Manage domains
> - Configure organizational settings
> - Complete the organization profile
> - Add a Microsoft partner or work with Microsoft FastTrack
> - Complete the subscription setup wizard
> - Plan and create a tenant
> - Edit an organizational profile
> - Plan and create subscriptions

Manage domains

When you create a Microsoft 365 subscription, the subscription tenancy is automatically assigned a custom onmicrosoft.com domain. The tenant name is in the format *name.onmicrosoft.com*, where *name* is the name you want to assign to your organization's tenancy. This name has to be unique, and no two organizations can share the same tenant name. When you create the tenancy, a check is performed against your proposed tenancy name. If a tenant with that name already exists, you will be required to select an alternative.

Although you're unlikely to actually use the onmicrosoft.com domain name after you have fully configured your organization's tenancy, it is important to note that you cannot change the tenant name after you configure your Microsoft 365 subscription. The tenant name chosen at setup remains with the subscription over the course of the subscription's existence and cannot be removed. Resist the temptation to assign an amusing name because your organization will be stuck with it even if it isn't the primary domain name used.

You can assign to the tenant a domain name that you own so that you don't have to use the tenant name on a regular basis. For example, you might sign up to a Microsoft 365 subscription with the tenant name *contoso.onmicrosoft.com*. Any account you create will use the contoso. onmicrosoft.com email suffix for the account's Office 365 Exchange mailbox. After you set up Microsoft 365, however, you can assign a custom domain name and use it as the primary email suffix. For example, assuming you owned the domain name contoso.com, you could configure your tenancy to use the custom domain name contoso.com with the contoso.onmicrosoft.com tenancy.

Microsoft 365 supports the addition of as many as 900 domains to a single subscription. You can use separate domain names with a subscription, such as contoso.com or tailwindtraders.com. You can also associate subdomains of a domain name, such as partners.tailwindtraders.com or australia.contoso.com.

Acquire a domain name

If your organization wants to use a new domain name with its Microsoft 365 tenancy, it can procure one with a registrar. When you do this, you can choose to have the registrar host the name server records for the domain or select your own name server records.

The vast majority of organizations will have already procured a domain name and have it hosted either with a specific domain registrar, their ISP, or even on their own DNS servers. To use a domain with Microsoft 365, the DNS servers used as name servers for the domain must support the following record types:

- **CNAME records** To fully support Skype for Business online, the name server DNS servers must be able to support multiple CNAME records in a DNS zone.

- **SPF/TXT records** These records enable you to configure sender protection framework records, which can be used to combat unsolicited commercial email. TXT records are also a way to verify domain ownership.

- **SRV records** SRV records are used for Skype for Business Online IM and presence integration using the Outlook Web App. They are also used for federation with Skype for Business Online users in different organizations, including for public internet connectivity with Microsoft accounts.

- **MX records** These records are used to route mail to Exchange Online mail servers.

Purchase a domain through Microsoft 365

In some regions, you can purchase a custom domain name from within Microsoft 365. When you do this, you're limited to the following top-level domains:

- .biz
- .com
- .info
- .me
- .mobi
- .net
- .org
- .tv
- .co.uk
- .org.uk

Purchasing a domain through Microsoft 365 can be advantageous in that the vast majority of DNS-related operations will be performed automatically for you. You shouldn't choose this option if your organization will continue to use email services outside Microsoft 365, however, because you won't be able to modify the appropriate MX records.

Configure a custom domain name

To configure Microsoft 365 to use a custom domain name, you must add the custom domain name to Microsoft 365. The account used to perform this action must be a global administrator of a business or enterprise plan.

To add a custom domain to Microsoft 365, perform the following steps:

1. In the left pane of the **Microsoft 365 admin center**, under **Settings**, select **Domains**. (See Figure 1-2.)

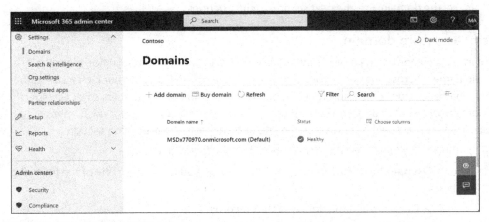

FIGURE 1-2 The Domains page

2. If your organization already has a domain, select **Add domain**.

> **NOTE** You can also buy a domain through Office 365 and GoDaddy. To do so, you select the Buy Domain button on the Domains page. When you buy a domain through GoDaddy, the entire process of assigning a custom domain to Microsoft 365 occurs automatically. If your organization's domain is already hosted elsewhere, however, you will have to confirm ownership of that domain by configuring special TXT or MX records that can be checked by the setup process.

The **New Domain** page opens.

3. In the **Domain name** box, type the name of the existing domain you want to configure and select **Use this domain**. (See Figure 1-3.)

FIGURE 1-3 Adding an existing domain in Microsoft 365

This begins the process of adding the domain. You will need to confirm ownership before you can use the domain. See the next section for instructions.

Verify a custom domain

You can use a custom domain name with Microsoft 365 only if your organization owns that domain name. Microsoft requires you to perform a series of DNS configuration changes to the domain name to prove that your organization owns and controls the domain. After you specify the domain you want to add, you verify it on the Domain Verification page, which opens automatically when you select Use This Domain. (Refer to step 3 in the preceding section.)

To confirm ownership of your organization's domain, follow these steps:

1. On the **Domain Verification** page (see Figure 1-4), you can choose one of the following options:

   - Add a TXT record to the domain's DNS records
   - If you can't add a TXT record, add an MX record to the domain's DNS records

■ Add a text file to the domain's website

In this case, choose **Add a TXT record to the domain's DNS records** and select **Continue**.

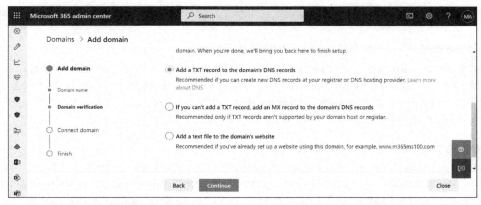

FIGURE 1-4 Verifying the domain

2. Follow the step-by-step instructions on the page that appears to add a TXT record to the domain to verify domain ownership. (See Figure 1-5.)

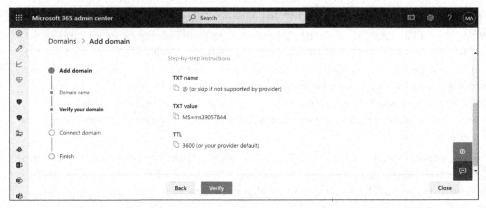

FIGURE 1-5 TXT record in details

3. Select **Verify**.

Microsoft 365 will attempt to confirm the presence of the record. Depending on how the DNS is configured, it may take as long as 15 minutes for the verification process to successfully complete.

NOTE If you are using GoDaddy as your DNS hosting provider, the Microsoft 365 setup process can add all the necessary Microsoft 365 services. Alternatively, you can perform the steps manually as outlined later in this chapter.

Configure workloads for a new domain name

By configuring a custom domain's purpose, you can choose how it will be used with a variety of Microsoft 365 services. For example, you might want to use one custom domain as an email suffix, another custom domain with SharePoint, and another for Teams. You can only configure a domain's purpose after you have verified the DNS zone.

EXCHANGE ONLINE–RELATED DNS RECORDS

When you provision Microsoft 365 for your organization, Microsoft ensures that the DNS records for your organization's tenant domain (the onmicrosoft.com domain) are configured properly so that email addresses using the tenant domain as an email domain suffix have mail routed properly.

For example, if you provision a Microsoft 365 tenant, and the tenant domain is contoso.onmicrosoft.com, then email sent to users at this email domain—such as an email sent to don.funk@contoso.onmicrosoft.com—will arrive at the correct location because Microsoft 365 will provision the appropriate DNS records automatically when the tenancy is provisioned.

When you add a custom domain to Microsoft 365, you must configure an appropriate set of DNS records to ensure that mail flows properly to Exchange Online mailboxes that use the custom domain. For example, if your custom domain is tailspintoys.com, you must configure DNS so that email will function properly for Exchange Online mailboxes configured to use the tailspintoys.com email domain. When properly configured, the user associated with the Exchange Online mailbox don.funk@tailspintoys.com will receive email sent from other hosts on the internet.

If your custom DNS zone is hosted by GoDaddy, Microsoft 365 can configure the appropriate DNS records for you automatically. If your custom DNS zone is hosted by another DNS hosting provider, you will have to manually configure DNS records. Specifically, you must configure the following DNS records:

- The Autodiscover CNAME record for Autodiscover service
- An MX record for mail routing
- A Sender Policy Framework (SPF) record to verify the identity of the mail server

These records are listed in Table 1-3. The specifics of records will be provided for you by the Microsoft DNS setup wizard. The MX record takes the form <customdnsname>.mail.protection.outlook.com and will vary depending on the custom domain name being registered.

TABLE 1-3 Microsoft 365 Exchange DNS records

Type	Priority	Host Name	Value	TTL
MX	0	@	<customdnsname>.mail.protection.outlook.com	1 hour
TXT	-	@	v=spf1 include:spf.protection.outlook.com -all	1 hour
CNAME	-	autodiscover	autodiscover.outlook.com	1 hour

MX RECORDS

You must configure an MX record in your custom domain to point to an Office 365 target mail server. The address of this target mail server will depend on the name of the custom domain and is described in the documentation as being in the form <mx token>.mail.protection.out-look.com. You can review the value for MX record by performing the following steps:

1. In the left pane of the **Microsoft 365 admin center**, under **Settings**, select **Domains**.
2. Select the custom domain you created.
3. The **Domain properties** page opens.
4. Locate the **MX record**. (See Figure 1-6.)

FIGURE 1-6 MX record in Azure DNS

To ensure that mail routes properly, you must configure the MX priority for the record to be a lower value than any other MX records configured for the custom domain. When mail is being routed, a check is performed to determine which MX record has the lowest value for the priority field. For example, an MX record with a priority of 10 will be chosen as a destination for mail routing over an MX record with a priority of 20.

SPF RECORDS

The Sender Policy Framework (SPF) record is a special TXT record that reduces the possibility of malicious third parties using the custom domain to send spam or other types of unwanted email. An SPF record is used to validate which email servers are authorized to send messages on behalf of the custom domain. The SPF record must be a TXT record, and the TXT value must include the following:

```
v=spf1 include:spf.protection.outlook.com -all
```

The record should also be set with a TTL value of 3600. Only one TXT record for an SPF should exist within a specific zone. If an SPF record is already present, append the Microsoft 365 values to the existing record rather than creating a new one.

AUTODISCOVER CNAME RECORDS

You must create a CNAME record that uses the autodiscover alias to point to the host name autodiscover.outlook.com so that Outlook clients' settings are automatically provisioned for Exchange Online. For example, if the custom domain you assigned to Microsoft 365 was tailspintoys.com, you would need to create the CNAME record autodiscover.tailspintoys.com and have it point to autodiscover.outlook.com.

EXCHANGE FEDERATION TXT RECORDS

If you are configuring federation between an on-premises Exchange deployment and Exchange Online, you must create two special TXT records that include a custom-generated domain-proof hash text.

The first record will include the custom domain name and the hash text, such as tailspintoys.com and Y96nu89138789315669824, respectively. The second record will include the name exchangedelegation with the custom domain name and custom-generated domain-proof hash text like exchangedelegation.tailspintoys.com and Y3259071352452626169.

EXCHANGE FEDERATION CNAME RECORDS

If you are configuring federation, you need an additional CNAME record to support federation with Office 365. This CNAME record will need the alias autodiscover.service, and it should also point to autodiscover.outlook.com.

> **MORE INFO   MICROSOFT 365 DNS RECORDS**
>
> You can learn more about DNS records for Microsoft 365 at *https://docs.microsoft.com/ microsoft-365/enterprise/external-domain-name-system-records*.

SKYPE FOR BUSINESS–RELATED DNS RECORDS

Skype for Business requires you to configure two types of DNS records if you have a custom domain. You must configure two SRV records and two CNAME records to get Skype for Business working properly with a custom domain.

SKYPE FOR BUSINESS ONLINE CNAME RECORDS

If you want to use Skype for Business with a custom domain, you also must create two separate CNAME records. The first CNAME record uses the alias sip and points to sipdir.online.lync.com. This CNAME record allows the client to find the Skype for Business service and assists in the process of signing in. The second CNAME record assists the Skype for Business mobile device client to find the Skype for Business service and also assists with sign-in. The alias for this record is lyncdiscover and the record target is webdir.online.lync.com. These records are listed in Table 1-4.

TABLE 1-4 Microsoft 365 Skype for Business CNAME DNS records

Type	Host Name	Value	TTL
CNAME	sip	sipdir.online.lync.com	1 hour
CNAME	lyncdiscover	webdir.online.lync.com	1 hour

SKYPE FOR BUSINESS ONLINE SRV RECORDS

Skype for Business Online requires two SRV records. The first record is used to coordinate the flow of data between Skype for Business clients. This record should have the following properties:

- **Service** _sip
- **Protocol** _TCP
- **Priority** 100
- **Weight** 1
- **Port** 443
- **Target** sipdir.online.lync.com

The second record is used by Skype for Business to share instant messaging features with clients other than Lync for Business by allowing SIP federation. This record should have the following properties:

- **Service** _sipfederationtls
- **Protocol** _TCP
- **Priority** 100
- **Weight** 1
- **Port** 5061
- **Target** sipfed.online.lync.com

These records are also listed in Table 1-5.

TABLE 1-5 Microsoft 365 Skype for Business SRV DNS records

Service	Protocol	Port	Target	Name	TTL
_sip	_tls	443	sipdir.online.lync.com	@	1 hour
_sipfederationtls	_tcp	5061	sipfed.online.lync.com	@	1 hour

Mobile Device Management for Microsoft 365 DNS records

If you are using mobile device management (MDM) for Microsoft 365, you must create two CNAME records, also known as *aliases*, so that devices can find the appropriate location to register. These two records are listed in Table 1-6.

TABLE 1-6 Microsoft 365 Mobile Device Management DNS records

Type	Host Name	Value	TTL
CNAME	enterpriseregistration	enterpriseregistration.windows.net	1 hour
CNAME	enterpriseenrollment	enterpriseenrollment.manage.microsoft.com	1 hour

Verify DNS settings

You can check DNS settings at any time. To do so, select the domain in the Microsoft 365 Admin Center, select Refresh, and note whether the domain status is listed as Healthy. (See Figure 1-7.) Microsoft 365 determines whether a domain is healthy by performing a query against the records required for the services you have chosen and validating that the results returned by the query match those required by Microsoft 365.

FIGURE 1-7 TXT record in Azure DNS

Set the default domain

Setting the default domain specifies which domain suffix will automatically be used with Microsoft 365 user accounts. You can select a default domain only if you have configured Microsoft 365 with at least one custom domain.

To set the default domain:

1. Sign into the **Microsoft 365 admin center** as a global admin.
2. In the left pane, under **Settings**, select **Domains**.
3. Select the domain that you want to set as the default domain.
4. On the domain's page, shown in Figure 1-8, select **Set as default**.

FIGURE 1-8 Listing of domains

Configure authoritative and internal relay domains

You can set the authoritative domain and internal relay domains in Exchange Online. An *authoritative domain* is the domain used with Microsoft 365 or, if Exchange is set to a hybrid configuration, where some mailboxes are located on-premises and others in the cloud. You use an internal relay domain when you have a connector to a separate set of mail servers you maintain on-premises.

To configure the authoritative domain for Exchange Online, perform the following steps:

1. Sign into the **Microsoft 365 admin center** as a global admin.
2. In the left pane, under **Admin centers**, select **Exchange**.

    The **Exchange admin center** opens.

3. Under **Mail Flow**, select **Accepted Domains**.

A list of accepted domains appears. (See Figure 1-9.)

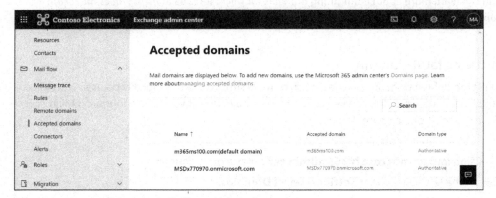

FIGURE 1-9 Accepted domains in Exchange Admin Center

4. Select the domain that you want to configure.

5. On the **Accepted domain** page, ensure that the **Authoritative** option button is selected. (See Figure 1-10.)

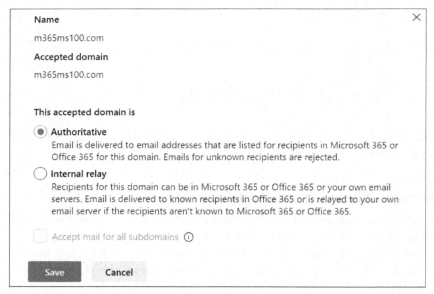

FIGURE 1-10 Configuring the Authoritative Domain

Configure user identities for the new domain name

When your Microsoft 365 organization adopts a new custom domain name, you will need to determine what steps you should take to allow users to leverage that domain name. For example, should all newly created user accounts be assigned that domain name for email and the UPN sign-in? Should existing user accounts be modified so that they use the new domain name for email and UPN sign-in? Should the new domain name simply be added as an alternative domain suffix to the existing organization email address? In this section you will learn what steps you can take to modify the primary address so that it uses a new domain name.

MANAGE EMAIL ADDRESSES

The default address, also known as the *primary address* and *reply-to address*, is the address that users employ to sign into Microsoft 365 resources, including Office 365, and to which recipients reply when they receive an email message from a user. You can view a user's primary email address in the Microsoft 365 Admin Center on the user's properties page. (See Figure 1-11.)

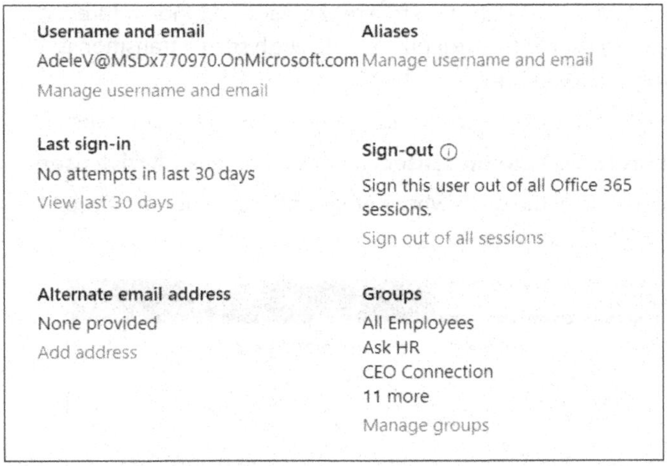

Username and email | Aliases
AdeleV@MSDx770970.OnMicrosoft.com | Manage username and email
Manage username and email

Last sign-in | Sign-out ⓘ
No attempts in last 30 days | Sign this user out of all Office 365 sessions.
View last 30 days | Sign out of all sessions

Alternate email address | Groups
None provided | All Employees
Add address | Ask HR
 | CEO Connection
 | 11 more
 | Manage groups

FIGURE 1-11 Locating a user's primary email address

You can change the primary email address if you have added another email address to a Microsoft 365 user account. (See Figure 1-12.) Be aware that changing the primary email address also changes the user name.

NOTE The email suffix for the primary address must be configured as an accepted domain for the Office 365 tenancy.

Manage username and email

If the primary email is also their username, then changing the primary email will also change their current username. An alias is another email address that people can use to email Adele Vance.

Primary email address and username

Username	Domains
AdeleV	@ m365ms100.com

Done

FIGURE 1-12 Changing a user account's primary email address

To perform a bulk email address update, you can use PowerShell. You might do this if, for example, the name of the organization changes. This step should be taken with extreme care. Supporting a small number of users through a transition to a new email and logon address is relatively simple, but supporting every user in the organization through such a transition is what might politely be termed "logistically intensive."

To update the email and logon domains of multiple users, perform the following steps:

1. In the left pane of the **Microsoft 365 admin center**, under **Users**, select **Active users**.

2. On the **Active Users** page, select all the users whose email and logon domains you want to update. (See Figure 1-13.)

FIGURE 1-13 Selecting multiple users

3. Open the **More** drop-down list and select **Change domains**.

4. In the **Change domains** panel, open the **Change domains** drop-down list, select one of the domains that has been added to Microsoft 365, and select **Save changes**. (See Figure 1-14.)

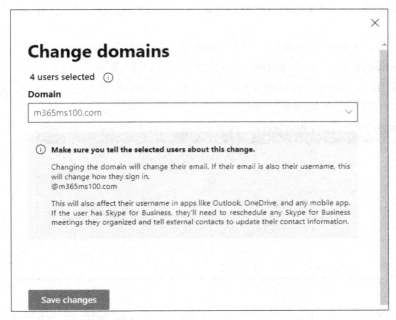

FIGURE 1-14 Select multiple users

You will be notified that email addresses and user names in apps associated with Microsoft 365 will need to be updated.

SET UP ADDITIONAL EMAIL ADDRESSES

Having additional email addresses enables mailboxes to receive messages from more than a single address. Also known as *proxy addresses* or *secondary addresses*, they can take any format and can use any domain name associated with the organization's Microsoft 365 tenancy. For example, Adele Vance's user account could have the primary user name and address as AdeleV@contoso.com, but it could also have the following addresses associated with the same Exchange mailbox:

- adele.vance@contoso.com
- adele.vance@tailwindtraders.com
- adeleV@fabrikam.com
- feedback@contoso.com
- suggestions@contoso.com

You can set up additional email addresses for an Office 365 account's Exchange Online mailbox using a variety of methods. To set up an additional email address for an Exchange Online mailbox using Exchange Admin Center, perform the following steps:

1. Sign in to the **Microsoft 365 admin center** with a user account with tenant administrator permissions.

2. In the left pane, under **Admin centers**, select **Exchange**.

3. In **Exchange admin center**, select **Recipients** and then select **Mailboxes**.

4. Select the recipient for whom you want to set up an additional email address. In Figure 1-15, the entry for Adele Vance is selected.

FIGURE 1-15 Selecting a recipient for an additional email address

5. On the **User mailbox properties** page, select **Manage email address types**, as shown in Figure 1-16.

FIGURE 1-16 The User Mailbox properties page

6. Select **Add email address type**.

7. On the **New email address** page, ensure that **SMTP** is selected and enter the new email address. You can also specify the new email address as the default reply-to address.

To set up an additional email address for an Exchange Online mailbox using the Microsoft 365 Admin Center, perform the following steps:

1. In the left pane of the **Microsoft 365 admin center**, under **Users**, select **Active users**.

2. Select the user for which you want to configure the additional email address.

   The User mailbox properties page opens.

3. Under **Aliases**, select **Manage username and email**.

4. On the **Manage username and email** page, under **Alias**, type the new email address in the **Username** and **Domains** boxes, and select **Save changes**. (See Figure 1-17.)

FIGURE 1-17 Setting up an additional email address

5. Optionally, to set the new email address as the primary email address, select the **ellipsis**, and then select **Change to primary email**.

You can also use the `Set-Mailbox` cmdlet to set up additional email addresses. For example, to add the email address berger.debra@m365ms100.com to Debra Berger's Exchange Online mailbox, issue the following command using PowerShell as a global administrator:

```
Set-Mailbox "Debra Berger" –EmailAddresses @{Add=berger.debra@m365ms100.com}
```

Implement a domain name strategy

As you learned earlier in this chapter, you can configure a Microsoft 365 subscription with as many as 900 domain names. These can be completely different domain names or subdomains of a given domain name.

Being able to associate as many as 900 domain names with a single subscription gives your organization a substantial number of options when it comes to implementing a domain name strategy. For example, you could configure each service associated with a Microsoft 365 subscription with a different domain name. In this case, if your organization owned the contoso.com domain, you might choose to have the following domain name configuration:

- **Contoso.com** Domain name associated with Exchange Online. Each user signs into Microsoft 365 using an account with a contoso.com UPN suffix.

- **Skype.contoso.com** Subdomain name associated with the Skype for Business services.

- **Mdm.contoso.com** Subdomain name associated with mobile device management functionality for Microsoft 365.

You might also choose to configure separate subdomains and provide them as alternate email domains used with secondary addresses for Exchange Online mailboxes. For example, you could use adele.vance@contoso.com as the primary email address for a mailbox but configure adele.vance@tailwindtraders.com as a proxy address. A single Adele Vance mailbox could then receive email addressed to multiple addresses.

EXAM TIP

Remember the types of DNS records that you can configure to verify ownership of a specific custom domain name.

Configure organizational settings

To configure the organizational settings, select Settings in the left pane of the Microsoft 365 Admin Center, and then select Org Settings. This opens the Org Settings page. This page has three tabs: Services, Security & Privacy, and Organization Profile. The Services tab, shown in Figure 1-18, enables you to configure the following:

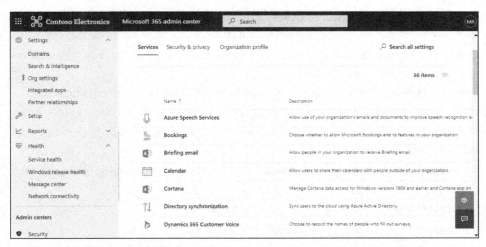

FIGURE 1-18 The Services tab of the Org Settings page

- **Azure Speech Services** Allow your organization's emails and documents to be used to improve speech-recognition accuracy.
- **Bookings** Enable Microsoft Bookings (a scheduling tool) and its features.
- **Briefing email** Specify whether people receive Briefing emails. These are generated by Outlook, which looks for actionable tasks and includes them in the email.
- **Calendar** Configure calendar-sharing for people outside your organization.
- **Cortana** Manage Cortana data access for Windows 10 versions 1909 and earlier.
- **Directory synchronization** Configure Azure AD synchronization.
- **Dynamics 365 Customer Voice** Specify whether people who fill out customer surveys will have their names stored.
- **Dynamics 365 Sales Insights – Analytics** Specify whether Dynamics 365 can generate insights based on user data.
- **Dynamics 365 Sales Insights – Connection Graph** Manage connection graph settings for Dynamics 365 Sales Insights.
- **Dynamics CRM** Manage organization Dynamics CRM settings.
- **Mail** Configure auditing, message tracking, and spam and malware protection for email.
- **Microsoft 365 Groups** Manage external sharing settings.
- **Microsoft Azure Information Protection** Configure Azure Information Protection settings.

- **Microsoft Communication to Users** Configure whether users in your organization will receive marketing messages from Microsoft.

- **Microsoft Forms** Manage whether the names of organization users who fill out forms will be shared externally.

- **Microsoft Graph Data Connect** Manage Microsoft Graph data connection settings.

- **Microsoft Planner** Configure whether users can publish plans and tasks to iCalendar.

- **Microsoft Rewards** Specify whether users can connect their Azure AD and Microsoft Rewards accounts.

- **Microsoft Search in Bing Home Page** Customize the Bing.com page for signed-in users.

- **Microsoft Teams** Configure Microsoft Teams settings.

- **Microsoft To Do** Configure Microsoft To Do settings.

- **Modern Authentication** Configure Exchange Online authentication settings at the organization level.

- **Multi-factor Authentication** Configure multifactor authentication settings for users.

- **MyAnalytics** Configure MyAnalytics settings.

- **News** Configure how organization news is sent and displayed.

- **Office Installation Options** Specify how often users receive feature updates and which Office apps users can install.

- **Office on the Web** Specify whether users can employ third-party storage services with Office on the Web.

- **Office Scripts** Configure automation settings for Office on the Web.

- **Productivity Score** Configure privacy controls for Productivity Score.

- **Reports** Manage privacy controls for reports in Microsoft 365 Admin Center.

- **SharePoint** Configure external sharing settings for SharePoint.

- **Sway** Specify sharing and content sources that can be configured for Sway.

- **User Consent to Apps** Set the level of consent that users can provide to allow apps access to organization data.

- **User-Owned Apps and Services** Configure user access to Office Store and Office 365 trials.

- **What's New in Office** Specify whether users will be notified about new Office features.

- **Whiteboard** Configure access to Microsoft Whiteboard and shared whiteboard collaboration settings.

The Security & Privacy tab, shown in Figure 1-19, allows you to configure the following:

FIGURE 1-19 The Security & Privacy tab of the Org Settings page

- **Bing data collection** Specify whether Bing can use organization search behavior to improve results.
- **Customer lockbox** Configure requirements for data access.
- **Password expiration policy** Configure the organization password policy.
- **Privacy profile** Set the organization's privacy statement.
- **Privileged access** Configure scoped access for privileged tasks and data access.
- **Self-service password reset** Configure self-service password reset settings.
- **Sharing** Configure settings related to external access to organization data.

Complete the organization profile

The Organization Profile tab, shown in Figure 1-20, allows you to configure the following:

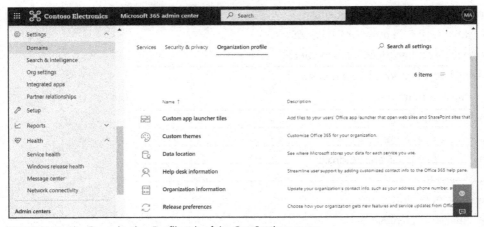

FIGURE 1-20 The Organization Profile tab of the Org Settings page

- **Custom app launcher tiles**   Configure tiles for the Office App launcher to enable users to easily access web and SharePoint sites.
- **Custom themes**   Configure themes for Office 365.
- **Data location**   Specify where data is stored for each Microsoft 365 service used by your organization.
- **Help desk information**   Enter customized contact information for the Office 365 help pane.
- **Organization information**   Enter organization information, including phone number and address.
- **Release preferences**   Specify how the organization will consume new features and service updates.

Add a Microsoft partner or work with Microsoft FastTrack

Microsoft FastTrack is a program that assists organizations in deploying and migrating to Microsoft 365. FastTrack can aid in the following areas:

- Core onboarding
- Microsoft 365 Apps
- Network health
- Azure Active Directory and Azure AD Premium
- Azure Information Protection
- Discover & Respond
- Insider Risk Management
- Microsoft 365 Defender
- Microsoft Cloud App Security
- Microsoft Defender for Endpoint
- Microsoft Defender for Identity
- Microsoft Defender for Office 365
- Microsoft Information Governance
- Microsoft Information Protection
- Microsoft Intune
- Exchange Online
- Microsoft Teams
- Outlook for iOS and Android
- Power BI
- Project Online
- SharePoint Online

- OneDrive
- Yammer Enterprise
- Windows 10
- Windows Virtual Desktop
- App Assure

> **MORE INFO** **FASTTRACK FOR MICROSOFT 365**
>
> You can learn more about Microsoft FastTrack at *https://docs.microsoft.com/fasttrack/ products-and-capabilities*.

Microsoft partners enable you to delegate control of parts of your tenancy to people outside your organization. To configure partner access, the partner must send an email request to a Microsoft 365 administrator for partner status, and the Microsoft 365 administrator must accept the invitation in the Microsoft 365 Admin Center. The administrator does this from the Partner Relationships page shown in Figure 1-21. (To access this page, select Settings in the left pane of the Microsoft 365 Admin Center and then select Partner Relationships.) This page also describes the relationship type and the roles assigned to the partner and enables you to remove partners and partner roles from your organization's tenancy.

FIGURE 1-21 The Partner Relationships page in the Microsoft 365 Admin Center

Microsoft 365 supports the following partner types:

- **Reseller**   Resells Microsoft products to organizations.
- **Delegated administrator**   Manages products and services for organizations. This type of partner is assigned the global administrator role in Azure AD for your tenancy and can create user accounts, assign and manage licenses, and perform password resets.

- **Reseller and delegated administrator** A combination of the reseller and delegated administrator partner types.
- **Partner** Is given a user account in your organization's tenancy and can be delegated rights.
- **Advisor** Can perform password resets and handle support incidents.
- **Line-of-business (LOB) partner** Can develop, submit, and manage LOB apps for your organization.

> **MORE INFO** **MANAGE MICROSOFT 365 PARTNERS**
>
> You can learn more about managing partner relationships at *https://docs.microsoft.com/ microsoft-365/commerce/manage-partners*.

Complete the subscription setup wizard

After you have created your subscription, you can configure it manually or use a subscription setup wizard. The subscription setup wizard includes steps for domain configuration, adding users, and installing Office.

To use the subscription setup wizard after deploying your subscription, follow these steps:

1. Select **Go to guided setup**, as shown in Figure 1-22.

FIGURE 1-22 Complete the subscription setup wizard

2. As shown in Figure 1-23, the wizard asks if you want to install Office. Select **Continue** to bypass this step.

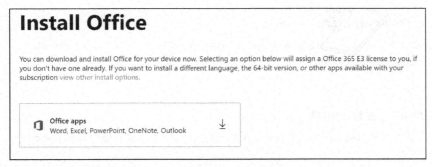

Install Office

You can download and install Office for your device now. Selecting an option below will assign a Office 365 E3 license to you, if you don't have one already. If you want to install a different language, the 64-bit version, or other apps available with your subscription view other install options.

> **Office apps**
> Word, Excel, PowerPoint, OneNote, Outlook

FIGURE 1-23 The Install Office page of the subscription setup wizard

3. The wizard asks if you want to use the default domain or configure the subscription to use a different domain. To use the default domain, select **Use this domain** and set up a custom domain later, as outlined earlier in this chapter.

4. On the **Add users and assign licenses** page (see Figure 1-24), you can add users to Microsoft 365. All users that you add during this step will be assigned a Microsoft 365 license.

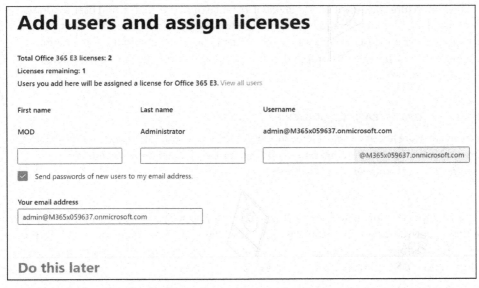

Add users and assign licenses

Total Office 365 E3 licenses: **2**
Licenses remaining: **1**
Users you add here will be assigned a license for Office 365 E3. View all users

First name	Last name	Username
MOD	Administrator	admin@M365x059637.onmicrosoft.com
		@M365x059637.onmicrosoft.com

☑ Send passwords of new users to my email address.

Your email address
admin@M365x059637.onmicrosoft.com

Do this later

FIGURE 1-24 Add users and assign licenses

5. If you are not using the default domain, configure domain DNS record options in the **How do you want to connect your domain?** page. If you are using the default domain, Microsoft will handle this for you. Either way, once you have provided this information, select **Continue**.

6. The wizard displays the **Microsoft Teams** page. You can skip this for now. Select **Continue** to complete the subscription setup wizard.

Plan and create a tenant

When planning a Microsoft 365 tenant, you must understand the difference between these three terms:

- **Organization**   A group—such as a business, an institution, or a government agency—that will use Microsoft 365 or another Microsoft cloud offering. Organizations are usually identified by one or more public domain names, such as tailwindtraders.com. An organization can have multiple subscriptions.

- **Subscription**   An agreement with Microsoft for one or more services. In the case of Microsoft 365, charges accrue to subscriptions based on per-user license fees. A subscription can only be associated with one Azure AD tenant.

- **Tenant**   A regional location that houses the infrastructure that provides cloud services. An Azure AD tenant is an individual instance of Azure AD hosting user accounts or groups. Microsoft 365 subscriptions are associated with an Azure AD tenant. Multiple Microsoft cloud offering subscriptions can be associated with the same Azure AD tenant. This is most often done so that a single identity provider can be used across multiple services.

The most important initial decisions that you will make about your Microsoft 365 tenancy will be the tenant name and the tenant region. You learned about tenant names and how the onmicrosoft.com domain you choose when creating the tenancy can never be removed, even if you add a custom DNS domain, as discussed earlier in this chapter.

The tenant region determines the following:

- Which Microsoft 365 services will be available to the subscription
- The taxes that will be included in the subscription fee
- The billing currency for the subscription
- The Microsoft data center that will host the resources allocated to the subscription

For example, if you select the United States as the tenant region, your organization's Microsoft 365 tenancy will be allocated resources in a U.S. data center. Selecting New Zealand currently means that your organization's Microsoft 365 tenancy will be allocated resources in a data center in Australia (until the New Zealand data center, opening soon, becomes available).

Unlike with other Microsoft 365 settings, you cannot change the tenant region after you have selected it. The only way to alter a tenant region is to cancel your existing subscription and create a new one.

Selecting the correct tenant is important from a compliance perspective. There are many stories of consultants in countries outside the United States setting up U.S. tenancies, only to find out later that they must re-create the tenancy because customer data is stored outside the associated organization's national borders.

> **MORE INFO** **WHERE TENANCY DATA IS STORED**
>
> You can learn more about where tenancy data is stored at *https://products.office.com/where-is-your-data-located*.

Although you cannot change the region of your tenancy, Microsoft does offer multi-geo capability. This functionality enables an organization to expand Microsoft 365 services across multiple geographic regions, thereby allowing specific data generated by a multinational organization to be stored in specific locations to meet legal requirements pertaining to data residency. To enable multi-geo functionality for a Microsoft 365 tenancy, the organization's account team must request it.

> **MORE INFO** **MICROSOFT 365 MULTI-GEO**
>
> You can learn more about Microsoft 365 multi-geo options at *https://docs.microsoft.com/microsoft-365/enterprise/microsoft-365-multi-geo*.

Microsoft offers customers the ability to move an existing tenant's data to a new region if a new data center opens in that region. For example, before 2015, Australian customers had their data stored in the Asia/Pacific data center. When the Australian data center became available, Microsoft offered customers with existing tenancies in the Asia/Pacific data center the option of migrating to the Australian one. However, if an Australian customer deployed a new tenancy today in a data center other than the one in Australia, they would not be able to request a migration because they already had the option of deploying to an Australian data center. At some point in the future, customers in New Zealand are likely to be offered the ability to move data to the New Zealand data center, which Microsoft has announced will be opened on the North Island.

> **MORE INFO** **MOVING DATA TO A NEW DATA CENTER**
>
> You can learn more about moving data to a new data center at *https://docs.microsoft.com/en-us/microsoft-365/enterprise/moving-data-to-new-datacenter-geos*.

Edit an organizational profile

To update your organization's name, address, phone, and technical contact information, you must have global administrator rights to the subscription. To make these modifications to the organization profile, perform the following steps:

1. In the left pane of the **Microsoft 365 admin center**, under **Settings**, select **Org settings**.

2. Select the **Organization profile** tab.

3. Select **Organization information**.

   The **Organization Information** pane opens. (See Figure 1-25.)

FIGURE 1-25 The Organization Information pane

4. Provide the following information:
   - Name
   - Street address
   - Apartment or suite
   - City
   - State or province
   - ZIP or postal code
   - Country or region
   - Phone
   - Technical contact
   - Preferred language

MORE INFO   **EDIT ORGANIZATION INFORMATION**

You can learn more about editing organization information at *https://docs.microsoft.com/en-us/microsoft-365/admin/manage/change-address-contact-and-more.*

Plan and create subscriptions

A *subscription* is an agreement with Microsoft to obtain one or more services. There are many Microsoft 365 subscription options. Before purchasing a subscription, you should assess your users' needs to determine which subscription is most suitable. It may be that you have several different groups of users in your organization who have separate needs. Because Microsoft 365 allows you to associate multiple subscriptions with a single tenancy, you can add subscriptions as necessary to a tenancy and assign licenses to users as appropriate.

You add subscriptions to a tenancy on the Purchase Services page. To access this page, select Purchase Services under Billing in the left pane of the Microsoft 365 Admin Center.

MORE INFO   **MULTIPLE SUBSCRIPTIONS**

You can learn more about subscriptions at *https://docs.microsoft.com/en-us/microsoft-365/commerce/licenses/subscriptions-and-licenses?view=o365-worldwide.*

Configure tenant wide workload settings

The principle of least privilege suggests that organizations will be more secure if privileged users are assigned the minimum level of administrative rights required to fulfill their roles. For example, rather than giving every IT support technician the Microsoft 365 global administrator role, users who are responsible only for changing passwords could be assigned the helpdesk administrator (password administrator) role and IT support technicians who are responsible for assigning licenses could be assigned the license administrator role. In this section you will learn about the Microsoft 365 administrative roles and how they can be used to manage specific workload settings.

Global administrator

Global administrators have the most permissions over a Microsoft 365 tenancy. A global administrator has the following permissions:

- View organization and user information
- Manage support tickets
- Reset user passwords
- Perform billing and purchasing operations
- Create and manage user views

- Create, edit, and delete users
- Create, edit, and delete groups
- Manage user licenses
- Manage domains
- Manage organization information
- Delegate administrative roles to others
- User directory synchronization

Users who have the global administrator role in the Microsoft 365 tenancy have the following roles in Exchange Online:

- Exchange Online administrator
- Company administrator
- SharePoint Online administrator
- Skype for Business Online administrator

Billing administrator

Members of the billing administrator role are responsible for making purchases, managing Microsoft 365 subscriptions, managing support tickets, and monitoring the health of Office 365 services. A billing administrator has the following permissions:

- View organization and user information
- Manage support tickets
- Perform billing and purchasing operations

Members of this role do not have any equivalent roles in Exchange Online, SharePoint Online, or Skype for Business Online.

Dynamics 365 service administrator

Users who hold the Dynamics 365 service administrator role can manage Dynamics 365 instances, including performing backup and recovery operations. These users can also perform Dynamics 365 copy and reset actions. Finally, they can open Microsoft support tickets and view the service dashboard and message center.

Customer Lockbox access approver

Members of the Customer Lockbox access approver role manage customer lockbox requests for the tenancy. They receive email notifications for Customer Lockbox requests. Users who hold this role can approve or deny requests using the Microsoft 365 Admin Center. They can also enable and disable the Customer Lockbox feature. Only users who hold the global administrator role can reset the password of users who hold the Customer Lockbox access approver role.

Exchange administrator

The Exchange administrator role is also known as the Exchange Online administrator role. Users who have been given the Exchange Online administrator role can manage mailboxes and anti-spam policies for their tenancy. This includes the ability to:

- Recover deleted items from mailboxes
- Configure how long deleted items will be retained before permanent deletion
- Configure mailbox sharing policies
- Configure Send As and Send on Behalf of delegates for a mailbox
- Configure anti-spam and malware filters
- Create shared mailboxes

> **MORE INFO** **EXCHANGE ONLINE ADMINISTRATOR**
>
> You can learn more about the Exchange administrator role at *https://docs.microsoft.com/ office365/admin/add-users/about-exchange-online-admin-role*.

Helpdesk (password) administrator

Members of the helpdesk (password) administrator role are responsible for resetting passwords for nonprivileged users and other members of the password administrator role. Members of this role can manage service requests and monitor service health. Members of this role have the following permissions:

- View organization and user information
- Manage support tickets
- Reset nonprivileged user passwords as well as passwords of other password administrators

> **NOTE** Members of this role cannot reset passwords of global administrators, user management administrators, or billing administrators.

- Manage the Exchange Online help desk administrator role
- Manage the Skype for Business Online administrator role

License administrator

Users assigned the license administrator role can add, remove, and update user license assignments. They can also manage group-based licensing, as well as configure the usage location for users. Users assigned this role cannot purchase or manage subscriptions, create or manage groups, or modify users beyond configuring usage location.

Skype for Business administrator

Users given the Skype for Business administrator role can perform the following tasks:

- Set up dial-in conferencing
- Set up PSTN calling
- Transfer phone numbers to Skype for Business Online
- Enable Skype Meeting Broadcast
- Allow users to contact external Skype for Business users
- Allow users to add external contacts from Skype
- Determine who can view the service's online presence
- Enable and disable mobile notifications
- Create customized meeting invitations
- View online reports for Skype for Business Online

Message center reader

Users assigned the message center reader role can view all posts made to the Microsoft 365 Message Center. Users assigned this role can also share these messages with other users by forwarding them through email. Finally, users with this role have read access to a subset of Admin Center resources, including users, groups, domains, and subscriptions.

Power BI service administrator

Users assigned the Power BI administrator role have access to Microsoft 365 and Office 365 Power BI usage metrics. These users can also manage the organization's usage of Power BI.

Reports reader

Users who hold the reports reader role can view all Microsoft 365 activity reports, as well as any reports that are published through the reporting application programming interfaces (APIs).

Service administrator

Members of the service administrator role can manage service requests and monitor the health of services. Before a global administrator can assign the service administrator role to a user, the user must be assigned administrative permissions to one of the Office 365 services, such as SharePoint Online or Exchange Online. Service administrators have the following permissions over the assigned service:

- View organization and user information
- Manage support tickets

SharePoint administrator

Also known as the SharePoint Online administrator, this role enables users to use the Share-Point Online Admin Center. Users who have this role can also perform the following tasks:

- Create and manage site collections
- Manage site collections and global settings
- Designate site collection administrators
- Manage site collection storage limits
- Manage SharePoint online user profiles

> **MORE INFO   SHAREPOINT ADMINISTRATOR**
>
> You can learn more about the SharePoint administrator role at *https://docs.microsoft.com/ sharepoint/sharepoint-admin-role*.

Teams communications administrator

Users who hold this role can manage the calling and meeting features of Teams. This includes assigning phone numbers and setting meeting policies. Users who hold this role can also use call analytics and troubleshooting tools.

Teams communications support engineer

Users who hold this role can troubleshoot communications issues in Teams. They can access call analytics tools and view call record information for all call participants.

Teams communications support specialist

Users who hold this role can troubleshoot communications issues in Teams. This role differs from the support engineer role in that the specialist can only view call record information for a specific user rather than all call participants.

Teams service administrator

Users who hold this role can administer all aspects of Microsoft Teams except the assignment of licenses. Users who hold this role can:

- Manage calling policies
- Manage messaging policies
- Manage meeting policies
- Use call analytics tools
- Manage users and their telephone settings
- Manage Microsoft 365 groups

User management administrator

Members of the user management administrator role can reset some user passwords, monitor service health, manage some user accounts and groups, and handle service requests. Members of this role have the following permissions:

- View organization and user information
- Manage support tickets
- Reset the passwords of all user accounts except those assigned the global administrator, billing administrator, and service administrator roles
- Create and manage user views
- Create, edit, and delete users and groups except users who are assigned global administrator privileges
- Manage user licenses
- Hold the Skype for Business Online administrator role

Delegated administrator

Delegated administrators are people outside the organization who perform administrative duties within the Office 365 tenancy. Administrators within the tenancy control who receives delegated administrator permissions. You can assign delegated administrator permissions only to users who have Office 365 accounts in their own tenancy.

When you configure delegated administration, you can choose one of the following permission levels:

- **Full administration**   The delegated administrator has the same privileges as a member of the global administrator role.
- **Limited administration**   The delegated administrator has the same privileges as a member of the helpdesk (password) administrator role.

> **MORE INFO   DELEGATED ADMINISTRATORS**
>
> You can learn more about delegated administrators at *https://support.office.microsoft.com/ article/Partners-Offer-delegated-administration-26530dc0-ebba-415b-86b1-b55bc06b073e*.

Manage role membership

To assign an administrative role to a Microsoft 365 user, open the Manage Admin Roles page of the user's properties. (See Figure 1-26.) Simply specify the administrative role that you want to assign and an alternate email address. (This enables you to perform password recovery if necessary.) You can only add Microsoft 365 users to a role. You cannot add a Microsoft 365 group to a role.

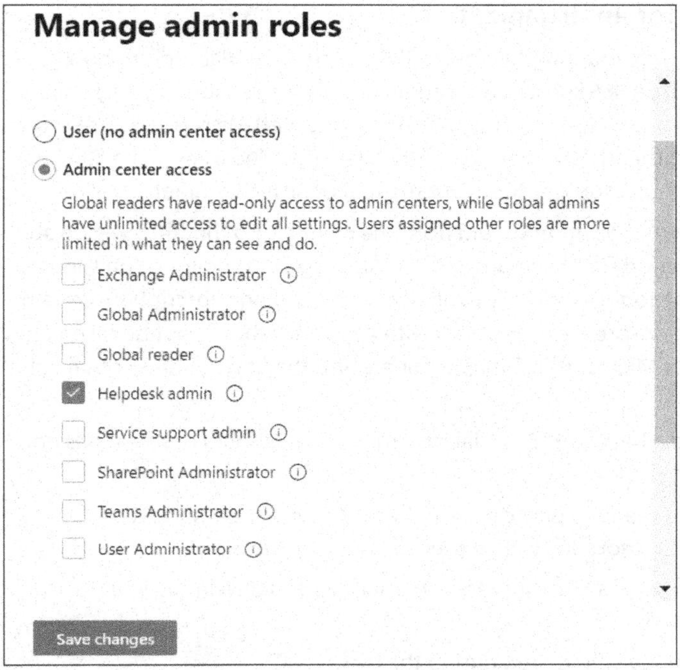

Manage admin roles

○ User (no admin center access)

◉ Admin center access

Global readers have read-only access to admin centers, while Global admins have unlimited access to edit all settings. Users assigned other roles are more limited in what they can see and do.

☐ Exchange Administrator ⓘ

☐ Global Administrator ⓘ

☐ Global reader ⓘ

☑ Helpdesk admin ⓘ

☐ Service support admin ⓘ

☐ SharePoint Administrator ⓘ

☐ Teams Administrator ⓘ

☐ User Administrator ⓘ

Save changes

FIGURE 1-26 Assigning the helpdesk administrator role

You can also use this page of a user's account to remove an assigned role. To do this, deselect the role that you want to remove and select Save.

You can view a list of users assigned a particular role by opening the Roles page in the Microsoft 365 Admin Center and selecting the role whose membership you want to view. Figure 1-27 shows the members of the helpdesk administrator role.

Helpdesk admin

General   **Assigned admins**   Permissions

Select users to reassign them to a different role or to remove them. If you're concerned about reducing their access, assign the global reader role as well.

Learn more about assigning admin roles

+ Add

Admin name	Last sign-in
Adele Vance AdeleV@m365ms100.com	No attempts in 30 days

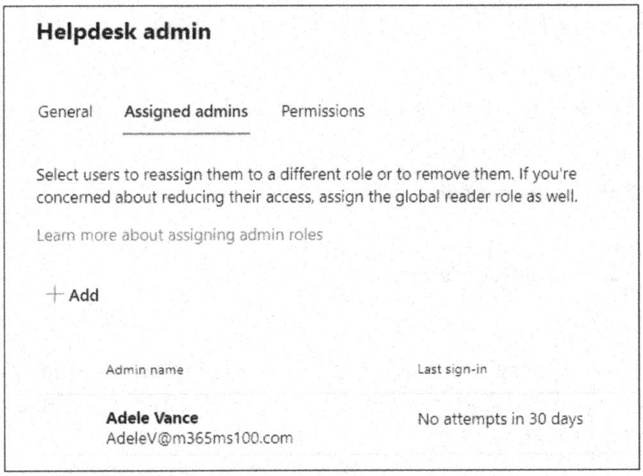

FIGURE 1-27 List of helpdesk administrators

Evaluate Microsoft 365 for an organization

Organizations that are considering adopting Microsoft 365 can create a trial subscription, which is available to existing Office 365 subscribers. A trial subscription enables the organization to create and use a Microsoft 365 tenancy as well as the associated Microsoft 365 services for a 30-day evaluation period. The trial period allows for 25 licenses. The trial can be converted to a traditional Microsoft 365 subscription after the trial period is complete.

Before initiating the trial, an organization should do some planning so that they will be able to use the 30-day evaluation period for maximum benefit. Although the organization should approach the trial as a pilot that could eventually evolve into an ongoing subscription, certain actions, such as integrating the on-premises directory with Azure AD, should not be taken until the organization is satisfied that Microsoft 365 is appropriate and that it will indeed obtain an ongoing subscription.

Specifically, before initiating a Microsoft 365 trial, an organization should ensure it has done the following:

- Identify 25 users who are ready to participate in the trial. These users should be representative of how Microsoft 365 will be used in your organization.
- Provide these users with separate computers with trial versions of Windows 10 Enterprise edition installed.
- Identify meaningful workloads to be run during the trial.

It is important to determine whether Microsoft 365 is appropriate for your organization during the trial. This means identifying any potential hurdles in the trial period rather than after Microsoft 365 has been fully adopted.

Creating a test plan or use case involves developing a formal process to describe how the pilot will proceed and how the results of the pilot will be assessed. The test plan should involve the following general phases:

- Deploying the Microsoft 365 tenancy that will be used for the pilot
- Creating user accounts for pilot users
- Configuring active use of email for pilot users
- Deploying Microsoft 365 Apps for enterprise software
- Enabling pilot user access to Microsoft 365 services
- Soliciting pilot user feedback about the experience

> **NOTE** Each organization's plans will be slightly different.

You must record pilot user feedback so that you can use it when evaluating how decisions made in the planning phase stack up against real-world outcomes. Doing so will enable you to make adjustments during the deployment phase.

You can migrate the email accounts of a small number of users from your on-premises environment to Microsoft 365 while keeping the majority of your existing mailboxes in the on-premises mail solution. This is called *simple domain sharing for SMTP email addresses*.

For example, consider this scenario:

- Your organization has provisioned the contoso.microsoftonline.com Office 365 tenancy.
- Your organization has its own on-premises mail solution, which uses the contoso.com email suffix.
- Your organization hosts its own DNS records on servers: dns1.contoso.com and dns2.contoso.com.
- An MX record in the contoso.com zone points to the host mailserver.adatum.com with a priority of 10.
- An SPF record in the contoso.com DNS zone has the value `v=spf1 mx include:contoso.com -all`.

To configure Office 365 so that some pilot users can receive email through Microsoft 365, while others still use the on-premises solution, take the following steps:

1. Update the SPF record to `v=spf1 mx include:contoso.com include:spf.protection.outlook.com -all`.
2. Confirm ownership within Microsoft 365 of the contoso.com DNS zone by configuring the appropriate TXT record.
3. Mark the domain as shared in Exchange Online. You do this on the **Mail Flow** page in **Exchange Admin Center**. (To access Exchange Admin Center from the Microsoft 365 Admin Center, select **Admin** in the pane on the left and then select **Exchange**.)
4. Set the domain as an **Internal Relay** domain.
5. Configure the on-premises mail solution to forward mail for each pilot user account to the contoso.microsoftonline.com mail domain. For example, the on-premises mailbox for the don.funk@contoso.com email account should forward all incoming email to don.funk@contoso.microsoftonline.com.
6. Configure each pilot user's account in Microsoft 365 to use the on-premises DNS zone mail domain. For example, Don Funk's Microsoft 365 user account should be configured with a reply-to address of don.funk@contoso.com.
7. Use Exchange Admin Center to migrate the contents of the pilot users' on-premises mailboxes.

MORE INFO TRIAL MICROSOFT 365

You can learn more about using the Microsoft 365 trial edition if you have an existing Office 365 subscription at *https://docs.microsoft.com/office365/admin/try-or-buy-microsoft-365*.

Upgrade existing subscriptions to Microsoft 365

Microsoft 365 is a combination of the following existing Microsoft products:

- Office 365
- Enterprise Mobility + Security (EMS)
- Windows 10

An organization that already has Office 365 subscriptions for its users can upgrade those subscriptions to Microsoft 365. Similarly, an organization that has both Office 365 and EMS subscriptions can upgrade them to include Microsoft 365 licenses.

You purchase additional services in the Purchase Services page. To access this page, select Billing in the left pane in the Microsoft 365 Admin Center and then select Purchase Services. (See Figure 1-28.) After you purchase the appropriate licenses, you can assign them to users.

> **NOTE** Microsoft's FastTrack for Microsoft 365 service provides information and advice on upgrading an existing deployment or performing a new deployment.

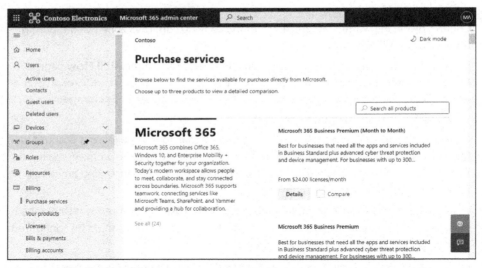

FIGURE 1-28 The Purchase Services page

Manage tenant subscriptions

You can manage Microsoft 365 tenant subscriptions from the Your Products page. To access this page, select Billing in the left pane in Microsoft 365 Admin Center and then select Your Products. (See Figure 1-29.)

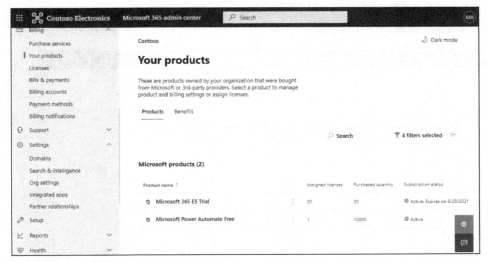

FIGURE 1-29 The Your Products page

Skill 1.3: Manage Microsoft 365 subscription and tenant health

This skill section deals with managing subscription and tenant health for a Microsoft 365 deployment. To master this skill, you will need to understand options when it comes to managing service health, as well as how to create and manage service requests, create a health response plan, monitor service health, create and review reports, schedule and review security and compliance reports, and schedule and review usage metrics.

> **This section covers the following topics:**
> - Manage service health alerts
> - Create an internal service health response plan
> - Monitor service health
> - Configure and review reports
> - Schedule and review security and compliance reports
> - Schedule and review usage metrics

Manage service health alerts

The Service Health dashboard shows you the health status of all services related to your organization's Microsoft 365 subscription. For example, the Service Health dashboard shown in Figure 1-30 shows that several services are in a healthy state and others are listed with advisories. To open this dashboard, select Health in the left pane of the Microsoft 365 Admin Center and then select Service Health.

FIGURE 1-30 The Service Health dashboard

Table 1-7 defines the various statuses associated with services.

TABLE 1-7 Microsoft 365 service status definitions

Status	Definition
Investigating	Microsoft is aware of the issue and is investigating its cause and scope of impact.
Service degradation	Microsoft has confirmed that an issue is present in a specific Microsoft 365 service or feature. This status is often assigned when a service is performing in a slower-than-normal fashion or when intermittent interruptions are occurring.
Service interruption	Microsoft is aware that significant disruption is occurring with the listed system.
Restoring service	Microsoft has determined the cause of the issue and is in the process of restoring full functionality.
Extended recovery	Microsoft has restored full functionality for most users, but some users may require more time before the fix reaches them.
Investigation suspended	Microsoft has requested additional information from customers to determine the cause of a disruption.
Service restored	Microsoft has confirmed that remediation actions have resolved the problem and that the service is in a healthy state. You can view service issues to learn details of the disruption.
Post-incident report published	Microsoft has published a detailed post-incident report that includes root cause information and steps that have been taken to ensure that the issue does not arise again.

The Service Health page includes several tabs along the top, including a History tab. Select this tab to display the status history of services over a specified period of time (30 days by default). Figure 1-31 shows the status history over the last 7 days. The information on this tab can help you diagnose issues that may have occurred previously that you were not aware of—for example, if you need to provide an explanation to a user as to why they were unable to access specific functionality over the weekend. Selecting each item provides further details.

FIGURE 1-31 The History tab of the Service Health page

Create an internal service health response plan

Microsoft provides a variety of methods to notify your organization of a service disruption beyond end users ringing the service desk to complain that they cannot get "the thing to work." You can monitor these service communication channels to become aware of potential issues and take steps to notify users before it affects them. Service communication channels include the following:

- **The Office 365 Admin App**   This app enables Microsoft 365 and Office 365 administrators to monitor service status from a mobile device. Tenant administrators can also use the app to view service health information and maintenance status updates.

- **Office 365 Management Pack for System Center Operations Manager**   Organizations that use System Center Operations Manager to monitor their environment can install the Office 365 Management Pack so that alerts are visible within the Operations Manager console. The management pack includes Subscription Health, Service Status, Active Incidents, and Resolved Incidents sections, as well as the Message Center.

- **Office 365 Service Communications API** This API enables you to interact with Office 365 service communications in a manner that suits your organization. This API provides a method for connecting existing monitoring tools to Office 365 service communications. The API allows you to monitor real-time service health, Message Center communications, and planned maintenance notifications.

MORE INFO **SERVICE HEALTH RESPONSE**

You can learn more about service health response at *https://docs.microsoft.com/office365/ servicedescriptions/office-365-platform-service-description/service-health-and-continuity*.

Monitor service health

Microsoft 365 provides administrators with information about upcoming maintenance events through planned maintenance notifications. You can view planned maintenance events in the Message Center. (See Figure 1-32.) To access this page, select Health in the left pane of the Microsoft 365 Admin Center and then select Message Center.

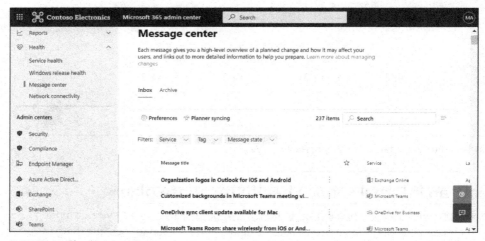

FIGURE 1-32 The Message Center

MORE INFO **MESSAGE CENTER**

You can learn more about the Message Center at *https://docs.microsoft.com/en-us/microsoft-365/admin/manage/message-center?view=o365-worldwide*.

Monitor license allocations

Microsoft 365 users require licenses to use Outlook, SharePoint Online, Skype for Business, and other services. Users who have been assigned the global administrator or user management administrator roles can assign licenses when creating new Microsoft 365 user accounts. They can also assign licenses to accounts created through directory synchronization or federation.

When a license is assigned to a user, the following occurs:

- An Exchange Online mailbox is created for the user.
- Edit permissions for the default SharePoint Online team site are assigned to the user.
- The user gains access to Skype for Business features associated with the license.
- For Microsoft 365 Apps for enterprise, the user will be able to download and install Microsoft Office on as many as five computers running Windows or macOS.

You can view the number of valid licenses and the number of those licenses that have been assigned on the Licenses page. You access this page by selecting Billing in the left pane of Microsoft 365 Admin Center and then selecting Licenses.

> **MORE INFO   ASSIGN LICENSES**
>
> You can learn more about assigning licenses at *https://docs.microsoft.com/microsoft-365/admin/add-users/add-users*.

EXAM TIP

Remember that an Exchange Online mailbox is created for a user when an Microsoft 365 license is assigned to that user.

Configure and review reports

You can integrate Microsoft 365 usage analytics with Power BI to visualize and analyze Microsoft 365 usage data. To enable Microsoft 365 usage analytics for Power BI, perform the following steps:

1. In the left pane of the **Microsoft 365 Admin Center**, under **Reports**, select **Usage**.
2. On the **Usage** page, in the **Microsoft 365 Usage Analytics** section, select **Get Started**.
3. On the **Reports** pane, shown in Figure 1-33, select the **Enable Power BI for usage analytics** check box. Then select **Save**.

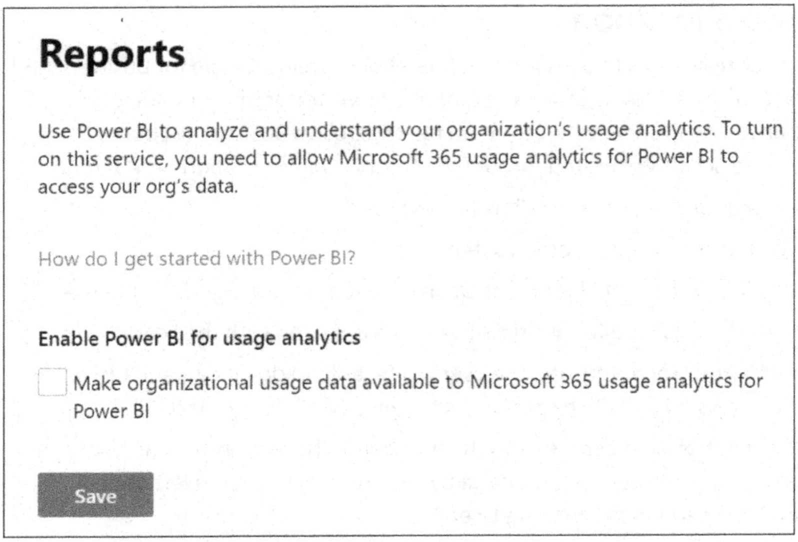

Reports

Use Power BI to analyze and understand your organization's usage analytics. To turn on this service, you need to allow Microsoft 365 usage analytics for Power BI to access your org's data.

How do I get started with Power BI?

Enable Power BI for usage analytics

☐ Make organizational usage data available to Microsoft 365 usage analytics for Power BI

Save

FIGURE 1-33 Power BI for usage analytics

To start the template app, follow these steps:

1. Copy the tenant ID. Alternatively, locate it in the Azure Active Directory Console.
2. Select **Go to Power BI**.
3. Sign into Power BI. Then select **Apps**.
4. Type **Microsoft 365** and select **Search in AppSource**.
5. On the **Power BI Apps** page, type **Microsoft 365**, select **Microsoft 365 Usage**, and then select **Get It Now**.

Microsoft 365 usage analytics includes the following reports:

- **Executive Summary** A high-level view of Microsoft 365 business adoption, usage, mobility, communication, collaboration, and storage
- **Overview** Includes Adoption, Usage, Communication, Collaboration, Storage, and Mobility reports
- **Activation and Licensing** Information about activations and the license types in use
- **Product Usage** Information on usage of Exchange, Microsoft 365 groups, OneDrive, SharePoint, Skype, Teams, and Yammer
- **User Activity** User activity reports for individual services

> **MORE INFO   USAGE ANALYTICS REPORT**
>
> You can learn more about usage analytics reports at *https://docs.microsoft.com/microsoft-365/admin/usage-analytics/usage-analytics*.

Schedule and review security and compliance reports

Certain Microsoft 365 reports reveal how security and compliance rules and technologies are used across your Microsoft 365 organization. You can view some of these reports from the Microsoft 365 Admin Center. Other reports are available in the Security & Compliance Center. (See Figure 1-34.)

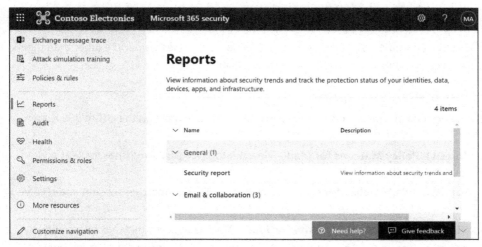

FIGURE 1-34 The Reports dashboard

Reports that relate to security and compliance are split across four categories:

- Auditing reports
- Data loss prevention (DLP) reports
- Protection reports
- Rules reports

You need one of the following roles to view reports in the Security & Compliance Center:

- **The security reader role in Exchange** This role is assigned by default to the organization management and security reader role groups.
- **The DLP compliance management role in the Security & Compliance Center** You must have this role to view DLP reports and policies. This role is assigned by default to the compliance administrator, organization management, and security administrator role groups.

> **MORE INFO SECURITY AND COMPLIANCE REPORTS**
>
> You can learn more about the Microsoft 365 security and compliance reports at *https://docs. microsoft.com/en-us/microsoft-365/compliance/reports-in-security-and-compliance.*

Auditing reports

The following security and compliance reports are available through the Security & Compliance Center:

- **Audit Log**   View user and administrator activity for the Microsoft 365 organization, including changes made to administrator role groups.
- **Azure AD**   View Azure AD reports, including reports for unusual or suspicious sign-in activity. This requires a paid Azure AD subscription.
- **Exchange Audit**   View and search for mailboxes accessed by people other than their owners. (Mailbox audit logging must be enabled.)

Data loss prevention reports

The following data loss prevention (DLP) reports are available through the Office 365 Admin Center:

- **Top DLP Policy Matches for Mail**   View the top DLP policy matches for sent and received email.
- **Top DLP Rule Matches for Mail**   View the top DLP rule matches for sent and received email.
- **DLP Policy Matches by Severity for Mail**   Track DLP policy matches by severity.
- **DLP Policy Matches, Overrides, and False Positives for Mail**   View DLP matches, overrides, and false positives for incoming and outgoing messages.

Protection reports

The following protection reports are available through the Microsoft 365 Admin Center:

- **Top Senders and Recipients**   View the top mail senders, mail recipients, spam recipients, and malware recipients across the Microsoft 365 subscription.
- **Top Malware for Mail**   View the amount of malware received through email for the reporting period.
- **Malware Detections**   View the amount of malware sent and received through the Microsoft 365 subscription for the reporting period.
- **Spam Detections**   View the amount of spam on the basis of the content being filtered or the original sending host being blocked.
- **Sent and Received Mail**   View the amount of sent and received mail categorized by good mail, malware, spam, and messages dealt with by rules.

Rules reports

The following rules reports are available through the Office 365 Admin Center:

- **Top Rule Matches for Mail**   View the number of messages based on sent and received transport rule matches.
- **Rule Matches for Mail**   View all rule matches for received and sent email.

Schedule and review usage metrics

Usage reports (see Figure 1-35) show how users in your organization are employing Microsoft 365 services. You can review reports over periods of 7 days, 30 days, 90 days, and 180 days. Reports are not generated immediately but become available after 48 hours.

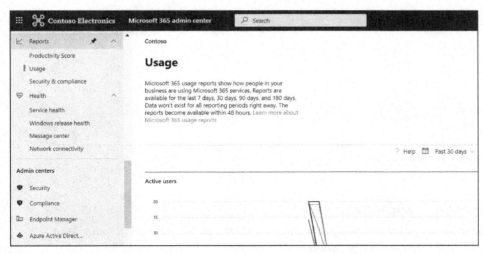

FIGURE 1-35 Usage reports

Users who hold the following roles can view these reports:

- Global administrator
- Exchange administrator
- SharePoint administrator
- Skype for Business administrator
- Report reader
- Teams service administrator
- Teams communications administrator

The following sections detail the types of usage reports that are available.

Email Activity report

The Email Activity report, shown in Figure 1-36, displays the number of send, receive, and read actions across the organization, with a per-user breakdown. You can use this report to get high-level information about email traffic at your organization, including the last activity date, and the number of send, receive, and read actions.

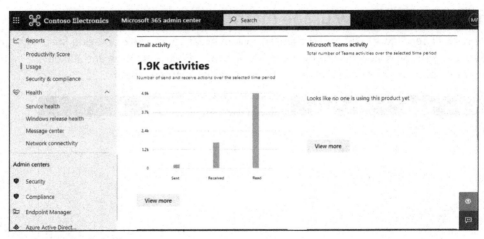

FIGURE 1-36 Email Activity report

MORE INFO **EMAIL ACTIVITY REPORT**

You can learn more about the Email Activity report at *https://docs.microsoft.com/en-us/microsoft-365/admin/activity-reports/email-activity*.

Mailbox Usage report

The Mailbox Usage report, shown in Figure 1-37, shows the total number of mailboxes, the total number of active user mailboxes, the amount of storage used across all mailboxes, and the mailboxes by quota status (good, warning issued, send prohibited, and send/receive prohibited). You can also view the number of deleted items, the last activity date, and the number of items in each user's mailbox.

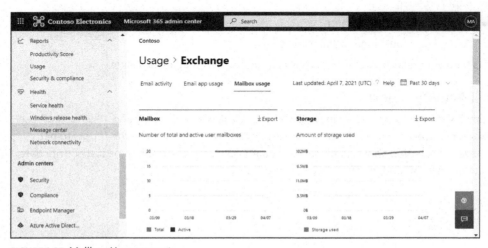

FIGURE 1-37 Mailbox Usage report

MORE INFO   MAILBOX USAGE REPORT

You can learn more about the Mailbox Usage report at *https://docs.microsoft.com/en-us/ microsoft-365/admin/activity-reports/mailbox-usage*.

Office Activations report

The Office Activations report provides data on users who have activated their Office 365 subscription on one or more devices. You can use it to track activations for Microsoft 365 Apps for Enterprise, Project, and Visio Pro for Office 365. You can also view activation information, including whether the product was activated on a computer running Windows or macOS, or on devices running the iOS or Android mobile operating system.

MORE INFO   OFFICE ACTIVATIONS REPORT

You can learn more about the Office Activations report at *https://docs.microsoft.com/ microsoft-365/admin/activity-reports/microsoft-office-activations?view=o365-worldwide*.

Active Users report

The Active Users report, shown in Figure 1-38, tracks the number of licenses being used across your organization. It also provides information about the products licensed by specific users. You can use this report to determine which products are not being fully used.

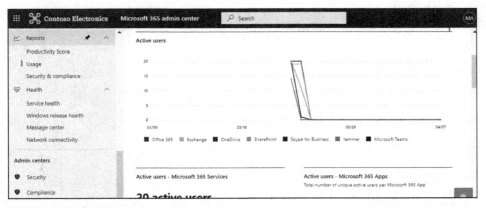

FIGURE 1-38 Active Users report

MORE INFO   ACTIVE USERS REPORT

You can learn more about the Active Users report at *https://docs.microsoft.com/en-us/ microsoft-365/admin/activity-reports/active-users?view=o365-worldwide*.

Email App Usage report

The Email App Usage report tracks the email app used by each user to access Exchange Online. This enables you to view the app usage profile of each user. This report tracks usage through Outlook on Windows, Outlook on Mac OSX, Outlook on the web, and mobile clients.

> **MORE INFO   EMAIL APP USAGE REPORT**
>
> You can learn more about the Email App Usage report at *https://docs.microsoft.com/en-us/ microsoft-365/admin/activity-reports/email-apps-usage*.

OneDrive Activity report

The OneDrive Activity report, also known as the OneDrive for Business Activity Report, enables you to view the activity of all Office 365 OneDrive users. This report, shown in Figure 1-39, provides information on the following:

- Last OneDrive activity
- Files viewed or edited
- Files synced
- Files shared internally
- Files shared externally

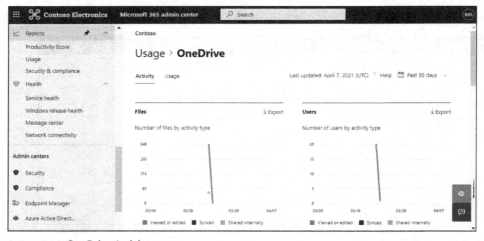

FIGURE 1-39 OneDrive Activity report

> **MORE INFO   ONEDRIVE ACTIVITY REPORT**
>
> You can learn more about the OneDrive Activity report at *https://docs.microsoft.com/ microsoft-365/admin/activity-reports/onedrive-for-business-activity-ww*.

OneDrive Usage report

The OneDrive Usage report, also known as the OneDrive for Business Usage report, provides a high-level overview of how files are used in your organization's OneDrive for Business subscription. The report, shown in Figure 1-40, provides details of the following:

- **URL**   The file's location within OneDrive for Business
- **Owner**   The Office 365 account associated with the file
- **Last activity date (UTC)**   The last date that the file was accessed
- **Files**   The number of files associated with the user
- **Active Files**   The number of the user's files actively in use
- **Storage used (MB)**   Storage consumed by the user's files

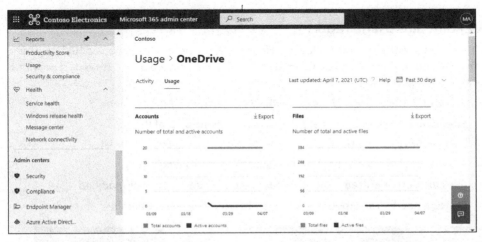

FIGURE 1-40 OneDrive Usage report

> **MORE INFO   ONEDRIVE USAGE REPORT**
>
> You can learn more about the OneDrive Usage report at *https://docs.microsoft.com/microsoft-365/admin/activity-reports/onedrive-for-business-usage*.

SharePoint Activity report

The SharePoint Activity report enables you to track how Microsoft 365 users in your organization interact with SharePoint Online. This report provides the following information on a per-user basis:

- **Last activity date**   The last time the user interacted with SharePoint Online
- **Files viewed or edited**   The number of files with which the user has interacted that were hosted on the organization's SharePoint Online instance

- **Files synced**   The number of files that have synchronized between devices used by the user and SharePoint Online
- **Files shared internally**   The number of files shared with other Office 365 users through SharePoint Online
- **Files shared externally**   The number of files shared through Office 365 with external users

> **MORE INFO   SHAREPOINT ACTIVITY REPORT**
>
> You can learn more about the SharePoint Activity report at *https://docs.microsoft.com/microsoft-365/admin/activity-reports/sharepoint-activity*.

SharePoint Site Usage report

The SharePoint Site Usage report, shown in Figure 1-41, provides information about how SharePoint sites in your organization's SharePoint Online deployment are used. This report provides you with the following information:

- **Site URL**   The address of the site within your SharePoint deployment
- **Site owner**   The Microsoft 365 user assigned ownership of the site
- **Last Activity date**   The last time activity was recorded against the site
- **Files**   The number of files stored on the SharePoint online site
- **Files viewed or edited**   Files that have recently been viewed or modified
- **Storage used**   The amount of storage consumed by files on the site

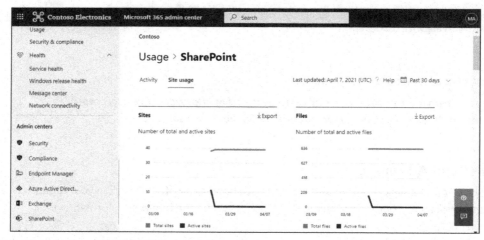

FIGURE 1-41 SharePoint Site Usage report

Skype for Business Activity report

The Skype for Business Activity report tracks Skype for Business activity on a per-user basis across your Office 365 organization. This includes information on the following:

- Last activity date
- Peer-to-peer calls
- Organized conferences
- The number of users who have participated in conferences

Skype for Business Peer-To-Peer Activity report

The Skype for Business Peer-To-Peer Activity report provides information about communication that occurs between individual Skype for Business users outside of Skype for Business conferences. This report tracks the following activity on a per-user basis:

- Last activity date
- Number of peer-to-peer instant messaging sessions
- Number of peer-to-peer audio conferences
- Number of peer-to-peer video conferences
- Number of peer-to-peer application-sharing sessions
- Number of peer-to-peer file transfers
- Number of minutes spent in peer-to-peer audio conferences
- Number of minutes spent in peer-to-peer video conferences

Skype for Business Conference Organizer Activity report

The Skype for Business Conference Organizer Activity Report tracks conferences initiated by your organization's Skype for Business users. This report presents the following information by user name:

- Last activity
- IM sessions organized
- Audio and video sessions organized
- Application-sharing conferences organized
- Web conferences organized
- Dial-in/out third-party conferences organized
- Total audio/video minutes of conferences organized
- Total number of minutes where Microsoft functioned as the dial-in audio conferencing provider
- Total number of minutes where Microsoft functioned as the dial-out audio conferencing provider

> **MORE INFO** **SKYPE FOR BUSINESS CONFERENCE ORGANIZER ACTIVITY REPORT**
>
> You can learn more about the Skype for Business Conference Organizer Activity report at *https://docs.microsoft.com/SkypeForBusiness/skype-for-business-online-reporting/conference-organizer-activity-report*.

Skype for Business Conference Participant Activity report

The Skype for Business Conference Participant Activity report provides information about the activity of a specific participant, rather than organizer, on Skype for Business. This report includes the following information on a per-user basis:

- Last activity date
- Number of IM conferences the user participated in
- Number of audio and video conferences the user participated in
- Number of application-sharing conferences that the user participated in
- Number of web conferences that the user participated in
- Number of dial-in/out third-party conferences that the user participated in using a third-party audio conferencing provider where Skype for Business was used for audio
- Total audio and video minutes

Yammer Activity report

The Yammer Activity report tracks how much users in your organization are interacting with Yammer. It provides information about the number of unique users posting to Yammer, how many users read a specific message, how many liked a specific message, and the general level of interaction across the organization.

Yammer Device Usage report

The Yammer Device Usage report provides data about the specific types of devices used to interact with the organization's Yammer instance. The report provides information on the following:

- Number of daily users by device type
- Number of users by device type
- Per-user device usage

Yammer Groups Activity report

The Yammer Groups Activity report tracks how users in your organization interact with Yammer groups. The report provides information on the number of groups created, as well as the following:

- Group name
- Group administrator
- Group type

- Connection to Office 365
- Last activity date
- Members
- Messages posted
- Messages read
- Messages liked

MORE INFO   **YAMMER GROUPS ACTIVITY REPORT**

You can learn more about the Yammer Groups Activity report at *https://docs.microsoft.com/office365/admin/activity-reports/yammer-groups-activity-report*.

Microsoft Teams User Activity report

The Microsoft Teams User Activity report provides information on how users in your organization interact with the tenancy's Microsoft Teams instance. Activities tracked by this report include the following:

- Channel messages
- Chat messages
- Calls
- Meetings
- Other activities

MORE INFO   **MICROSOFT TEAMS USER ACTIVITY REPORT**

You can learn more about the Microsoft Teams User Activity report at *https://docs.microsoft.com/office365/admin/activity-reports/microsoft-teams-user-activity*.

Microsoft Teams Device Usage report

The Microsoft Teams Device Usage report provides information about the specific devices that Microsoft 365 users are employing to interact with the tenancy's Microsoft Teams instance. The report tracks the following operating systems and devices:

- Windows
- Mac
- Web
- iOS
- Android Phone
- Windows Phone

MORE INFO **MICROSOFT TEAMS DEVICE USAGE REPORT**

You can learn more about the Microsoft Teams Device Usage report at *https://docs.microsoft.com/office365/admin/activity-reports/microsoft-teams-device-usage*.

EXAM TIP

The best way to learn about the reports available in Microsoft 365 is to access them through your organization's subscription or to create your own trial subscription and to investigate them there.

Skill 1.4: Plan migration of user and data

This section deals with migrating data from an existing on-premises deployment to Microsoft 365 and Office 365. To master this skill, you will need to understand how to identify data that needs to be migrated, how to identify mailboxes to migrate, how to migrate them, how to migrate users and groups, and how to import PST (personal storage table) files.

> **This section covers the following topics:**
> - Identify data to be migrated and migration methods
> - Identify users and mailboxes to be migrated and migration methods
> - Plan migration of on-premises users and groups
> - Import PST files

Identify data to be migrated and migration methods

Each organization will have a different set of challenges when it comes to identifying which data should be migrated from their on-premises environment to Microsoft 365. This is because each organization's data is unique, and the data that is critical to one organization might be seen as trivial to another. When assessing which data needs to be migrated to Microsoft 365, consider the following questions:

- **What on-premises data is critical to the organization?**   Planning a migration to Microsoft 365 gives an organization a chance to assess whether all the data it retains actually needs to be retained.

- **What data needs to be moved from the on-premises environment to Microsoft 365?** Not every file and folder needs to be migrated to Microsoft 365. For example, it might be that files stored on file servers that haven't been accessed for the last two years need not be migrated.

- **What data will remain on-premises?** Moving to Microsoft 365 doesn't mean that all data must be removed from on-premises locations. There may be compliance reasons, especially in countries that do not have Microsoft data centers, dictating that certain types of data must remain within specific geographic boundaries and cannot be stored in Microsoft's cloud.

- **Where is the data currently located?** For example, does your organization use file shares? Do you want to move all file share data across to SharePoint Online, or will you implement a solution such as Azure File Sync? Is the data located on end-user computers?

After you have identified which data needs to be migrated to Microsoft 365, you can determine the appropriate method to perform that migration. You will learn about migration methods later in this chapter.

Move Data to SharePoint Online

There are a variety of methods to migrate data from an on-premises environment to SharePoint Online:

- **SharePoint Migration Tool** Use this to migrate files from on-premises SharePoint document libraries, lists, and regular file shares to SharePoint Online.

- **OneDrive sync client** Drag and drop files on a client computer and have those files sync with either OneDrive for Business or SharePoint Online.

- **Manual upload** Manually upload files one at a time to the SharePoint Online tenant.

> **MORE INFO MIGRATING SHAREPOINT DATA TO SHAREPOINT ONLINE**
>
> You can learn more about migrating SharePoint data to SharePoint Online at *https://docs.microsoft.com/sharepointmigration/migrate-to-sharepoint-online*.

Migrate known local folders to OneDrive for Business

Many organizations have known folders, such as Documents folders, directed to an on-premises file share. To migrate these files to Office 365, you can use a group policy to redirect them from the on-premises file share to OneDrive—*if* the organization's computers are members of Active Directory Domain Services (AD DS) domains.

In organizations where computers are not members of AD domains, you will have to use more intensive manual methods to move files into OneDrive folders. This process is manual because in non-domain environments, where users have more freedom to configure their computers as they see fit rather than being subject to domain policy, they are more likely to store their files in idiosyncratic locations.

When known folders, such as the Documents folder, are redirected to OneDrive, users continue to use them in the normal manner. In the background, however, the contents of the known folders are automatically synced with OneDrive. With this method, a group policy dictates whether the OneDrive folder is configured on the target computer. If not, known folders, such as the Documents folder, will not be redirected.

When you have redirected known folders, shortcuts to those folders will point to the new location linked with OneDrive. The existing folder structure will still be in place, and the contents of those folders will remain in the original location. Similarly, if known folders are currently redirected to network shares, you will have to migrate data from that location to OneDrive after you redirect the known folders to OneDrive. Microsoft recommends scripts that use XCopy or Robocopy to perform this task. You can only use this strategy if OneDrive files are being stored in the default location, which is %userprofile%\OneDrive - <TenantName>. If OneDrive files are being stored in another location, you cannot use the known folder redirection strategy.

As mentioned, the known folder redirection strategy requires that computers be members of an AD DS domain. But there's another option: downloading and installing OneDrive group policy objects on a domain controller. These objects are the ADML and ADMX files, and they are located in the OneDrive installation directory of a computer with the OneDrive client installed: (%localappdata%\Microsoft\OneDrive\BuildNumber\adm\). To do this, follow these steps:

1. Open the **Group Policy Management Editor**.

2. In the pane on the left, navigate to the **User Configuration\Policies\Administrative Templates\OneDrive** folder.

3. Double-select the **Prevent Users from Changing the Location of Their OneDrive Policy** setting in the pane on the right.

4. Select the **Enabled** option button in the dialog box that opens. Then select **OK**. This will block users from moving their OneDrive folder.

5. To create a new environment variable, navigate to the **User Configuration\Preferences\ Windows Settings** folder in the left pane in the **Group Policy Management Editor**.

6. Double-select the **Environment** setting in the pane on the right.

   The New Environment Properties dialog box opens with the General tab displayed. (See Figure 1-42.)

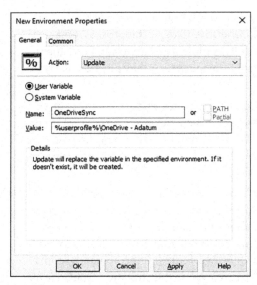

FIGURE 1-42 New environment setting

7. In the **Name** box, type **OneDriveSync**.

8. In the **Value** box, type **%userprofile%\\<SyncFolder>**, where <SyncFolder> is the name of your default folder. (In the example in Figure 1-42, the default folder name is OneDrive – Adatum.)

9. Select the **Common** tab and then select **Targeting**.

   The Targeting Editor opens. (See Figure 1-43.)

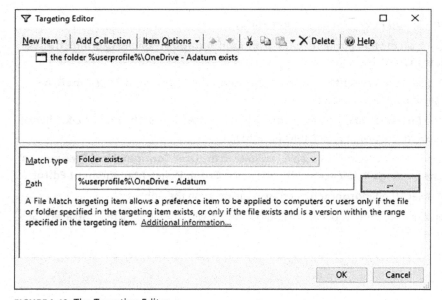

FIGURE 1-43 The Targeting Editor

10. Select **New Item** and choose **File Match** from the list that opens.

11. Open the **Match Type** drop-down list and choose **Folder Exists**.

12. In the **Path** box, type **%userprofile%\\<SyncFolder>**, where <SyncFolder> is the name of your OneDrive folder.

13. Select **OK** once to close the Targeting Editor and again to close the New Environment Properties dialog box.

14. Navigate to the **User Configuration\Policies\Windows Settings\Folder Redirection\ Documents** folder in the left pane of the **Group Policy Management Editor**.

15. Double-select the **Basic – Redirect Everyone's Folder to the Same Location** setting.

    The Documents Properties dialog box opens with the Target tab displayed. (See Figure 1-44.)

FIGURE 1-44 Document redirection policy

16. Open the **Target Folder Location** drop-down list and choose **Redirect to the Following Location**.

17. In the **Root Path** box, type **%OneDriveSync%\Documents**.

18. Select the **Settings** tab.

19. Deselect the **Move the Contents of Documents to the New Location** check box and select **OK**.

    You do this because if there are files in both locations with the same name, you might lose data. If there are no files in the new location, you can leave this setting enabled, and files will be migrated without the need for scripts.

20. Repeat steps 14 through 19 to redirect other known folders, such as Pictures, Music, Videos, Downloads, and others.

MORE INFO   REDIRECTING FOLDERS

You can learn more about redirecting known folders to OneDrive for Business at *https://docs.microsoft.com/onedrive/redirect-known-folders*.

MORE INFO   MIGRATING ORGANIZATION DATA TO OFFICE 365 ENTERPRISE

You can learn about migrating organization data to Microsoft 365 Enterprise: *https://docs.microsoft.com/microsoft-365/enterprise/migrate-data-to-office-365*.

Identify users and mailboxes to be migrated and migration methods

Adopting Microsoft 365 and Office 365 enables organizations to determine whether all users and mailboxes that exist in the on-premises environment will be required in the cloud-hosted environment.

Which users and mailboxes can be migrated will depend on the organization and its needs. Organizations must also keep in mind that user mailboxes in an Office 365 Enterprise E1 subscription cannot exceed 50 GB in size, and that user mailboxes in an Office 365 Enterprise E3 and E5 subscription cannot exceed 100 GB. (The Office 365 Enterprise E3 and E5 subscriptions allow archive mailboxes of unlimited size, however.) Organizations with users whose mailboxes exceed 100 GB may have to migrate some data to online archive mailboxes as they migrate those users to Exchange Online.

As with migrating data, there may be regulatory and compliance reasons why certain mailboxes in a hybrid deployment must be kept on on-premises Exchange deployments—for example, if the data needs to be kept within specific national boundaries. This can be a challenge when deploying Microsoft 365 in countries that do not have Microsoft data centers.

MORE INFO   MIGRATING EMAIL ACCOUNTS TO OFFICE 365

You can learn more about migrating email accounts at *https://docs.microsoft.com/Exchange/mailbox-migration/mailbox-migration*.

As for what method to use, there are several options:

- Remote move migration
- Staged migration
- Cutover migration
- Minimal hybrid or express migration
- Internet Message Access Protocol (IMAP) migration

These are discussed in the following sections.

Remote move migration

You use remote move migration when you have an Exchange hybrid deployment. In a hybrid deployment, an on-premises Exchange server coexists with Exchange Online. You must use a hybrid deployment and the remote move migration method if you will be migrating more than 2,000 Exchange Server 2010, Exchange Server 2013, Exchange Server 2016, or Exchange Server 2019 mailboxes to Exchange Online.

A hybrid deployment offers the following advantages:

- User accounts are managed through on-premises tools.
- Directory synchronization connects your on-premises Exchange deployment with Exchange Online.
- Users can use single sign-on to access their mailbox, whether the mailbox is hosted on the on-premises Exchange deployment or on Exchange Online.
- Email is routed securely between the on-premises Exchange server and Exchange Online.
- It offers free calendar sharing between users with mailboxes hosted on the on-premises Exchange server and mailboxes hosted on Exchange Online.

Before performing a remote move migration, you must meet the following prerequisites:

- A hybrid deployment must have already been configured between your on-premises Exchange deployment and Exchange Online.
- You must have been assigned the appropriate permissions. For mailbox moves in a hybrid deployment, this means you must have an account that has been assigned the organization management or recipient management role.
- You must have deployed the Mailbox Replication Service Proxy (MRSProxy) on all on-premises Exchange 2013, Exchange 2016, and Exchange 2019 client access servers. The client access role is hosted on mailbox servers in Exchange 2019.

After these prerequisites have been met, you can move mailboxes from your on-premises Exchange deployment to Exchange Online by performing the following steps:

1. Create a migration endpoint. Migration endpoints host connection settings for an on-premises Exchange deployment running the MRSProxy service.

2. Enable the **MRSProxy** service. The MRSProxy service is hosted on on-premises client access servers. You can enable this service from the **Exchange Admin Console** by selecting the client access server, editing the properties of the EWS virtual directory, and ensuring that **MRSProxy Enabled** is selected.

3. Move mailboxes. You can do so by using the Office 365 tab in the **Exchange Admin Center** on the on-premises Exchange deployment by creating a new migration batch or by using Windows PowerShell. When moving mailboxes, you move some—not all—at a time, in groups called *batches*.

4. Remove the completed migration batches. When the migration of a batch is complete, remove the data migrated using the batch from its original location by using Exchange Administration Center or Windows PowerShell.

5. Reenable offline access for Outlook on the Web. If users have been migrated from an on-premises Exchange deployment to Office 365, you must reset the **Offline Access** setting in their browser.

> ***MORE INFO***   **REMOTE MOVE MIGRATION**
>
> You can learn more about remote move migration at *https://docs.microsoft.com/exchange/ hybrid-deployment/move-mailboxes*.

Staged migration

In a staged migration, you migrate mailboxes from your on-premises Exchange Server to Office 365 in batches. You should opt for a staged migration in the following circumstances:

- Your organization has more than 2,000 on-premises mailboxes hosted in Exchange 2007. You cannot use a staged migration to migrate mailboxes from Exchange 2010 or later. (Exchange 2007 is no longer publicly supported by Microsoft as of mid-2017 and requires a specific support agreement.)

- Your organization intends to completely move its messaging infrastructure to Office 365.

- Your available migration period is in the timeframe of several weeks to several months.

- After migration is complete, you will still manage user accounts with on-premises management tools and have account synchronization performed with Azure AD.

- The primary domain name for your on-premises Exchange deployment must be configured as a domain associated with the tenancy in Office 365.

Staged migration involves the following general steps:

1. Create a CSV file that includes a row for every user who has an on-premises mailbox that you want to migrate. This is not every user in the organization, but just those who you will migrate in a particular batch.

2. Create a staged migration batch using **Exchange Admin Center** or **Windows PowerShell**.

3. Trigger the migration batch.

   Exchange Online performs the following steps:

   - Verify that directory synchronization is enabled and functioning. Directory synchronization migrates distribution groups, contacts, and mail-enabled users.

   - Verify that a mail-enabled user exists in Office 365 for every user listed in the batch CSV file.

- Convert the Office 365 mail-enabled user to an Exchange Online mailbox for each user in the migration batch.
- Configure mail forwarding for the on-premises mailbox.
- It sends you a status report informing you of which mailboxes have migrated successfully and which mailboxes have not. Successfully migrated users can start using Exchange Online mailboxes.

4. Convert the mailboxes of successfully migrated on-premises users to mail-enabled users in the on-premises Exchange deployment.

5. Configure a new batch of users to migrate and delete the current migration batch.

6. When all users have been migrated, assign licenses to Office 365 users, configure MX records to point to Exchange Online, and create an autodiscover record that points to Office 365.

7. Decommission the on-premises Exchange deployment.

> **MORE INFO** **STAGED MIGRATION**
>
> You can learn more about staged migrations at *https://docs.microsoft.com/exchange/mailbox-migration/what-to-know-about-a-staged-migration*.

Cutover migration

In a cutover migration, all mailboxes in an on-premises Exchange deployment are migrated to Office 365 in a single migration batch. Cutover migrations migrate global mail contacts as well as distribution groups. Cutover migrations are suitable when:

- You intend for all mailboxes to be hosted in Office 365 when the migration completes.
- You intend to manage user accounts using Office 365 tools.
- You want to perform the migration period in less than a week.
- Your organization has fewer than 2,000 mailboxes.
- Your on-premises messaging solution is Exchange Server 2010 or later.
- The primary domain name used for your on-premises Exchange deployment is configured as a domain associated with the tenancy in Office 365.

You can perform a cutover migration from the Exchange Admin Center or by using Windows PowerShell.

The cutover migration method involves the following general steps, performed by an administrator:

1. Create a series of empty mail-enabled security groups in Office 365.

2. Connect Office 365 to the on-premises Exchange deployment. In other words, create a migration endpoint.

3. Create and start a cutover migration batch using Exchange Admin Center or Windows PowerShell.

   Exchange Online performs the following steps:

   - It queries the address book of the on-premises Exchange deployment to identify mailboxes, distribution groups, and contacts.

   - It provisions new Exchange Online mailboxes.

   - It creates distribution groups and contacts within Exchange Online.

   - It migrates mailbox data—including email messages, contacts, and calendar items— from each on-premises mailbox to the corresponding Exchange Online mailbox.

   - It sends you a report that includes the number of successful and failed migrations. The migration report includes automatically generated passwords for each new Exchange Online mailbox. Users are forced to change their password the first time they sign in to Office 365.

   - Incremental synchronization occurs every 24 hours, updating Exchange Online with any new items created in the on-premises mailboxes.

4. When all migration issues have been resolved, change the MX records to point to Exchange Online.

5. Once mail flow to Exchange Online has been successfully established, delete the cutover migration batch. This terminates synchronization between the on-premises mailboxes and Office 365.

6. Perform post-migration tasks, such as assigning Office 365 licenses, creating an autodiscover DNS record, and decommissioning on-premises Exchange deployments.

MORE INFO **CUTOVER MIGRATION**

You can learn more about cutover migrations at *https://docs.microsoft.com/exchange/mailbox-migration/cutover-migration-to-office-365*.

Minimal hybrid or express migration

Minimal hybrid or express migration is appropriate for organizations that are running Exchange 2010 or later, that have a migration timetable shorter than a few weeks, and that do not intend to have an ongoing directory service configuration. For example, this method would be appropriate for an organization that intends to retire its on-premises AD DS infrastructure after migration is complete.

Performing a minimal hybrid migration involves the following steps:

1. Sign into the Microsoft 365 account using global administrator credentials.

2. In the **Microsoft 365 Admin Center**, add the domain that you use for your on-premises Exchange deployment by configuring a TXT record (or by signing into GoDaddy if your organization uses that registrar) and verify that the TXT record is properly configured.

3. Select **Setup** in the left pane of the **Microsoft 365 Admin Center**. Then select **Data Migration**.

4. On the **Data Migration** page, start the **Exchange Hybrid Configuration Wizard**.

5. Connect to the on-premises Exchange deployment and choose the **Minimal Hybrid Configuration** option.

6. Select **Synchronize Users and Passwords One at a Time**.

7. When prompted, install **Azure AD Connect** with the default options.

   Synchronization will occur once and then be turned off.

8. Configure Office 365 licenses for migrated users.

9. Migrate the user mailbox data.

10. Update the DNS MX records to point away from the on-premises Exchange deployment to Exchange Online.

> *MORE INFO* **MINIMAL HYBRID MIGRATION**
>
> You can learn more about minimal hybrid migrations at *https://docs.microsoft.com/exchange/mailbox-migration/use-minimal-hybrid-to-quickly-migrate*.

IMAP migration

IMAP migration uses the IMAP protocol to move the contents of on-premises user mailboxes to Exchange Online. This type of migration is suitable when the on-premises mail server is not running Exchange Server but is instead running an alternate mail server solution.

IMAP migration is supported for the following on-premises messaging solutions:

- Courier-IMAP
- Cyrus
- Dovecot
- UW-IMAP

IMAP migrations involve the following general steps, performed by a tenant administrator:

1. Create Office 365 user accounts and assign them Exchange Online user licenses to provide the user accounts with Exchange Online mailboxes.

2. Create a CSV file that contains a row for each on-premises user who will be migrated to Exchange Online using IMAP and includes each user's password. Microsoft recommends that you reset user passwords for on-premises IMAP mailbox users to simplify this process.

3. Create and trigger an IMAP migration batch from the Migration dashboard shown in Figure 1-45. (To access this dashboard, select **Setup** in the left pane of the **Microsoft 365 Admin Center** and then select **Data Migration**.) You can also do this through Windows PowerShell.

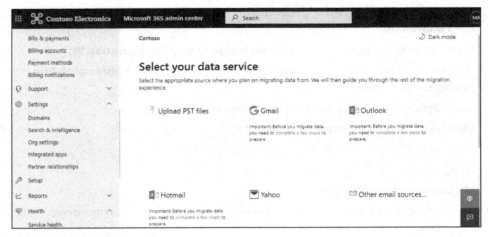

FIGURE 1-45 Select data service

When the migration batch is initiated, the following actions occur:

- Exchange Online creates a migration request for each user in the CSV file. Each migration request includes the credentials for the user in the on-premises IMAP messaging system.

- Messages from each user's IMAP mailbox are copied to the corresponding Exchange Online mailbox until all data is migrated.

- Exchange Online sends an email to the administrator informing them of the status of the migration. This email contains statistics about the number of mailboxes successfully migrated, how many could not be migrated, and any error reports.

- Exchange Online and the IMAP messaging system are synchronized every 24 hours to move any new messages from the on-premises environment to Exchange Online.

4. When all migration issues have been resolved, update MX records to point to Exchange Online.

5. When mail is flowing to Exchange Online, delete the migration batches.

> **MORE INFO   IMAP MIGRATION**
>
> You can learn more about IMAP migration at *https://docs.microsoft.com/exchange/mailbox-migration/migrating-imap-mailboxes/migrating-imap-mailboxes*.

Migration comparison

Table 1-8 lists the differences between the various methods you can use to migrate from an on-premises messaging environment to Exchange Online.

TABLE 1-8 Migration type comparison

On-premises Messaging Environment	Number of Mailboxes	Will User Accounts Be Managed On-Premises?	Migration Method
Exchange 2010 to Exchange 2019	Less than 2,000	No	Cutover migration
Exchange 2010	Less than 2,000	No	Staged migration
Exchange 2010	More than 2,000	Yes	Staged migration or remote move migration in hybrid deployment
Exchange 2010 or Exchange 2019	More than 2,000	Yes	Remote move migration in hybrid deployment
Non-Exchange on-premises messaging system	No maximum	Yes	IMAP migration

> **MORE INFO   MAILBOX MIGRATION**
>
> You can learn more about mailbox migration at *https://docs.microsoft.com/exchange/ mailbox-migration/decide-on-a-migration-path*.

Plan migration of on-premises users and groups

Most organizations already have an on-premises identity solution that hosts user and groups accounts: AD DS. When planning the migration of on-premises users and groups, you must grasp the following concepts:

- User categories
- Groups
- When bulk import is appropriate

It is also important to recognize that migration is different from hybrid coexistence. In a hybrid coexistence scenario, your organization retains its on-premises AD environment. In a migration scenario, your organization moves from an on-premises AD environment to Azure AD host accounts, with the on-premises AD environment decommissioned.

> **NOTE**   It is possible to use Azure AD Connect to synchronize accounts to Azure AD and then decommission your on-premises environment. This technique, and other information about Azure AD Connect and hybrid coexistence, is covered in Chapter 2.

Understand user categories

Not every user account in your organization's on-premises AD instance is the same. Although the vast majority of on-premises user accounts are used to sign on to workstations and access resources, a small number of accounts are used for different purposes, the most straightforward example being service accounts. Before migrating accounts, you should determine the following:

- **Is the user account still active?** Unless your organization has an effective user deprovisioning strategy, there will likely be accounts in AD that are associated with people who are no longer employed by your organization. There is no reason to migrate inactive user accounts from an on-premises AD environment to Microsoft 365.

- **Should the account be migrated to Microsoft 365?** Some user accounts exist for specific purposes—for example, to act as service accounts or as administrative accounts for specific services or workloads that will not be migrated to Microsoft 365. Service accounts and accounts used for specific on-premises workloads are unlikely to be required once your organization migrates to Microsoft 365.

Use the bulk import process

If your organization is planning to completely migrate to Azure AD as the primary identity provider and to decommission AD, you might choose to perform a bulk import of user accounts rather than attempt manual creation. If the organization that you are migrating has only a small number of users, it may be simpler to manually create those users using the Microsoft 365 administration tools. But if you must migrate a larger number, for which the manual creation process would be both laborious and tedious, you might instead choose to perform a bulk import.

The bulk import process enables you to import a list of users from a specially formatted CSV file into Microsoft 365. This CSV file must have the following fields in the first row:

- User Name
- First Name
- Last Name
- Display Name
- Job Title
- Department
- Office Number
- Office Phone
- Mobile Phone
- Fax
- Address
- City
- State or Province

- ZIP or Postal Code
- Country or Region

Each of these fields must be on the first line and each must be separated by a comma. Both a sample and a blank CSV file can be downloaded from the Bulk Add Users page.

After you have populated the CSV file with the account information you want to import, complete this operation by performing the following steps:

1. In the left pane of the **Microsoft 365 admin center**, under **Users**, select **Active Users**.

2. Select **Add Multiple Users**.

3. On the **Select a CSV File** page, shown in Figure 1-46, select the specially formatted file that has the user account information and select **Next**.

FIGURE 1-46 Select a CSV file

4. On the **Import Multiple Users** page, specify whether the users are allowed to sign in and access services, as well as the user location. Then select **Next**.

The Results page displays a list of users created and temporary passwords assigned.

Use soft delete

Some accounts that you migrate to Microsoft 365 may not be necessary. Similarly, there may be user accounts created during the trial or pilot Microsoft 365 deployment that are no longer appropriate once existing user accounts are migrated to Office 365. You can delete these accounts.

There are several ways to delete Microsoft 365 user accounts. Whether the user account is permanently deleted, termed a *hard delete*, or is moved to the Azure AD Recycle Bin, termed a *soft delete*, depends on the method used to delete the account.

You can use the following methods to delete a Microsoft 365 user account:

- **From the Microsoft 365 Admin Center** Under Users in the left pane of the Microsoft 365 Admin Center, select Active Users. Then select the user you want to delete, and select Delete User in the list of tasks associated with that user.
- **Using the `Remove-MsolUser` cmdlet** This is located in the Azure AD module for Windows PowerShell.
- **From the Exchange Admin Center** This is located in Exchange Online.
- **From the on-premises AD DS instance** If directory synchronization is configured, you can delete the user account when you remove it from the AD DS instance.

You can view a list of soft deleted users in the Deleted Users page in Microsoft 365 Admin Center. To do so, select Users in the left pane, and then select Deleted Users. (See Figure 1-47.) Soft-deleted users remain visible for 30 days and can be recovered during this period. After this period expires, the user account is permanently deleted and cannot be recovered.

FIGURE 1-47 List of deleted Microsoft 365 users

To recover a soft-deleted user (assuming you are within the 30-day timeframe), follow these steps:

1. Select the user account in the **Deleted Users** page in the M**icrosoft 365 admin center**.
2. Select **Restore**.

   When you restore an account, you will be asked whether to autogenerate a new password for the user or assign a password yourself, and whether you want to have the user change their password when they sign on. (See Figure 1-48.)

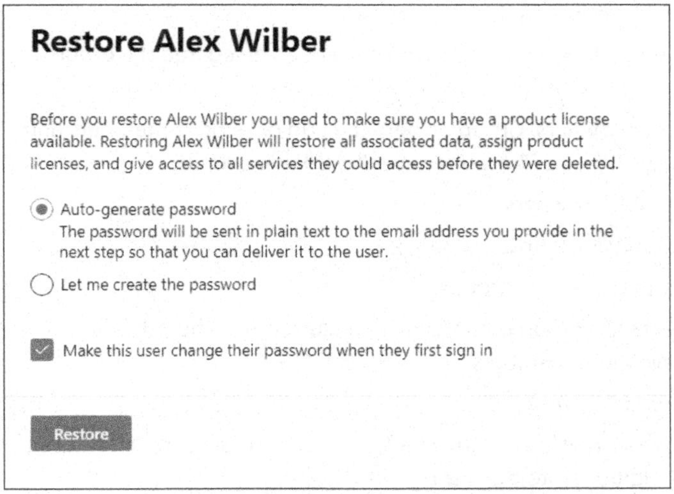

Restore Alex Wilber

Before you restore Alex Wilber you need to make sure you have a product license available. Restoring Alex Wilber will restore all associated data, assign product licenses, and give access to all services they could access before they were deleted.

◉ Auto-generate password
   The password will be sent in plain text to the email address you provide in the next step so that you can deliver it to the user.

○ Let me create the password

☑ Make this user change their password when they first sign in

`Restore`

FIGURE 1-48 Restoring a soft-deleted user account

3. Choose the desired option and select **Restore**.

> **MORE INFO   DELETING USER ACCOUNTS IN MICROSOFT 365**
>
> You can learn more about deleting Microsoft 365 user accounts at *https://docs.microsoft.com/azure/active-directory/active-directory-users-delete-user-azure-portal*.

Migrate groups to Microsoft 365

On-premises groups come in a variety of types and scopes. For the purposes of migrating to Microsoft 365, group scope—which can be domain local, domain global, or universal—isn't relevant. This is because if you have chosen to migrate users to Azure AD and decommission your organization's on-premises directory, you're unlikely to be concerned whether a group is visible in other domains in an AD forest, because you intend to retire that particular security construct.

Office 365 groups enable you to set up a collection of resources that a set of users can share. Resources might include a shared calendar, SharePoint Online document library, or shared Exchange Online mailbox.

Groups can be configured as public or private. Content in a public group is visible to anyone who has an account in the tenancy. Content in a private group is visible only to members of that group.

There are three methods through which Office 365 groups can be provisioned:

- **Open**   The default method of provisioning Office 365 groups. This enables Microsoft 365 users to create their own groups as needed.

- **IT-led**   Users can request a group from IT.
- **Controlled**   Group creation is limited to users who have been delegated the group creation role.

Each group can have one or more owners. Group owners can add or remove members and perform basic group curation tasks. Office 365 groups have the following limits:

- A group can have as many as 100 owners.
- A user can create as many as 250 groups.
- A tenancy can have as many as 500,000 groups.
- One thousand users can access a group conversation concurrently, although it is possible for a group to have more members.
- A user can be a member of 1,000 groups.
- A group can store as many as 1 TB of data with an additional 10 GB per subscribed user. It is possible to purchase additional storage for a group.
- A group mailbox has a size limit of 50 GB.

> **MORE INFO   UNDERSTANDING MICROSOFT 365 GROUPS**
>
> You can learn more about Microsoft 365 groups at *https://support.office.com/article/learn-about-office-365-groups-b565caa1-5c40-40ef-9915-60fdb2d97fa2*.

Import PST files

Importing PST files to Office 365 mailboxes enables you to move your organization's existing email messages to Exchange Online. Using the Intelligent Import feature, you can specify which items stored in PST files will be imported into Exchange Online. Importing PST files also allows you to ensure that your organization can meet compliance obligations, as messages will be available for discovery searches—something that is more challenging when email is stored on each person's individual computer in a separate PST file. Finally, importing PST files ensures that users have access to their existing messages no matter which device they use to interact with Exchange. If messages are stored in an offline PST file, and the user doesn't have access to the computer that hosts that PST file, they will not have access to those messages. PST files from Outlook 2007 and later can be imported to Exchange Online.

You import PST files into Office 365 using the network upload method. You can do this by directly uploading the files or by shipping an encrypted hard drive to Microsoft and having them import the data directly. When you ship an encrypted hard drive to Microsoft, Microsoft uploads the data to Azure within 10 days of receiving it before returning the physical device to you.

To import PST files, perform the following steps:

1. In **Exchange Online**, ensure that the organization management group is assigned the mailbox import export role.

2. On the **Import** page in the **Security & Compliance Center**, available under **Data Compliance**, create a shared access signature (SAS) key, also known as the SAS URL.

   This key provides the necessary permission and location to upload PST files to an Azure storage location, which will be in the same region as your Microsoft 365 organization.

3. Download and install the PST import tools, including the AzCopy tool.

4. Use AzCopy with the SAS URL to upload one or more PST files to Azure.

5. Use **Azure Storage Explorer** to review the list of PST files that have been successfully transferred to Office 365.

6. Create a mapping file that maps uploaded PST files to Office 365 mailboxes. This file must be in CSV format.

7. On the **Import** page of the **Security & Compliance Center**, create a PST import job.

   When you create this job, you specify the mapping file. You will be given the opportunity to configure a filter to control which data is actually imported into mailboxes.

8. Run the job to import the data into the appropriate Office 365 mailboxes.

The user account used to create the import jobs in the Office 365 import service must be assigned the mailbox import export role in Exchange Online. You can add this role to the organization management role group. Alternatively, you can create a new role group, assign this role, and then add user accounts to the group.

In addition to having this role, the account used to perform this task must be assigned the mail recipients role in Exchange Online—available to the organization management and recipient management role groups—or be a global administrator for the Microsoft 365 deployment.

PST files uploaded using the network upload method are stored in an Azure Blob storage container named *ingestiondata*. The PST files will remain in this blob storage for 30 days after the most recent import job has been created in the Security & Compliance Center. If you upload PST files using the network upload method but do not create an import job within 30 days, the PST files will be deleted.

PST import has the following additional caveats and characteristics:

- PST import occurs at approximately 24 GB per day, but jobs run in parallel. For example, importing five 24 GB PST files will take roughly the same amount of time as importing twenty 24 GB PST files.

- Multiple PST files can be imported to the same mailbox simultaneously.

- If a PST file stores any mailbox items that exceed 150 MB in size, those individual large items will not be imported into the Office 365 mailbox. Items smaller than 150 MB in size will still be imported, even though the larger items are skipped.

- Original message metadata isn't modified during the import process.

- Import is not supported if a PST file has more than 300 levels of nested folders.

- PST files can be imported into online archive mailboxes.

- PST files cannot be imported into Exchange Online public folders.

> **EXAM TIP**
>
> Remember the process that is used to import PST files into Exchange Online mailboxes.

Thought experiment

In this thought experiment, you will demonstrate your skills and knowledge of the topics covered in this chapter. You can find the answers to this thought experiment in the next section.

You have been asked to provide some advice to Fabrikam, a small manufacturing business that has migrated to Microsoft 365. Fabrikam needs your advice because the person responsible for its IT department recently left the company. Upon their departure, this person handed over the credentials of all their Microsoft 365 accounts to the CEO.

The CEO also reports to you that there have been license problems. The company initially purchased a 50-license subscription. Since then, 10 new users have been employed to replace 10 people who left the company over the last few months. The employees who departed still have Microsoft 365 accounts.

Fabrikam has signed up for a Microsoft 365 subscription and is currently using the tenant name Fabrikam.onmicrosoft.com. Fabrikam wants to assign its custom domain, Fabrikam.com, to Microsoft 365 and to have Microsoft DNS servers host this zone. With this information in mind, answer the following questions:

1. What kind of DNS record must be added to confirm ownership of the Fabrikam.com DNS zone?

2. Which DNS records must be modified to have Microsoft DNS servers host the Fabrikam.com DNS zone?

3. Describe the nature of at least one user account that will have global administrator rights for Fabrikam's Office 365 subscription.

4. What methods can be used to resolve the license conflicts?

Thought experiment answers

This section contains the answers to the thought experiment and explains why each answer is correct.

1. A TXT record must be added to confirm ownership of the Fabrikam.com DNS zone.

2. The NS records for the zone must be modified to allow Microsoft to host the Fabrikam.com DNS zone.

3. The first user account created for a subscription will be assigned global administrator privileges. This will be the user account of the IT staff member who recently left and who set up Microsoft 365.

4. The license conflict can be resolved by either manually removing licenses from the 10 users who have left the organization or by deleting their user accounts.

Chapter summary

- When you create a Microsoft 365 subscription, the subscription tenancy is automatically assigned a custom onmicrosoft.com domain.

- No two organizations can share the same tenant name.

- The tenant name chosen at setup remains with the subscription over the course of the subscription's existence.

- You can assign a domain name that you own to the tenant so that you don't have to use the onmicrosoft.com tenant name.

- To use a domain with Microsoft 365, the DNS servers used as name servers for the domain must support CNAME, SPF/TXT, SRV, and MX records.

- You can confirm ownership of a domain by configuring special TXT or MX records.

- Setting the default domain configures which domain suffix will automatically be used with Microsoft 365 user accounts.

- Changing the primary email address also changes the user name.

- You can perform a bulk email address update using PowerShell.

- Additional email addresses allow mailboxes to receive messages from more than a single address and can use any domain name associated with the organization's Microsoft 365 tenancy.

- A Microsoft 365 endpoint is a URL or IP address that hosts a specific Microsoft 365 or Office 365 service.

- Microsoft places each Microsoft 365 and Office 365 endpoint into one of three categories: optimize, allow, and default. Optimize requires minimum disruptions caused by latency and availability. Allow endpoints are less problematic, and default endpoints do not require optimization.

- Privileged access management allows you to configure policies that apply just-in-time administrative principles to sensitive administrative roles.

- Cloud authentication occurs against Azure AD. Use it with a password hash with a single sign-on and pass-through authentication with single sign-on.

- Federated authentication can occur using AD FS or a third-party authentication provider.

- Mail reports allow you to view how Office 365 mailboxes are used.

- Usage reports allow you to view information about browsers, operating systems, and license consumption.
- Skype for Business reports allow you to see how Skype for Business is being used in the organization.
- SharePoint reports allow you to see how SharePoint is being used with the Office 365 subscription.
- Data loss prevention (DLP) reports allow you to view how DLP rules and policies are being applied to message traffic.
- The Service Health dashboard is available from the Microsoft 365 Admin Center, allowing you to determine the status of the various elements of Microsoft 365, including fault history and planned maintenance.
- Users assigned the global administrator role have access to all administrative features.
- Users assigned the billing administrator role can make purchases, manage subscriptions, manage support tickets, and monitor service health.
- Users assigned the helpdesk (password) administrator role can reset the passwords of most Office 365 user accounts (except those assigned the global administrator, service administrator, or billing roles).
- Users assigned the service administrator role can manage service requests and monitor service health.
- You can assign and remove licenses by editing an Office 365 user's properties.
- Deleting a user removes all licenses assigned to that user.
- Pilot users should be a representative sample of your organization.
- You can use the SharePoint Migration Tool to migrate on-premises SharePoint document libraries, lists, and regular file shares to SharePoint Online.
- The OneDrive client allows you to drag and drop files on a client computer and have those files sync either with OneDrive for Business or SharePoint Online.
- You can use the bulk import method to import a CSV file of user identities into Azure AD.

CHAPTER 2

Manage user identity and roles

A key aspect of deploying Microsoft 365 is ensuring that user identity is configured properly. When this is done, users can seamlessly access resources in the on-premises environment as well as in the Microsoft 365 environment. If it is not done correctly, users must juggle different accounts, depending on whether the accessible resources are hosted locally or in the cloud.

In this chapter, you will learn about designing an identity strategy, how to plan identity synchronization with Azure AD Connect, how to manage that synchronization, how to manage Azure AD identities, and how to manage Azure AD user roles.

Skills in this chapter:

- Skill 2.1: Design identity strategy
- Skill 2.2: Plan identity synchronization by using Azure AD Connect
- Skill 2.3: Manage identity synchronization by using Azure Active Directory
- Skill 2.4: Manage Azure AD identities
- Skill 2.5: Manage user roles

Skill 2.1: Design identity strategy

This skill deals with designing a strategy related to on-premises and cloud-based identity. To master this skill, you'll need to understand how to determine your organization's requirements when it comes to synchronization, what an appropriate identity-management solution is, and what type of authentication solution is appropriate for your environment.

> **This section covers the following topics:**
> - Evaluate requirements and solution for synchronization
> - Evaluate requirements and solution for identity management
> - Evaluate requirements and solution for authentication

Evaluate requirements and solution for synchronization

Synchronization is the process of replicating on-premises identities, such as users and groups, to the cloud. Synchronization is necessary only when an on-premises identity provider is present. In some synchronization models, every on-premises identity is replicated to the cloud. In other models, only a subset of the on-premises identities is replicated.

Another consideration in evaluating synchronization requirements is determining what information about a user's identity needs to be synchronized to the cloud. Depending on the model chosen, some or all of the properties of those on-premises identities can be replicated. For example, some organizations store sensitive private data about employees within Active Directory. Only replicating what is necessary is especially important given the increasing regulation of data involving personal information.

Should an organization choose, it is possible to perform a complete replication of every aspect of an Active Directory object to the cloud. For example, an organization can deploy a domain controller, SharePoint Farm, System Center, and Exchange Server in Azure infrastructure-as-a-service (IaaS) virtual machines (VMs). You can have those VMs connected via VPN or an ExpressRoute connection to an on-premises Active Directory instance. In this scenario, the Azure IaaS VMs would essentially function as an expensive branch office site running in the Azure cloud.

When evaluating requirements and a solution for synchronization, consider the following questions:

- Which identities need to be replicated to the cloud?
- How often do those identities need to be replicated to the cloud?
- What properties of those identities need to be replicated to the cloud?

Which identities to replicate?

Deployment of Microsoft 365 gives organizations an ability to assess their existing identity needs. If an organization has been using Active Directory for a long time, it's likely that objects don't need to be replicated to the cloud and probably don't need to be in the on-premises Active Directory instance. It's a good idea, before implementing any Microsoft 365 replication scheme, to do a thorough audit of all the objects present within the on-premises directory and to clean out those that are no longer required.

Another issue to address is whether every on-premises identity needs to be present in Azure Active Directory. Many organizations take a phased approach to the introduction of Microsoft 365, migrating small groups of users to the service at a time rather than every user in the organization all at once. Users who are only present in the on-premises directory service won't need to have Microsoft 365 licenses assigned to them.

There are also special account types that are commonly present in an on-premises Active Directory instance that do not need to be, or simply cannot be, replicated to Azure Active Directory. For example, there is no need to replicate service accounts or accounts that are used for specific administrative purposes for on-premises resources, such as the management of an on-premises SQL Server database server or other workload.

Another challenge to consider is that many on-premises environments are more compli-cated than a single Active Directory domain. Some organizations have multidomain Active Directory forests. In addition, since it is a recommended Microsoft secure administrative prac-tice, an increasing number of large organizations have multiforest deployments—for example, an Enhanced Security Administrative Environment (ESAE) forest to store privileged accounts for the production forest.

User accounts are not the only identity that an organization may want to replicate to the cloud. It may be necessary to replicate some groups to the cloud because these groups may be useful in mediating access to Microsoft 365 workloads. For example, if your organization already has a local security group that is used to collect together members of the accounting team, you may want that group also present as a method of mediating access to resources and workloads within Microsoft 365.

How often to replicate?

When evaluating requirements and a solution for synchronization, you need to answer several important questions. For example, how often do the properties of an on-premises identity change and how soon must those changes be present within Azure Active Directory?

You don't want a user who changes his or her password to have to wait 24 hours before that new password can be used against cloud identities. Similarly, if you deprovision a user account because a person's employment with the organization has terminated, you'll want that action to be reflected in limiting access to Microsoft 365 workloads, rather than the user account hav-ing continued access for some time after the user's on-premises identity has been disabled.

Although there can be bandwidth considerations around identity synchronization, the majority of such traffic is going to be the replication of changes, also known as *delta*, rather than constant replications of the entire identity database. The amount of bandwidth consumed by delta identity synchronization traffic is often insignificant compared to the bandwidth con-sumed by other Microsoft 365 workloads and services.

Which properties to replicate?

Active Directory has been present at some organizations for almost two decades. One of the original selling points of Active Directory was that it could store far more information than just user names and passwords. Because of this, many organizations use Active Directory to store a substantive amount of information about personnel, including telephone numbers, the user's position within the organization, and the branch office where the user works.

When considering a synchronization solution, determine which on-premises Active Direc-tory attribute information needs to be replicated to Azure Active Directory. For example, you may have an application running in Azure that needs access to the Job Title, Department, Company, and Manager attributes, as shown in Figure 2-1.

FIGURE 2-1 Which attributes to replicate

Evaluate requirements and solutions for identity management

Evaluating the requirements and solutions for identity management first involves determining what your organization's source of authority is. The source of authority is the directory service that functions as the primary location for the creation and management of user and group accounts. You can choose between having an on-premises Active Directory instance function as a source of authority, or you can have Azure Active Directory function as the source of authority.

Even though Azure Active Directory is present in a hybrid deployment, the source of authority will be the on-premises Azure AD instance. Hybrid deployment accounts are used for authentication and authorization purposes with existing on-premises resources as well as Microsoft 365 workloads.

Source of authority is a very important concept when it comes to creating users and groups in an environment where Azure AD Connect is configured to synchronize an on-premises Active Directory with the Azure Active Directory instance that supports the Microsoft 365 tenancy. When you create a user or group in the on-premises Active Directory instance, the on-premises Active Directory instance retains authority over that object. Objects created within the on-premises Active Directory instance that are within the filtering scope of objects synchronized via Azure AD Connect will replicate to the Azure Active Directory instance that supports the Microsoft 365 tenancy.

Newly created on-premises user and group objects will only be present within the Azure Active Directory instance that supports the Microsoft 365 tenancy after synchronization has occurred. You can force synchronization to occur using the Azure AD Connect Synchronization Service Manager tool.

Evaluate requirements and solution for authentication

When evaluating authentication requirements, determine whether your organization wants to still rely on the traditional combination of user name and password or move toward more sophisticated and secure authentication techniques, such as multifactor authentication. When making this determination, many organizations will decide that more secure technologies are appropriate for sensitive accounts, such as those used for administrative tasks, and that the traditional method of user name and password will be sufficient for the majority of standard users.

Microsoft and Office 365 support a technology known as *modern authentication*. Modern authentication provides a more secure authentication and authorization method than traditional authentication methods. Modern authentication can be used with Microsoft 365 hybrid deployments that include Exchange Online and Teams. All Office and Microsoft 365 tenancies created after August 2017 that include Exchange Online have modern authentication enabled by default. Modern authentication includes a combination of the following authentication and authorization methods, as well as secure access policies:

- **Authentication methods**   Multifactor authentication, Client Certificate Authentication, and Active Directory Authentication Library (ADAL)
- **Authorization methods**   Microsoft's implementation of Open Authorization (OAuth)
- **Conditional access policies**   Mobile application management (MAM) and Azure Active Directory Conditional Access

***MORE INFO* HYBRID MODERN AUTHENTICATION**

You can learn more about hybrid modern authentication at the following address: https://docs.microsoft.com/en-us/microsoft-365/enterprise/hybrid-modern-auth-overview.

EXAM TIP

Remember the Azure AD Connect prerequisites.

Skill 2.2: Plan identity synchronization by using Azure AD Connect

This skill section deals with planning the implementation of identity synchronization using Azure AD Connect as the synchronization solution. To master this skill, you'll need to draw on some of the information you learned about in the previous skill as well as how to implement an appropriate Azure AD Connect sign-on option.

> **This section covers the following topics:**
> - Design directory synchronization
> - Implement directory synchronization with directory services, Federation services, and Azure endpoints by using Azure AD Connect

Design directory synchronization

Azure AD Connect is designed to streamline the process of configuring connections between on-premises deployment and an Azure AD instance. The Azure Active Directory Connect tool is designed to make the process of configuring synchronization between an on-premises Active Directory deployment and Azure Active Directory as frictionless as possible.

Azure Active Directory Connect can automatically configure and install simple password synchronization or Federation/single sign-on, depending on your organizational needs. When you choose the Federation with AD FS option, Active Directory Federation Services is installed and configured, as well as a web application proxy server to facilitate communication between the on-premises AD FS deployment and Microsoft Azure Active Directory.

The Azure Active Directory Connect tool supports the following optional features, as shown in Figure 2-2:

- **Exchange hybrid deployment** This option is suitable for organizations that have an Office 365 deployment in which there are mailboxes hosted both on-premises and in the cloud.

- **Exchange Mail Public Folders** This feature allows organizations to synchronize mail-enabled public folder objects from an on-premises Active Directory environment to Microsoft 365.

- **Azure AD app and attribute filtering** Selecting this option gives you the ability to be more selective about which attributes are synchronized between the on-premises environment and Azure AD.

- **Password synchronization** This synchronizes a hash of the user's on-premises password with Azure AD. When the user authenticates to Azure AD, the submitted password is hashed using the same process, and if the hashes match, the user is authenticated.

Each time the user updates their password on-premises, the updated password hash synchronizes to Azure AD.

- **Password writeback** Password writeback allows users to change their passwords in the cloud and have the changed password written back to the on-premises Active Directory instance.
- **Group writeback** With this option, changes made to groups in Azure AD are written back to the on-premises AD instance.
- **Device writeback** Here, information about devices registered by the user in Azure AD is written back to the on-premises AD instance.
- **Directory extension attribute sync** This option allows you to extend the Azure AD schema based on extensions made to your organization's on-premises Active Directory instance.

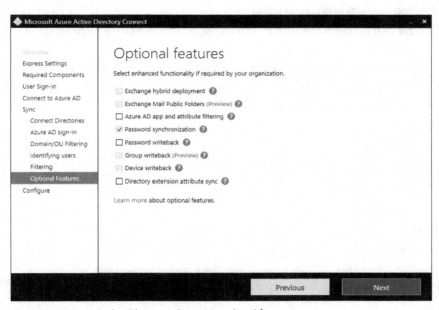

FIGURE 2-2 Azure Active Directory Connect optional features

> *MORE INFO* **AZURE ACTIVE DIRECTORY CONNECT**
>
> You can learn more about Azure Active Directory Connect at https://docs.microsoft.com/en-us/azure/active-directory/hybrid/whatis-hybrid-identity.

Clean up existing Active Directory objects

Before you deploy Azure AD Connect, it is prudent to ensure that your on-premises Active Directory environment is healthy. You should also have an excellent understanding of the current state of the Active Directory environment. This should include performing an audit to determine the following:

- Do any Active Directory objects use invalid characters?
- Do any Active Directory objects have incorrect Universal Principal Names (UPNs)?
- What are the current domain and forest functional levels?
- Are any schema extensions or custom attributes in use?

Before deploying Azure AD Connect, you should also ensure that you have performed the following tasks:

- Remove any duplicate proxyAddress attributes.
- Remove any duplicate userPrincipalName attributes.
- Ensure that blank or invalid userPrincipalName attribute settings have been altered so that the setting contains only a valid UPN.
- Ensure that for user accounts the cn and samAccountName attributes have been assigned values.
- Ensure that for group accounts, the member, alias, and displayName (for groups with a valid mail or proxyAddress attribute) are populated.
- Ensure that the following attributes do not contain invalid characters:
  - sn
  - samAccountName
  - givenName
  - displayName
  - mail
  - proxyAddress
  - mailNickName

UPNs that are used with Office 365 can only contain the following characters:

- Letters
- Numbers
- Periods
- Dashes
- Underscores

Rather than having to perform this operation manually, Microsoft provides some tools that allow you to automatically remediate problems that might exist with attributes before deploying Azure AD Connect.

IdFix

The IdFix tool, which you can download from Microsoft's website, allows you to scan an Active Directory instance to determine if any user accounts, group accounts, or contacts have problems that will cause them not to synchronize between the on-premises instance of Active Directory and the Microsoft 365 instance of Azure Active Directory. IdFix can also perform repairs on objects that would otherwise be unable to sync. IdFix runs with the security context of the currently signed-on user. This means that if you want to use IdFix to repair objects in the forest that have problems, the security account you use to run IdFix must have permissions to modify those objects. The IdFix tool is shown in Figure 2-3, displaying an account detected with an incorrectly configured userPrincipalName attribute.

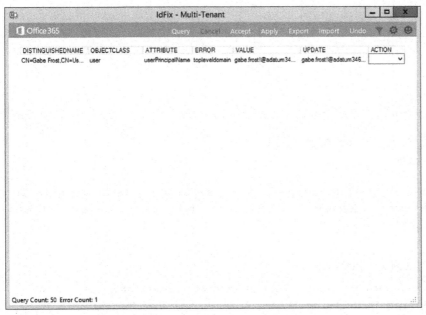

FIGURE 2-3 IdFix finds a user with a problematic UPN.

> **MORE INFO   IDFIX**
>
> You can download IdFix at the following address: *https://microsoft.github.io/idfix/*.

ADModify.NET

ADmodify.NET is a tool that allows you to make changes to specific attributes for multiple objects. If you are using ADSIEdit or the Advanced mode of the Active Directory Users and Computers console, you are able to modify the attribute of only one object at a time. For example, Figure 2-4 shows ADModify.NET used to modify the format of the userPrincipalName attribute for a number of user accounts so that it conforms to a specific format.

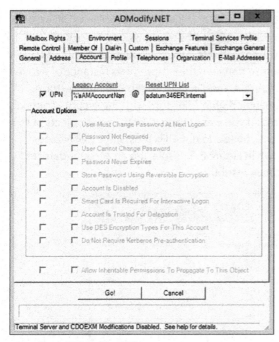

FIGURE 2-4 ADModify.NET

You can also use ADModify.NET to perform other system administration tasks, such as configuring a large number of accounts so that users have to change their password at next logon or to disable multiple accounts.

> **MORE INFO   ADMODIFY.NET**
>
> You can learn more about ADModify.NET at *https://archive.codeplex.com/?p=admodify*. At present ADModify.NET is located on CodePlex. At some point in the future, perhaps by the time you are reading this, it will be hosted on Github.

Use UPN suffixes and nonroutable domains

Before performing synchronization between an on-premises Active Directory environment and an Azure Active Directory instance used to support a Microsoft 365 tenancy, you must ensure that all user account objects in the on-premises Active Directory environment are configured with a value for the UPN suffix that can function for both the on-premises environment and Microsoft 365.

This is not a problem when an organization's internal Active Directory domain suffix is a publicly routable domain. For example, a domain name such as contoso.com or adatum.com that is resolvable by public DNS servers will suffice. Things become more complicated when the organization's internal Active Directory domain suffix is not publicly routable. For example, Figure 2-5 shows the adatum346ER.internal nonroutable domain.

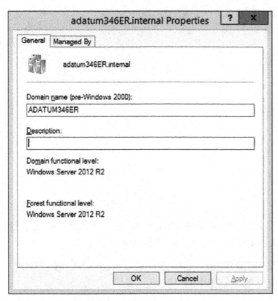

FIGURE 2-5 Nonroutable domain

If a domain is nonroutable, the default routing domain, such as adatum346ER.onmicrosoft.com, should be used for the Microsoft 365 UPN suffix. This requires modifying the UPN suffix of accounts stored in the on-premises Active Directory instance. Modification of the UPN after initial synchronization has occurred is not supported. So, you need to ensure that on-premises Active Directory UPNs are properly configured before performing initial synchronization using Azure AD Connect.

Perform the following steps to add a UPN suffix to the on-premises Active Directory in the event that the Active Directory domain uses a nonroutable namespace:

1. Open the **Active Directory Domains and Trust** console and select **Active Directory Domains and Trusts**.
2. On the **Action** menu, select **Properties**.
3. On the **UPN Suffixes** tab, enter the UPN suffix to be used with Microsoft 365. Figure 2-6 shows the UPN suffix of epistemicus.com.

FIGURE 2-6 Routable domain

4. Once the UPN suffix has been added in Active Directory Domains and Trusts, you assign the UPN suffix to user accounts. You can do this in one of three ways:

- Manually, as shown in Figure 2-7, by using the **Account** tab of the user's **Properties** dialog box in **Active Directory Users and Computers**.

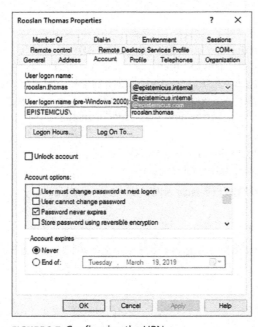

FIGURE 2-7 Configuring the UPN

- Using tools like ADModify.NET to reset the UPNs of multiple accounts, as shown in Figure 2-8.

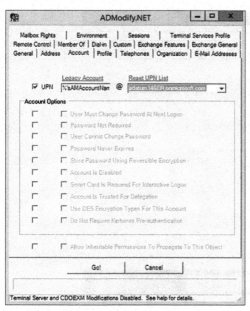

FIGURE 2-8 ADModify.NET

- Using Microsoft PowerShell scripts to reset the UPNs of multiple user accounts. For example, the following script resets UPN suffixes of all user accounts in the epistemicus.internal domain to epistemicus.onmicrosoft.com:

```
Get-ADUser -Filter {UserPrincipalName -like "*@epistemicus.internal"}
-SearchBase

"DC=epistemicus,DC=internal" |

ForEach-Object {

$UPN =

$_.UserPrincipalName.Replace("epistemicus.internal","epistemicus.
onmicrosoft.com")

Set-ADUser $_ -UserPrincipalName $UPN

}
```

Implement directory synchronization with directory services, Federation services, and Azure endpoints by using Azure AD Connect

Azure AD Connect supports a variety of user sign-in options, which are related to the method you use to synchronize directory information from Active Directory Domain Services to Azure AD. You configure which sign-in option you will use when setting up Azure AD Connect, as shown in

Figure 2-9. The default method, password sync, is appropriate for the majority of organizations that will use Azure AD Connect to synchronize identities to the cloud.

FIGURE 2-9 User sign-in

Password synchronization

Hashes of on-premises Active Directory user passwords synchronize to Azure AD, and changed passwords immediately synchronize to Azure AD. Actual passwords are never sent to Azure AD and are not stored in Azure AD. This allows for single sign-on for users of computers that are joined to an Active Directory domain that synchronizes to Azure AD. Password synchronization also allows you to enable password writeback for self-service password reset functionality through Azure AD.

Pass-through authentication

When authenticating to Azure AD, the user's password is validated against an on-premises Active Directory domain controller. Passwords and password hashes are not present in Azure AD. Pass-through authentication allows for on-premises password policies to apply. Pass-through authentication requires that Azure AD Connect have an agent on a computer joined to the domain that hosts the Active Directory instance that contains the relevant user accounts. Pass-through authentication also allows single sign-on for users of domain-joined machines.

With pass-through authentication, the user's password is validated against the on-premises Active Directory controller. The password doesn't need to be present in Azure AD in any form. This allows for on-premises policies, such as sign-in hour restrictions, to be evaluated during authentication to cloud services.

Pass-through authentication uses a simple agent on a Windows Server 2012 R2, Windows Server 2016, Windows Server 2019, or Windows Server 2022 domain-joined machine in the on-premises environment. This agent listens for password-validation requests. It doesn't require any inbound ports to be open to the internet.

You can also enable single sign-on for users on domain-joined machines that are on the corporate network. With single sign-on, enabled users only need to enter a user name to help them securely access cloud resources.

Active Directory Federation

Active Directory Federation allows users to authenticate to Azure AD resources using on-premises credentials. It also requires the deployment of an Active Directory Federation Services infrastructure. This is the most complicated identity synchronization configuration for Microsoft 365 and is only likely to be implemented in environments with complicated identity configurations.

> *MORE INFO* **AZURE AD CONNECT SIGN-IN OPTIONS**
>
> To learn more about sign-in options, consult the following article: *https://docs.microsoft.com/ en-us/azure/active-directory/connect/active-directory-aadconnect-user-signin*.

Azure Endpoints

The Azure AD Connect endpoint V2 API provides performance improvements over the original endpoint API. The V2 API supports syncing groups with more than 250,000 members. If you want to use the V2 API endpoint, Azure AD Connect must be upgraded to or installed as version 1.5.30.0 or later.

If your organization has deployed an earlier version of Azure AD Connect, the V1 API might still be in use. To switch to the V2 API, perform the following steps:

1. On the server on which Azure AD Connect is installed, open the **PowerShell prompt** as an administrator.
2. Disable the sync scheduler by running the following PowerShell command:
   ```
   Set-ADSyncScheduler -SyncCycleEnabled $false
   ```
3. Import the new PowerShell module that will be made available with the installation of the updated version of Azure AD Connect using the following command:
   ```
   Import-Module 'C:\Program Files\Microsoft Azure AD Sync\Extensions\
   AADConnector.psm1'
   ```
4. Switch to using the V2 endpoint by running the following commands:
   ```
   Set-ADSyncAADConnectorExportApiVersion 2
   Set-ADSyncAADConnectorImportApiVersion 2
   ```
5. Reenable the sync scheduler by running the following command:
   ```
   Set-ADSyncScheduler -SyncCycleEnabled $true
   ```

EXAM TIP

Remember the difference between password sync and pass-through authentication.

Skill 2.3: Manage identity synchronization by using Azure Active Directory

This skill section deals with the process of managing identity synchronization with Azure AD Connect once it has been deployed. To master this skill, you need to understand how to moni-tor Azure AD Connect Health, manage Azure AD Connect synchronization, configure object filters, and configure password synchronization.

> **This section covers the following topics:**
> - Configure directory synchronization by using Azure AD Connect
> - Monitor Azure AD Connect Health
> - Manage Azure AD Connect synchronization
> - Configure object filters
> - Configure password synchronization
> - Implement multiforest AD Connect scenarios

Configure directory synchronization by using Azure AD Connect

To configure Azure AD Connect synchronization, install the Azure AD Connect software and then run the Azure AD Connect Installation Wizard. The process of installing Azure AD Con-nect is simply a matter of installing the appropriate MSI file on a Windows Server computer in an environment that meets the necessary prerequisites. After the software is installed, you use the Azure AD Connect Setup Wizard to perform initial configuration. If you want to change any of the Azure AD Connect synchronization settings, you run the Setup Wizard again. You also have the option of using PowerShell or the Synchronization Service Manager to configure synchronization settings, which you'll learn about later in this section.

Meeting the Azure AD Connect installation requirements

Before installing Azure AD Connect, you should ensure that your environment, Azure AD Connect computer, and account used to configure Azure AD Connect meet the software, hardware, and privilege requirements. So, you need to ensure that your Active Directory environment is configured at the appropriate level, that the computer on which you will run Azure AD Connect has the appropriate software and hardware configuration, and that the account used to install Azure AD Connect has been added to the appropriate security groups.

> **MORE INFO   AZURE AD CONNECT PREREQUISITES**
>
> You can learn more about Azure AD Connect prerequisites here: *https://docs.microsoft.com/en-us/azure/active-directory/hybrid/how-to-connect-install-prerequisites*.

Azure AD and Office 365 requirements

Before you can install and configure Azure AD Connect, you must ensure that you have configured an additional domain for Office 365. By default, an Azure AD tenant will allow 50,000 objects; however, when you add and verify an additional domain, this limit increases to 300,000 objects. If you require more than 300,000 objects in your Azure AD instance, you can open a support ticket with Microsoft. If you require more than 500,000 objects in your Azure AD instance, you'll need to acquire an Azure AD Premium or Enterprise Mobility and Security license.

On-premises Active Directory environment requirements

Azure AD Connect requires that the on-premises Active Directory environment be configured at the Windows Server 2003 forest functional level or higher. The forest functional level is dependent on the minimum domain functional level of any domain in a forest. For example, if you have five domains in a forest, with four of them running at the Windows Server 2012 R2 domain functional level and one of them running at the Windows Server 2003 domain functional level, then Windows Server 2003 will be the maximum forest functional level.

Because Windows Server 2003 is no longer supported by Microsoft without a custom support agreement, your organization should have domain controllers running at least Windows Server 2008. Microsoft security best practice is to have domain controllers deployed with Microsoft's most recent version of the server operating system, so in theory you should have domain controllers running Windows Server 2016 or later. To support Azure AD Connect password writeback functionality, you'll need domain controllers running either Windows Server 2008 R2 or Windows Server 2008 with all service packs applied as well as hotfix KB2386717.

You can check the forest functional level by using the Active Directory Domains and Trusts console. To do this, perform the following steps:

1. Open the **Active Directory Domains and Trusts** console.
2. Select the **Active Directory Domains and Trusts** node.
3. On the **Actions** menu, select **Raise forest functional level**.

The **Raise forest functional level** dialog box displays the current functional level and, if possible, provides you with the option of upgrading the forest functional level. Figure 2-10 shows the forest functional level configured at Windows Server 2012 R2, which is the highest possible forest functional level for an organization where all domain controllers are running the Windows Server 2012 R2 operating system. If all the domain controllers are running the Windows Server 2016 operating system, it is possible to raise the domain and forest functional level to Windows Server 2016. Note that domains with exclusively Windows Server 2019 and Windows Server 2022 domain controllers can only be raised to the Windows Server 2016 domain and forest functional level.

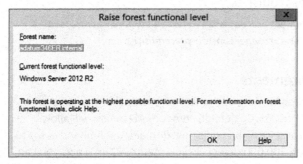

FIGURE 2-10 Forest functional level

You can also check the forest functional level by using the following Microsoft PowerShell command:

```
(Get-ADForest).ForestMode
```

Azure AD Connect Server requirements

Azure AD Connect is software that you install on a computer that manages the process of synchronizing objects between the on-premises Active Directory and the Azure Active Directory instance that supports the Microsoft 365 tenancy. You can install Azure AD Connect on computers running the following operating systems:

- Windows Server 2008 (x86 and x64)
- Windows Server 2008 R2 (x64)
- Windows Server 2012 (x64)
- Windows Server 2012 R2 (x64)
- Windows Server 2016 (x64)
- Windows Server 2019 (x64)
- Windows Server 2022 (x64)

Azure AD Connect cannot be installed on Windows Server 2003. Given that Windows Server 2003 is no longer supported by Microsoft, and that you are a diligent administrator, you will of course not have Windows Server 2003 in your environment.

Azure AD Connect has the following requirements:

- It must be installed on a Windows Server instance that has the GUI version of the operating system installed. You cannot install Azure AD Connect on a computer running the Server Core operating system.

- You can deploy Azure AD Connect on a computer that is either a domain controller, a member server, or, if you use the custom options, a stand-alone server.

- If installing on versions of Windows Server before Windows Server 2012, ensure that all service packs, updates, and relevant hotfixes are applied. (As a diligent administrator, you have already done this, so it presumably is not necessary to remind you.)

- If you want to use the password synchronization functionality, you need to ensure that Azure AD Connect is deployed on Windows Server 2008 R2 SP1 or later.

- The server hosting Azure AD Connect requires .NET Framework 4.5.1 or later.

- The server hosting Azure AD Connect requires Microsoft PowerShell 3.0 or later.

- The server hosting Azure AD Connect must not have PowerShell Transcription enabled through Group Policy.

- If you are deploying Azure AD Connect with Active Directory Federation Services, you must use Windows Server 2012 R2 or later for the web application proxy and Windows remote management must be enabled on the servers that will host AD FS roles.

- If global administrators will have multifactor authentication (MFA) enabled, then the URL *https://secure.aadcdn.microsoftonline-p.com* must be configured as a trusted site.

Connectivity requirements

The computer with Azure AD Connect installed must be a member of a domain in the forest that you want to synchronize, and it must have connectivity to a writable domain controller in each domain of the forest you want to synchronize on the following ports:

- **DNS**   TCP/UDP port 53
- **Kerberos**   TCP/UDP port 88
- **RPC**   TCP port 135
- **LDAP**   TCP/UDP port 389
- **SSL**   TCP port 443
- **SMB**   TCP port 445

The computer with Azure AD Connect installed must be able to establish communication with the Microsoft Azure servers on the internet over TCP port 443. This computer can be located on an internal network as long as it can initiate communication on TCP port 443. It does not need a publicly routable IP address. The computer hosting Azure AD Connect always initiates synchronization communication to Microsoft Azure. Microsoft Azure Active Directory does not initiate synchronization communication to the computer hosting Azure AD Connect on the on-premises network.

Although you can install Azure AD Connect on a domain controller, Microsoft recommends that you deploy Azure AD Connect on a computer that does not have the domain controller role. If you are going to be replicating more than 50,000 objects, Microsoft recommends that you deploy SQL Server on a computer that is separate from the computer that will host Azure AD Connect. If you plan to host the SQL Server instance on a separate computer, ensure that communication is possible between the computer hosting Azure AD Connect and the computer hosting the SQL instance on TCP port 1433.

If you are going to use a separate SQL Server instance, ensure that the account used to install and configure Azure AD Connect has systems administrator rights on the SQL instance and that the service account used for Azure AD Connect has public permissions on the Azure AD Connect database.

Hardware requirements

The hardware requirements of the computer that hosts Azure AD Connect depend on the number of objects in the Active Directory environment that you need to sync. The greater the number of objects that you need to sync, the steeper the hardware requirements. Table 2-1 provides a guide to the requirements, with all configurations requiring at least a 1.6 GHz processor.

TABLE 2-1 Azure AD Connect computer hardware requirements

Number of Objects in Active Directory	Memory	Storage
Fewer than 10,000	4 GB	70 GB
10,000–50,000	4 GB	70 GB
50,000–100,000	16 GB	100 GB
100,000–300,000	32 GB	300 GB
300,000–600,000	32 GB	450 GB
More than 600,000	32 GB	500 GB

During the planning phase, a new Microsoft 365 tenancy has a limit of 50,000 objects. However, once the first domain is verified, this limit is increased to 300,000 objects. Organizations that need to store more than 300,000 objects in an Azure Active Directory instance that supports a Microsoft 365 tenancy should contact Microsoft Support.

SQL Server requirements

When you deploy Azure AD Connect, you have the option of having Azure AD Connect install a SQL Server Express instance, or you can choose to have Azure AD Connect leverage a full instance of SQL Server. SQL Server Express is limited to a maximum database size of 10 GB. In terms of Azure AD Connect, this means that Azure AD Connect is only able to manage 100,000 objects. This is likely to be adequate for all but the largest environments.

For environments that require Azure AD Connect to manage more than 100,000 objects, you'll need to have Azure AD Connect leverage a full instance of SQL Server. Azure AD Connect can use all versions of Microsoft SQL Server, from Microsoft SQL Server 2008 with the most recent service pack to SQL Server 2019. SQL Azure, however, is not supported as a database for Azure AD Connect. If deploying a full instance of SQL Server to support Azure AD Connect, ensure that the following prerequisites are met:

- **Use a case-insensitive SQL collation** Case-insensitive collations have the _CI_ identifier included in their name. Case-sensitive collations (those that use the _CS_ designation) are not supported for use with Azure AD Connect.

- **You can only use one sync engine per SQL instance** If you have an additional Azure AD Connect sync engine, or if you are using Microsoft Identity Manager in your environment, each sync engine requires its own separate SQL instance.

Installation account requirements

The accounts that you use to install and configure Azure AD Connect have the following requirements:

- The account used to configure Azure AD Connect must have the administrator permission in the Microsoft 365 tenant. If you create a service account in Microsoft 365 to use in place of the account with tenant administrator permissions, be sure to configure the account with a password that does not expire.

- The account used to install and configure Azure AD Connect must have enterprise administrator permissions within the on-premises Active Directory forest if you will be using express installation settings. This account is required only during installation and configuration. Once Azure AD Connect is installed and configured, this account no longer needs enterprise administrator permissions. A best practice is to create a separate account for Azure AD Connect installation and configuration and to temporarily add this account to the enterprise administrators group during the installation and configuration process. After Azure AD Connect is installed and configured, this account can be removed from the enterprise administrators group. You should not attempt to change the account used after Azure AD Connect is set up and configured, since Azure AD Connect always attempts to run using the original account.

- The account used to install and configure Azure AD Connect must be a member of the local administrators group on the computer on which Azure AD Connect is installed.

Installing Azure AD Connect

Installing Azure AD Connect with express settings is appropriate if your organization has a single Active Directory forest and you want to use password sync for authentication. The Azure AD Connect express settings are appropriate for most organizations. To obtain Azure AD Connect, download it from the following website: *https://www.microsoft.com/en-us/download/details.aspx?id=47594*.

To install Azure AD Connect with Express settings, perform the following steps:

1. Double-click on the **AzureADConnect.msi** file that you downloaded from the Microsoft download center and select **Run** on the security warning shown in Figure 2-11.

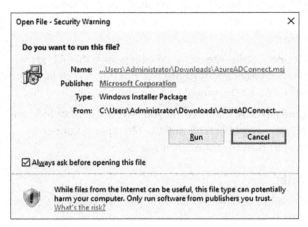

FIGURE 2-11 File security warning

2. Windows installs Azure AD Connect on your computer. When the installation is complete, you will be presented with the splash screen. Agree to the license terms and privacy notice, shown in Figure 2-12, and select **Continue**.

FIGURE 2-12 The Welcome to Azure AD Connect page in the Azure AD Connect Setup Wizard

3. If your organization has an internal nonroutable domain, you will need to use custom settings. Figure 2-13 shows the nonroutable domain epistemicus.internal in use. To use custom settings, select **Customize**.

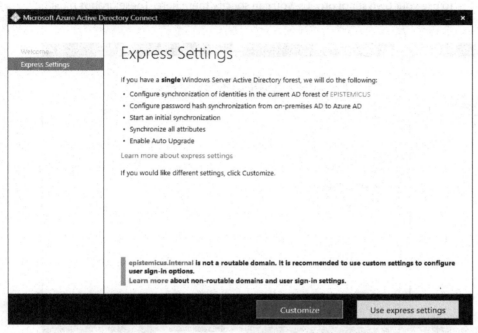

Express Settings

If you have a **single** Windows Server Active Directory forest, we will do the following:

- Configure synchronization of identities in the current AD forest of EPISTEMICUS
- Configure password hash synchronization from on-premises AD to Azure AD
- Start an initial synchronization
- Synchronize all attributes
- Enable Auto Upgrade

Learn more about express settings

If you would like different settings, click Customize.

epistemicus.internal **is not a routable domain. It is recommended to use custom settings to configure user sign-in options.**
Learn more **about non-routable domains and user sign-in settings.**

Customize | Use express settings

FIGURE 2-13 The Express Settings page in the Azure AD Connect Setup Wizard

4. On the **Install required components** page, shown in Figure 2-14, choose from the following options:

- **Specify A Custom Installation Location** Choose this option if you want to install Azure AD Connect in a separate location, such as on another volume.

- **Specify An Existing SQL Server** Choose this option if you want to specify an alternate SQL server instance. By default, Azure AD Connect will install a SQL Server Express instance.

- **Use An Existing Service Account** You can configure Azure AD Connect to use an existing service account. By default, Azure AD Connect will create a service account. You can configure Azure AD Connect to use a group managed service account if you are installing Azure AD Connect on a computer running Windows Server 2012 or later. You'll need to use an existing service account if you are using Azure AD Connect with a remote SQL Server instance or if communication with Azure will occur through a proxy server that requires authentication.

- **Specify Custom Sync Groups**   When you deploy Azure AD Connect, it creates four local groups on the server that hosts the Azure AD Connect instance: the administrators group, operators group, password reset group, and browse groups. If you want to use your own set of groups, you can specify them here. These groups must be local to the host server and not a member of the domain.

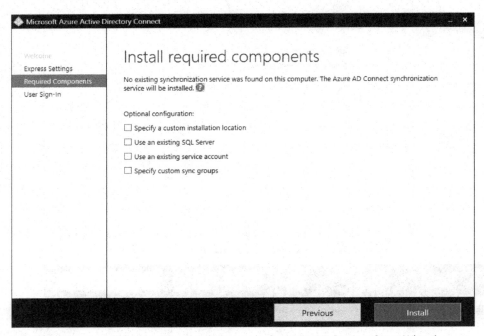

FIGURE 2-14 The Install Required Components page in the Azure AD Connect Setup Wizard

5. Once you have specified which custom options you require—and you can select none if you want, but you have to perform a custom installation because you have a non-routable domain on-premises—select **Install**.

6. On the **User Sign-in** page, specify what type of sign-in you want to allow. You can choose between the following options, the details of which were covered earlier in this chapter (except for PingFederate, which is a third-party tool and not addressed by the MS-100 exam). Most organizations choose password sync since it is the most straightforward.

- Password synchronization

- Pass-through authentication

- Federation with AD FS

- Federation with PingFederate

- Do not configure
- Enable Single sign-on

7. On the **Connect to Azure AD** page, provide the credentials of a global administrator account. Microsoft recommends that you use an account in the default onmicrosoft.com domain associated with the Azure AD instance you will be connecting to. If you choose the Federation with AD FS option, ensure that you do not sign in using an account in a domain that you will enable for Federation. Figure 2-15 shows sign-in with a password sync scenario.

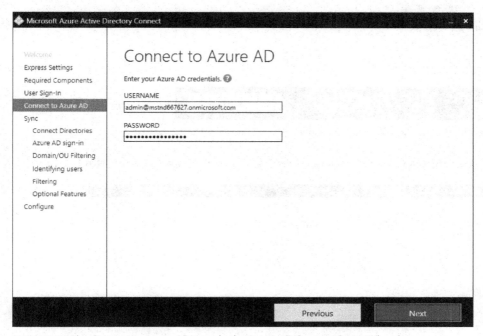

FIGURE 2-15 The Connect to Azure AD page in the Azure AD Connect Setup Wizard

8. After Azure AD Connect has connected to Azure AD, you will be able to specify the directory type to synchronize as well as the forest. Select **Add Directory** to add a specific forest. When you add a forest by selecting **Add Directory**, you will need to specify the credentials of an account that will perform periodic synchronization. Unless you are certain that you have applied the minimum necessary privileges to an account, you should provide enterprise administrator credentials and allow Azure AD Connect to create the account, as shown in Figure 2-16. Doing so will ensure that the account is assigned only the privileges necessary to perform synchronization tasks.

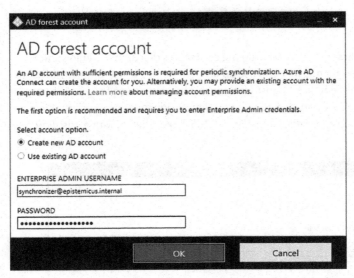

FIGURE 2-16 The AD Forest Account page in the Azure AD Connect Setup Wizard

9. After the credentials have been verified, as shown in Figure 2-17, select **Next**.

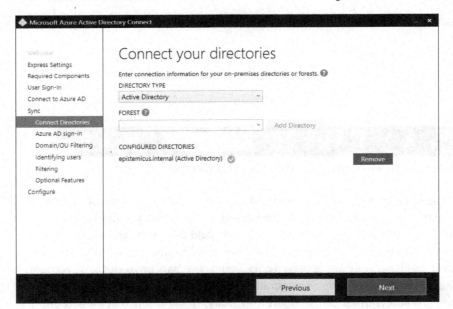

FIGURE 2-17 The Connect Your Directories page in the Azure AD Connect Setup Wizard

10. On the **Azure AD sign-in configuration** page, shown in Figure 2-18, review the UPN suffix and then inspect the on-premises attribute to use as the Azure AD user name. You'll need to ensure that accounts use a routable Azure AD user name.

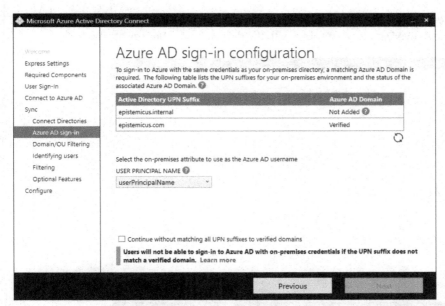

FIGURE 2-18 The Azure AD Sign-In Configuration page in the Azure AD Connect Setup Wizard

11. On the **Domain and OU filtering** page, shown in Figure 2-19, select whether you want to sync all objects or just objects in specific domains and OUs.

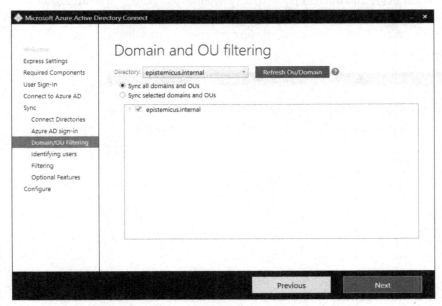

FIGURE 2-19 The Domain and OU Filtering page in the Azure AD Connect Setup Wizard

12. On the **Uniquely identifying your users** page, shown in Figure 2-20, specify how users are to be identified. By default, users should have only one representation across

all directories. If users exist in multiple directories, you can have matches identified by a specific Active Directory attribute, with the default being the mail attribute.

FIGURE 2-20 The Uniquely Identifying Your Users page in the Azure AD Connect Setup Wizard

13. On the **Filter users and devices** page, specify whether you want to synchronize all users and devices or only members of a specific group. Figure 2-21 shows members of the Microsoft 365 pilot users group being configured so that their accounts will be synchronized with Azure.

FIGURE 2-21 The Filter Users and Devices page in the Azure AD Connect Setup Wizard

14. On the **Optional features** page, shown in Figure 2-22, select any optional features that you want to configure. These features include the following:

- Exchange hybrid deployment
- Exchange Mail Public Folders
- Azure AD app and attribute filtering
- Password hash synchronization
- Password writeback
- Group writeback
- Device writeback
- Directory extension attribute sync

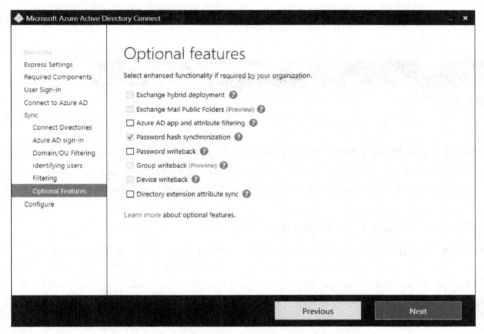

FIGURE 2-22 The Optional Features page in the Azure AD Connect Setup Wizard

15. On the **Ready to configure** page, shown in Figure 2-23, you can choose to start synchronization or enable staging mode, where synchronization will prepare to be run but will not synchronize any data with Azure AD.

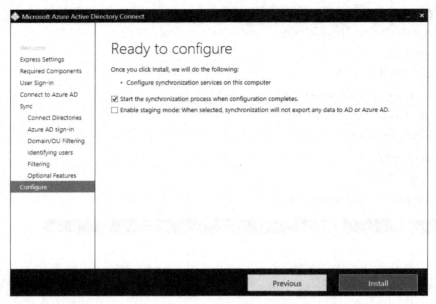

FIGURE 2-23 The Ready To Configure page in the Azure AD Connect Setup Wizard

---

MORE INFO   **AZURE AD CONNECT CUSTOM INSTALLATION**

To install Azure AD Connect with the custom settings, consult the following article: *https://docs.microsoft.com/en-us/azure/active-directory/hybrid/how-to-connect-install-custom*.

Identifying synchronized attributes

Azure AD Connect synchronizes some, but not all, attributes from the on-premises Active Directory instance to the Azure Active Directory instance that supports a Microsoft 365 tenancy. Depending on whether the object is a user account, group account, or mail-enabled contact object, there 143 separate attributes that synchronize. These attributes are listed in Table 2-2.

TABLE 2-2 List of attributes synchronized by Azure AD Connect

accountEnabled	MsExchArchiveGUID	msExchTeamMailboxOwners
Assistant	MsExchArchiveName	msExchTeamMailboxSharePointLinkedBy
altRecipient	msExchArchiveStatus	msExchTeamMailboxSharePointUrl
authoring	msExchAssistantName	msExchUCVoiceMailSettings

C	msExchAuditAdmin	msExchUsageLocation
Cn	msExchAuditDelegate	msExchUserHoldPolicies
Co	msExchAuditDelegateAdmin	msOrg-IsOrganizational
company	msExchAuditOwner	msRTCSIP-ApplicationOptions
countryCode	MsExchBlockedSendersHash	msRTCSIP-DeploymentLocator
department	msExchBypassAudit	msRTCSIP-Line
description	MsExchBypassModeration FromDLMembersLink	msRTCSIP-OwnerUrn
displayName	MsExchBypassModerationLink	msRTCSIP-PrimaryUser Address
dLMemRejectPerms	msExchCoManagedByLink	msRTCSIP-UserEnabled
dLMemSubmitPerms	msExchDelegateListLink	msRTCSIP-OptionFlags
ExtensionAttribute1	msExchELCExpirySuspensionEnd	objectGUID
ExtensionAttribute10	msExchELCExpirySuspensionStart	oOFReplyToOriginator
ExtensionAttribute11	msExchELCMailboxFlags	otherFacsimileTelephone
ExtensionAttribute12	MsExchEnableModeration	otherHomePhone
ExtensionAttribute13	msExchExtensionCustomAttribute1	otherIpPhone
ExtensionAttribute14	msExchExtensionCustomAttribute2	otherMobile
ExtensionAttribute15	msExchExtensionCustomAttribute3	otherPager
ExtensionAttribute2	msExchExtensionCustomAttribute4	otherTelephone
ExtensionAttribute3	msExchExtensionCustomAttribute5	pager
ExtensionAttribute4	MsExchGroupDepartRestriction	photo
ExtensionAttribute5	MsExchGroupJoinRestriction	physicalDeliveryOfficeName
ExtensionAttribute6	msExchHideFromAddressLists	postalCode
ExtensionAttribute7	MsExchImmutableID	postOfficeBox
ExtensionAttribute8	msExchLitigationHoldDate	PreferredLanguage
ExtensionAttribute9	msExchLitigationHoldOwner	proxyAddresses
Facsimiletelephonenumber	MsExchMailboxGuid	PublicDelegates
givenName	msExchMailboxAuditEnable	pwdLastSet
GroupType	msExchMailboxAuditLogAgeLimit	reportToOriginator

hideDLMembership	MsExchModeratedByLink	ReportToOwner
homephone	MsExchModerationFlags	samAccountName
Info	MsExchRecipientDisplayType	sn
Initials	msExchRecipientTypeDetails	St
ipPhone	MsExchRemoteRecipientType	streetAddress
L	msExchRequireAuthToSendTo	targetAddress
legacyExchangeDN	MsExchResourceCapacity	TelephoneAssistant
Mail	MsExchResourceDisplay	telephoneNumber
mailnickname	MsExchResourceMetaData	thumbnailphoto
managedBy	MsExchResourceSearchProperties	title
Manager	msExchRetentionComment	unauthOrig
Member	msExchRetentionURL	url
middleName	MsExchSafeRecipientsHash	userAccountControl
Mobile	MsExchSafeSendersHash	userCertificate
msDS-HABSeniorityIndex	MsExchSenderHintTranslations	UserPrincipalName
msDS-PhoneticDisplayName	msExchTeamMailboxExpiration	userSMIMECertificate

> *MORE INFO* **ATTRIBUTES SYNCHRONIZED BY AZURE AD CONNECT**
>
> You can learn more about which attributes are synchronized by Azure AD Connect at *https://docs.microsoft.com/en-us/azure/active-directory/connect/active-directory-aadconnectsync-attributes-synchronized*.

Monitor Azure AD Connect Health

Azure AD Connect Health is a tool available in the Azure Active Directory Admin Center, shown in Figure 2-24, that allows you to monitor the health of synchronization between your organization's on-premises directory and Azure Active Directory.

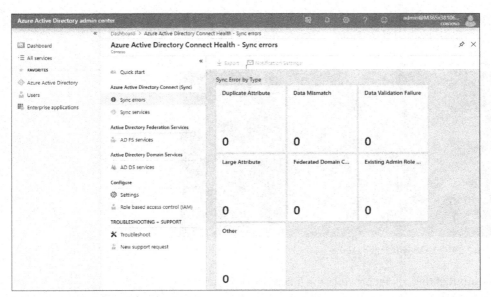

FIGURE 2-24 Azure AD Connect Health

You can use Azure AD Connect Health to view information about the following:

- **Synchronization errors** These include duplicate attributes, data mismatches, data validation failure, large attributes, Federated domain change, and existing admin role conflicts.

- **Synchronization services** This handles information about which services are synchronizing with Azure Active Directory.

- **AD FS services** This is information about AD FS when Azure AD Connect is configured for Federation, including information about errors and issues.

- **AD DS services** This is information about domains and forests connected to Azure Active Directory.

> *MORE INFO* **AZURE AD CONNECT HEALTH**
>
> You can learn more about Azure AD Connect Health at *https://docs.microsoft.com/en-us/ azure/active-directory/hybrid/whatis-azure-ad-connect*.

Manage Azure AD Connect synchronization

You can manage synchronization using a variety of tools, including PowerShell cmdlets that are part of the ADSync PowerShell module. This module is automatically installed on a computer when you install Azure AD Connect.

To view the current configuration of the scheduler, you can run the `Get-ADSyncScheduler` cmdlet. The output of this cmdlet is shown in Figure 2-25.

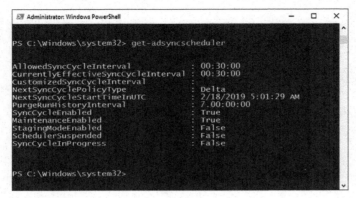

FIGURE 2-25 Get-ADSyncScheduler

The output of this cmdlet provides the following information:

- **AllowedSyncCycleInterval** Minimum intervals between sync cycles supported by Microsoft. If you sync more often than this interval, your configuration will be deemed unsupported.

- **CurrentlyEffectiveSyncCycleInterval** The schedule that currently applies.

- **CustomizedSyncCycleInterval** Used when you have a custom schedule applied.

- **NextSyncCyclePolicyType** Specifies whether the next sync is a full synchronization or a delta synchronization.

- **NextSyncCycleStartTimeInUTC** The time when the next sync cycle will occur according to the schedule.

- **PurgeRunHistoryInterval** Specifies how long the logs should be kept.

- **SyncCycleEnabled** Specifies whether the scheduler is running an import, sync, or export process as part of its execution.

- **MaintenanceEnabled** Specifies if the maintenance process is enabled.

- **StagingModeEnabled** Lists whether the staging mode is enabled.

- **SchedulerSuspended** Specifies whether synchronization is suspended.

- **SyncCycleInProgress** Specifies whether synchronization is actually occurring.

You can use the `Set-ADSyncScheduler` cmdlet to configure the following settings that are displayed when you run the `Get-ADSyncScheduler` cmdlet:

- CustomizedSyncCycleInterval

- NextSyncCyclePolicyType

- PurgeRunHistoryInterval

- SyncCycleEnabled

- MaintenanceEnabled

MORE INFO **MANAGING THE SCHEDULER**

You can learn more about managing the Azure AD Connect scheduler at *https://docs. microsoft.com/en-us/azure/active-directory/hybrid/how-to-connect-sync-feature-scheduler.*

By default, synchronization occurs between the on-premises instance of Active Directory and Azure Active Directory every 30 minutes. In some cases, however, you'll make a change to a user account or create a collection of user accounts and want to get those changes or new accounts up into the Azure Active Directory instance that supports the Office 365 tenancy as fast as possible. You can force synchronization by running the Azure AD Connect Wizard again, or you can use the Synchronization Service Manager.

To perform a full synchronization using the Synchronization Service Manager, follow these steps:

1. Open the **Synchronization Service Manager** by selecting **Synchronization Service** in the **Start** menu or by running the miisclient.exe file in the C:\Program Files\ Microsoft Azure AD Sync\UIShell folder.

2. Select the **Connectors** tab.

3. On the **Connectors** tab, select the name of your Active Directory domain service, as shown in Figure 2-26.

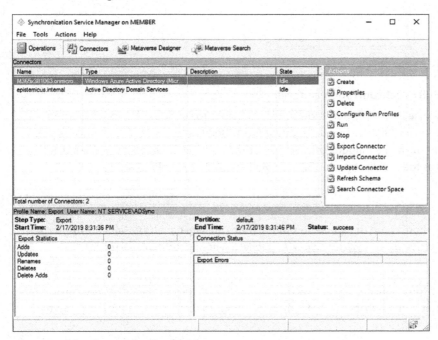

FIGURE 2-26 Synchronization Service Manager

4. In the **Actions** pane, select **Run**.

5. The **Run Connector** dialog box contains a list of synchronization options (see Figure 2-27):
    - **Full Synchronization**   Performs a full synchronization
    - **Delta Import**   Imports changed schema and objects
    - **Delta Synchronization**   Synchronizes only objects that have changed since the last sync
    - **Export**   Writes data from the Azure instance to the on-premises instance
    - **Full Import**   Suitable for initiating the first full synchronization or the first full synchronization after you have changed the filtering parameters

FIGURE 2-27 Full synchronization

6. Select **Full Synchronization** and select OK.

You can also use the Synchronization Service Manager to configure extensive filtering options. However, for tasks such as configuring OU-based filtering, Microsoft recommends that you first attempt to configure filtering using the Azure AD Connect Setup Wizard and rely on a tool such as the Synchronization Service Manager only if problems arise.

MORE INFO   **SYNCHRONIZATION SERVICE MANAGER**

You can learn more about the Synchronization Service Manager at *https://docs.microsoft.com/ en-us/azure/active-directory/hybrid/how-to-connect-sync-service-manager-ui*.

You can also force synchronization by using the Start-ADSyncCycle cmdlet. You can use this cmdlet to trigger either a delta or a full synchronization. To force a delta sync cycle, run the following command:

```
Start-ADSyncCycle -PolicyType Delta
```

To trigger a full sync cycle, run this command:

```
Start-ADSyncCycle -PolicyType Initial
```

Configure object filters

When you use Azure AD Connect to synchronize on-premises Active Directory to an Azure Active Directory instance, the default setting is to have all user accounts, group accounts, and mail-enabled contact objects synchronized up to the cloud. For some organizations, synchronizing everything is exactly what they want. Other organizations want to be more selective about which objects are synchronized from the on-premises Active Directory environment to the Azure Active Directory instance that supports the Office 365 tenancy.

With Azure AD Connect, you can choose to filter based on the following options, as shown in Figure 2-28:

- **Domain based**   In a forest with multiple domains, you can configure filtering so that only objects from some domains, and not others, are filtered.
- **Organizational unit (OU) based**   With this filtering type, you choose which objects are filtered based on their location within specific organizational units.

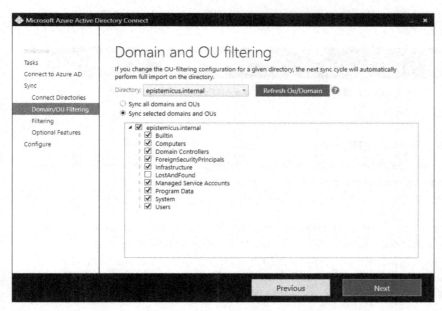

FIGURE 2-28 The Domain and OU Filtering page in the Azure AD Connect Setup Wizard

You can also configure filtering on the basis of group membership, as shown in Figure 2-29. You can configure separate group-based filters for each forest or domain synchronized using Azure AD Connect.

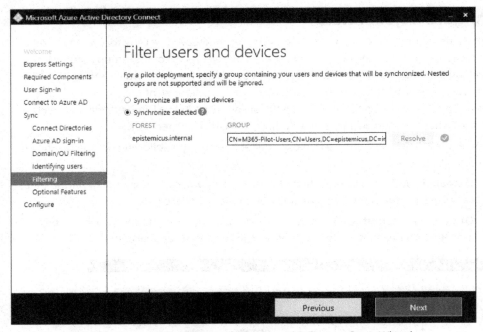

FIGURE 2-29 The Filter Users and Devices page in the Azure AD Connect Setup Wizard

---

MORE INFO **CONFIGURE FILTERING**

You can learn more about Azure AD sync filtering at *https://docs.microsoft.com/en-us/azure/ active-directory/hybrid/how-to-connect-sync-configure-filtering*.

Although Azure AD Connect will address most organizations' synchronization requirements, the most comprehensive tool you can use to filter synchronization is the Synchronization Rules Editor, shown in Figure 2-30. You can use this tool to modify existing synchronization rules but also to create new rules. Rather than configuring synchronization on a per-domain or per-OU basis, you can tailor rules for individual objects and specific Active Directory attributes.

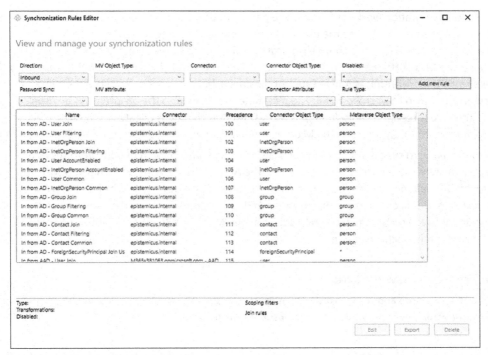

FIGURE 2-30 Synchronization Rules Editor

> **MORE INFO**   **SYNCHRONIZATION RULES EDITOR**
>
> You can learn more about the Synchronization Rules Editor at *https://docs.microsoft.com/
> en-us/azure/active-directory/connect/active-directory-aadconnectsync-change-the-
> configuration*.

Configure password synchronization

Password sync allows the synchronization of user account passwords from an on-premises
Active Directory to the Azure Active Directory instance that supports the Office 365 tenancy.
The advantage of this is that users can sign in to Microsoft 365 using the same password that
they use to sign in to computers on the on-premises environment. Password sync does not
provide single sign-on or Federation.

When you enable password sync, the on-premises password complexity policies override
password complexity policies configured for the Azure Active Directory instance that supports
the Microsoft 365 tenancy. This means that any password that is valid for an on-premises user
will be valid within Microsoft 365, even if it would not be normally.

Password expiration works as follows: The password of the account of the cloud user object is set to never expire. Each time the user account password is changed in the on-premises Active Directory instance, this change replicates to the Azure Active Directory instance that supports the Microsoft 365 tenancy. This means that it is possible for a user account's password to expire on the on-premises Active Directory instance, but that user can still use the same password to sign in to Microsoft 365. The next time they sign in to the on-premises environment, they are forced to change their password, and that change replicates to the Azure Active Directory instance that supports the Microsoft 365 tenancy.

When password sync is enabled and you disable a user's account in the on-premises Active Directory instance, the user's account in the Azure Active Directory instance that supports the Microsoft 365 tenancy is disabled within a few minutes. If password sync is not enabled and you disable a user account in the on-premises Active Directory instance, the user's account in the Azure Active Directory instance that supports the Microsoft 365 tenancy is not disabled until the next full synchronization.

> **MORE INFO PASSWORD SYNC**
>
> You can learn more about password sync at *https://docs.microsoft.com/en-us/azure/active-directory/hybrid/how-to-connect-password-hash-synchronization*.

Implement multiforest AD Connect scenarios

The Azure Active Directory Connect tool supports synchronization from multiple on-premises Active Directory forests to a single Azure Active Directory instance. Multiple-forest synchronization to a single Azure AD instance is supported only when a single Azure AD Connect server is in use. Microsoft does not support multiple Azure AD Connect servers synchronizing with a single Azure AD instance, whether one or multiple forests are being synchronized.

By default, Azure AD Connect assumes that:

- A user has a single enabled account. Also, the forest where this account is located must host the directory that is used to authenticate the user. This assumption is used in both password sync and Federation scenarios. On the basis of this assumption, the UserPrincipalName and sourceAnchor/immutableID attributes are drawn from this forest.

- Each user has a single mailbox, and the forest that hosts that mailbox is the best source of attributes visible in the Exchange global address list (GAL). If a user doesn't have an associated mailbox, any configured forest can function as the source for the attribute values.

- If a user account has a linked mailbox, there will be an account in an alternate forest used for the sign-in process.

The key to synchronizing user accounts from multiple forests is that only one user account from all synchronized forests should represent the user. This means that the synchronization engine should have a way to determine when accounts in separate forests represent the same user. You can configure how the Azure AD Connect sync engine identifies users on the Uniquely Identifying Your Users page, shown in Figure 2-31, using one of the following options:

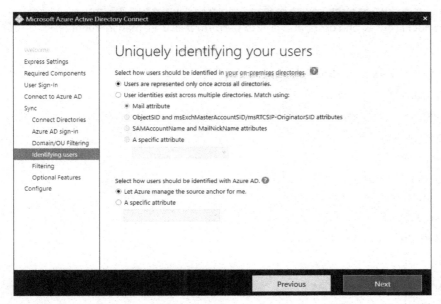

FIGURE 2-31 The Uniquely Identifying Your Users page in the Azure AD Connect Setup Wizard

- Matching users using the mail attribute
- Matching users using `ObjectSID` and `msExchangeMasterAccountSID/msRTCIP-OriginatorSID` attributes
- Matching users using the `SAMAccountName` and `MailNickName` attributes
- Specifying a custom attribute on which to match names

MORE INFO **MULTIFOREST SYNCHRONIZATION**

You can learn more about multiforest synchronization and supported topologies for Azure AD Connect at *https://docs.microsoft.com/en-us/azure/active-directory/hybrid/ plan-connect-topologies*.

EXAM TIP

Remember what tools you can use to trigger synchronization.

Skill 2.4: Manage Azure AD identities

This skill deals with the management of identities within Azure Active Directory. This is of primary importance when Azure Active Directory functions as the source of authority. To master this skill, you'll need to understand how to plan for the use of Azure AD identities; how to deploy self-service password reset; how to manage access reviews, Azure AD groups, Azure AD passwords, product licenses, and users; and how to perform bulk user-management tasks.

> **This section covers the following topics:**
> - Plan Azure AD identities
> - Implement and manage Azure AD self-service password reset
> - Manage access reviews
> - Manage groups
> - Manage passwords
> - Manage product licenses
> - Manage users
> - Perform bulk user management

Plan Azure AD identities

In hybrid environments, you'll manage identities primarily using on-premises management tools such as Active Directory Users and Computers. In environments where Azure AD forms the primary source of authority, you can use the Microsoft 365 Admin Center to manage user identities. You can also use the Azure Active Directory Admin Center, as shown in Figure 2-32, or you can use Azure CLI or PowerShell.

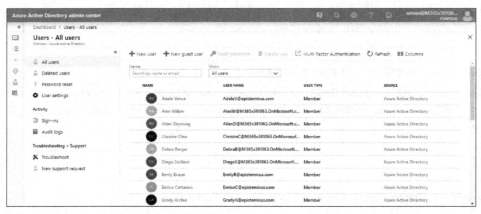

FIGURE 2-32 Azure Active Directory Admin Center

When planning the use of Azure identities, you'll need to consider the following questions:

- **What UPN will be used with the identity for login to Microsoft 365 resources?** You can change the UPN suffix to any domain that is configured and authorized for use with the directory.

- **What authentication and authorization options will be required to access Microsoft 365 resources?** Will users need to regularly change their passwords? Will users be required to perform multifactor authentication?

- **What roles will be assigned to users?** Will you need to assign Azure AD roles to specific users? What method will you use to perform this task?

- **Will Azure AD groups be used?** What strategy will you use to manage collections of users into groups? Will your organization use a group naming convention?

You'll learn more about how to perform user-management tasks later in this chapter.

Implement and manage Azure AD self-service password reset

Something that is challenging to deploy in an on-premises environment but that is relatively straightforward to deploy in an environment that uses Azure AD as a source of identity authority, is self-service password reset. A self-service password reset allows users to reset their own password when they forget that password rather than having to contact the service desk and have a member of the IT staff perform the task for them.

To enable self-service password reset, perform the following steps:

1. Open the **Azure Active Directory portal** at *https://aad.portal.azure.com* with an account that has tenant administrator permissions.

2. In the **Azure Active Directory admin center**, select the **Users** node. This will open the **Users** blade, as shown in Figure 2-33.

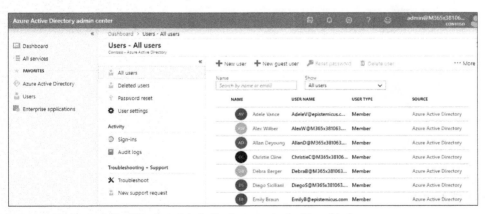

FIGURE 2-33 Azure Active Directory Admin Center open to the Users blade

3. In the **Users** blade of the **Azure Active Directory Admin Center**, select **Password Reset**.

4. On the **Password reset – Properties** page, select **All**, as shown in Figure 2-34, to enable the self-service password reset for all Microsoft 365 users.

FIGURE 2-34 Enabling self-service password reset

Once self-service password reset is enabled, users will be prompted for additional information the next time that they sign in, which will be used to verify their identity if they use the self-service password reset tool. Users can reset their passwords by navigating to the website *https://passwordreset.microsoftonline.com*, shown in Figure 2-35, and completing the form.

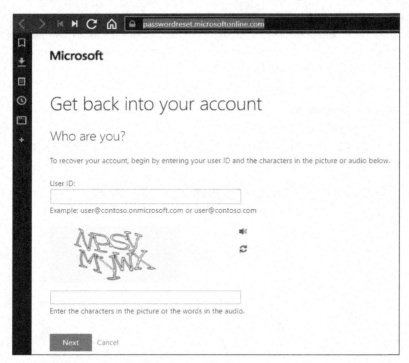

FIGURE 2-35 Resetting a password

Manage access reviews

You can review a user's access to Microsoft 365 resources through the Azure Active Directory Admin Center. To perform this task, open the user's properties page and select the **Sign-ins** section of the **User Management** blade. Figure 2-36 shows the sign-in activity of the administrator account used to manage a Microsoft 365 tenancy.

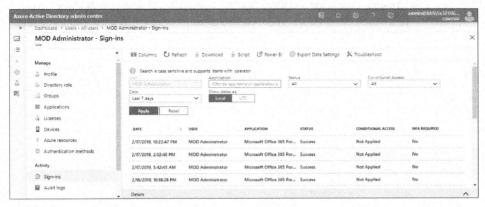

FIGURE 2-36 Viewing sign-in activity

The Audit Logs node enables you to review the actions performed by accounts. Figure 2-37 shows that actions performed by the account used for Microsoft 365 tenancy administration are recorded for review.

FIGURE 2-37 The Audit Logs node

Manage groups

Groups enable you to collect users together and then assign them privileges and access to workloads or services. Rather than assign privileges and access to workloads or services directly to users, you can assign these rights to a group, and then indirectly assign them to users by adding the user accounts to the appropriate group. Using groups in this way is a long-standing administrative practice because it allows you to determine a user's level of access and rights by looking at the user's group memberships rather than checking each workload and service to determine if the user account has been assigned rights to that service. You can use the Azure Active Directory Admin Center to manage groups.

Azure AD supports two group types:

- **Office 365 groups**   Used for collaboration between users. These users can be inside or external to the organization. Each Office 365 group has an associated email address, shared workspace for conversations, shared location for files, calendar events, and a planner.

- **Security groups**   Used to grant access to specific Microsoft 365 resources, such as SharePoint sites. Security groups can contain user accounts as well as device accounts. Device-related groups are most often used with services such as Intune.

Figure 2-38 shows the selection of group types when creating a group.

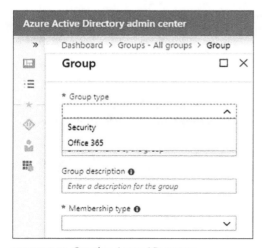

FIGURE 2-38 Creating Azure AD groups

Group membership for both group types can be configured as assigned or dynamic. When the assigned option is selected, membership is managed manually. When the dynamic option is selected, group membership is determined based on the results of a query against user or device attributes. For example, suppose you have a user located in a specific department or city who is managed by a specific person. That user could automatically be put in a specific group. Figure 2-39 shows an Office 365 group with dynamic membership, where users who are associated with the marketing department are automatically assigned membership to the Marketing group.

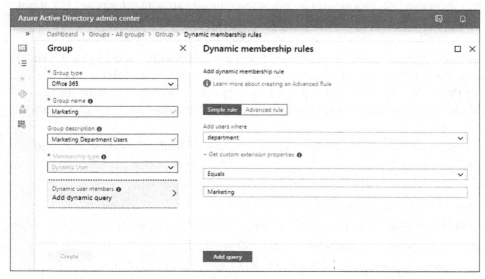

FIGURE 2-39 Office 365 dynamic group membership

Source of authority is important when modifying users and groups. Modifications that occur in the on-premises Active Directory overwrite the current state of the objects within the Azure Active Directory instance that supports the Microsoft 365 tenancy. The only exception to this rule is with the assignment of licenses, which only occurs using the Microsoft 365 Admin Center or PowerShell tools.

Modifications made to on-premises user and group objects will be present only within the Azure Active Directory instance that supports the Microsoft 365 tenancy after synchronization has occurred. By default, synchronization occurs every 30 minutes. You can force synchronization to occur using the Synchronization Service Manager tool or by using PowerShell.

With deletion, the concept of source of authority again is very important. When you want to delete a user or group account created in the on-premises Active Directory instance, you should use tools such as Active Directory Users and Computers or the Active Directory Admin Center to remove that user. When you delete a user or group using this method, the user will be deleted from the on-premises Active Directory instance and then, when synchronization occurs, from the Azure Active Directory instance that supports the Microsoft 365 tenancy.

When you delete a user from Microsoft 365, their account remains in the Azure Active Directory Recycle Bin for 30 days. This means you can recover the account online should you need to do so. If you delete a user from your on-premises Active Directory environment but have enabled the on-premises Active Directory Recycle Bin, recovering the user from the on-premises Active Directory Recycle Bin will recover the user account in Microsoft 365. If you don't have the Active Directory Recycle Bin enabled, you will need to create another account with a new GUID.

In some cases, synchronization doesn't work properly and objects that are deleted from the on-premises Active Directory instance are not deleted from the Azure Active Directory instance that supports the Microsoft 365 tenancy. In this circumstance you can use the `Remove-MsolUser`, `Remove-MsolGroup`, or `Remove-MsolContact` PowerShell cmdlets to manually remove the orphaned object.

You can use the following PowerShell commands from the AzureAD module to manage Azure AD groups:

- `Get-AzureADGroup` Provides information about Azure AD groups
- `New-AzureADGroup` Creates a new Azure AD group
- `Set-AzureADGroup` Configures the properties of an Azure AD group
- `Remove-AzureADGroup` Removes an Azure AD group
- `Add-AzureADGroupMember` Adds a user to an Azure AD group
- `Remove-AzureADGroupMember` Removes a user from an Azure AD group
- `Add-AzureADGroupOwner` Adds a user as an owner of an Azure AD group and gives the user limited group-management privileges
- `Remove-AzureADGroupOwner` Removes a user as owner of an Azure AD group.

> **MORE INFO AZURE AD GROUPS**
>
> You can learn more about Azure AD groups at *https://docs.microsoft.com/en-us/azure/active-directory/fundamentals/active-directory-groups-view-azure-portal*.

Manage passwords

The only thing people forget more often than where they put their keys is what their password is. As someone who supports Microsoft 365, it's more likely than not that if you haven't enabled self-service password reset, or even if you have, you're going to have to reset user passwords on a semi-regular basis.

To reset a Microsoft 365 user password, perform the following steps:

1. In the **Microsoft 365 admin center**, select the user whose password you want to reset in the list of active users by selecting the check box next to the user's name.
2. On the user's properties page, select the **Reset password** button, as shown in Figure 2-40.

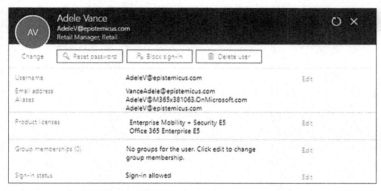

FIGURE 2-40 Reset Password button

3. On the **Reset password** page, shown in Figure 2-41, choose whether to autogenerate a password or create a password, and select whether the password needs to be changed when the user next signs in.

FIGURE 2-41 Password reset

4. Provide the new password to the user through a secure channel, such as in person or over the phone.

You can also reset a user's password through PowerShell using the `Set-MsolUserPassword` cmdlet with this syntax:

```
Set-MsolUserPassword -UserPrincipalName <UPN> -NewPassword <NewPassword>
-ForceChangePassword $True
```

Finally, you can configure a password expiration policy for all users by performing the following steps:

1. In the **Microsoft 365 admin center**, select **Security & privacy** under **Settings**, as shown in Figure 2-42.

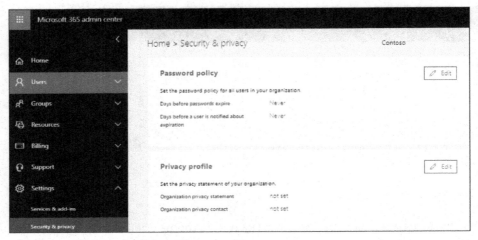

FIGURE 2-42 Security and privacy settings

2. Next to **Password policy**, select **Edit**.

3. On the **Password policy** page, shown in Figure 2-43, you can choose to have passwords never expire or you can configure passwords to expire after a specific number of days. You can also configure the number of days before a user will be informed that their password will expire.

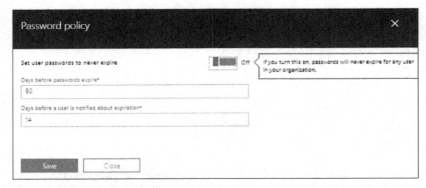

FIGURE 2-43 The Password Policy page

MORE INFO   **RESET USER PASSWORDS**

You can learn more about resetting Microsoft 365 user passwords at *https://docs.microsoft.com/en-us/microsoft-365/admin/add-users/reset-passwords*.

Manage product licenses

Users require licenses to use Microsoft 365 services and products. To assign a license to a user, perform the following steps:

1. In the **Microsoft 365 admin center**, select the **Active users** node under **Users**, as shown in Figure 2-44.

FIGURE 2-44 The Active Users node

2. Select the check box next to the user to whom you want to assign a license. This will bring up the user's properties page, as shown in Figure 2-45.

FIGURE 2-45 User properties page

3. On the user's properties page, select **Edit** next to **Product licenses**.

4. Use the **Location** drop-down menu to choose your location. Then assign licenses as needed: Enterprise Mobility and Security, Office 365 Enterprise, and Windows 10 Enterprise, as shown in Figure 2-46.

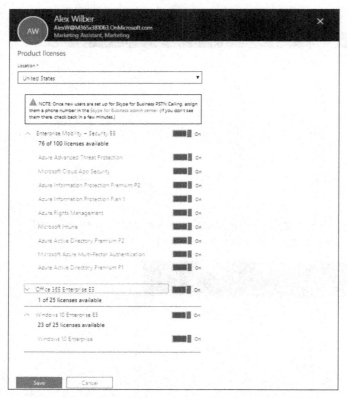

FIGURE 2-46 The Product Licenses page

5. Select **Save** to assign the licenses to the user.

User accounts created in Microsoft 365 by the synchronization process will not automatically be assigned Microsoft 365 licenses. This means that when you are creating new user accounts in the on-premises environment after you've initially configured Azure AD Connect, you'll also need to use Microsoft 365 Admin Center or PowerShell to provision those accounts with Microsoft 365 licenses.

One of the simplest methods to assign licenses to a large number of accounts is by using PowerShell. To do so, you need to first ensure that a usage location is set for each unlicensed user, and then assign a license using the proper SKU identifier.

To determine which Microsoft 365 users have not been properly configured with a license, run the following PowerShell command:

```
Get-MsolUser -UnlicensedUsersOnly
```

To assign all unlicensed users to a specific location, use the following command, where `<location>` is the location to which you want to assign the unlicensed users:

```
Get-MsolUser -UnlicensedUsersOnly | Set-MsolUser -UsageLocation <location>
```

You'll need to apply the account SKU ID to each account. You can do this by first by assigning SKU information to a variable with the following command:

```
$Sku=Get-MsolAccountSku
```

Once you have this information, you can use the following command to apply the appropriate account SKU ID to correctly license each account:

```
Get-MsolUser -UnlicensedUsersOnly | Set-MsolUser -AddLicenses $Sku.AccountSkuID
```

> **MORE INFO**   **ASSIGN LICENSES TO USERS**
>
> You can learn more about assigning licenses to users at *https://docs.microsoft.com/en-us/ microsoft-365/admin/add-users/add-users*.

Manage users

You can use the Microsoft 365 Admin Center, the Azure Active Directory Admin Center, or Azure PowerShell to manage Azure AD user accounts. The Azure Active Directory Admin Center gives you a greater set of options for managing the properties of user accounts than the Microsoft 365 Admin Center because you can edit extended user properties, as shown in Figure 2-47.

FIGURE 2-47 A user's Profile page

To create a new Azure AD user, perform the following steps:

1. In the **Azure AD admin center**, select **Users – All users** and then select **New user**.
2. In the **New user** blade, shown in Figure 2-48, provide the following information:

   - **Name**   The user's actual name.
   - **User name**   The user's sign-in name in UPN format.
   - **Profile**   The user's first name, last name, job title, and department.
   - **Properties**   The user's source of authority. By default, if you are creating the user using the Azure Active Directory Admin Center or the Microsoft 365 Admin Center, this will be Azure Active Directory.
   - **Groups**   The groups the user should be a member of.
   - **Directory role**   Whether the account has user, global administrator, or a limited administrator role.
   - **Password**   The automatically generated password. With the Show Password option, you can transmit the password to the user through a secure channel.

FIGURE 2-48 The User page for creating new users

You can also use the Azure Active Directory Admin Center to perform the following user administrator tasks:

- Update profile information
- Assign directory roles
- Manage group membership
- Manage licenses
- Manage devices

- Manage access to Azure resources
- Manage authentication methods

MORE INFO **USING AZURE AD POWERSHELL TO MANAGE USERS**

You can learn more about Azure AD PowerShell cmdlets for managing users at https://docs. microsoft.com/en-us/powershell/azure/active-directory/new-user-sample.

Perform bulk user management

The best tools for performing bulk user management are the Azure AD–related PowerShell commands. You can use the following commands, some of which are shown in Figure 2-49, to script bulk user-management tasks:

- `New-AzureADUser` Create a new Azure AD user.
- `Get-AzureADUser` Retrieve information about one or more Azure AD users.
- `Set-AzureADUser` Configure the properties of an Azure AD user.
- `Remove-AzureADUser` Remove an Azure AD user account.
- `Get-AzureADUserMembership` View group membership for a specific Azure AD user.
- `Set-AzureADUserPassword` Manage Azure AD user passwords.

```
PS C:\Windows\system32> get-command -noun AzureADUs*

CommandType     Name                                    Version    Source
-----------     ----                                    -------    ------
Cmdlet          Get-AzureADUser                         2.0.2.4    AzureAD
Cmdlet          Get-AzureADUserAppRoleAssignment        2.0.2.4    AzureAD
Cmdlet          Get-AzureADUserCreatedObject            2.0.2.4    AzureAD
Cmdlet          Get-AzureADUserDirectReport             2.0.2.4    AzureAD
Cmdlet          Get-AzureADUserExtension                2.0.2.4    AzureAD
Cmdlet          Get-AzureADUserLicenseDetail            2.0.2.4    AzureAD
Cmdlet          Get-AzureADUserManager                  2.0.2.4    AzureAD
Cmdlet          Get-AzureADUserMembership               2.0.2.4    AzureAD
Cmdlet          Get-AzureADUserOAuth2PermissionGrant     2.0.2.4    AzureAD
Cmdlet          Get-AzureADUserOwnedDevice              2.0.2.4    AzureAD
Cmdlet          Get-AzureADUserOwnedObject              2.0.2.4    AzureAD
Cmdlet          Get-AzureADUserRegisteredDevice         2.0.2.4    AzureAD
Cmdlet          Get-AzureADUserThumbnailPhoto           2.0.2.4    AzureAD
Cmdlet          New-AzureADUser                         2.0.2.4    AzureAD
Cmdlet          New-AzureADUserAppRoleAssignment        2.0.2.4    AzureAD
Cmdlet          Remove-AzureADUser                      2.0.2.4    AzureAD
Cmdlet          Remove-AzureADUserAppRoleAssignment     2.0.2.4    AzureAD
Cmdlet          Remove-AzureADUserExtension             2.0.2.4    AzureAD
Cmdlet          Remove-AzureADUserManager               2.0.2.4    AzureAD
Cmdlet          Revoke-AzureADUserAllRefreshToken       2.0.2.4    AzureAD
Cmdlet          Set-AzureADUser                         2.0.2.4    AzureAD
Cmdlet          Set-AzureADUserExtension                2.0.2.4    AzureAD
Cmdlet          Set-AzureADUserLicense                  2.0.2.4    AzureAD
Cmdlet          Set-AzureADUserManager                  2.0.2.4    AzureAD
Cmdlet          Set-AzureADUserPassword                 2.0.2.4    AzureAD
Cmdlet          Set-AzureADUserThumbnailPhoto           2.0.2.4    AzureAD
```

FIGURE 2-49 User-related PowerShell cmdlets

MORE INFO **USER-MANAGEMENT POWERSHELL CMDLETS**

You can learn more about Azure AD PowerShell cmdlets for managing users at *https://docs. microsoft.com/en-us/powershell/module/azuread/?view=azureadps-2.0#users*.

> **EXAM TIP**
>
> Remember which PowerShell cmdlets you use to add and remove users from groups.

Skill 2.5: Manage user roles

This skill section deals with managing user roles within Azure Active Directory. To master this skill, you'll need to understand how to plan Azure AD roles, allocate roles, configure administrative accounts, configure Azure AD RBAC, delegate administrator rights, manage administrator roles, and plan security and compliance roles.

> **This section covers the following topics:**
> - Plan user roles
> - Manage admin roles
> - Allocate roles for workloads
> - Manage role allocations by using Azure AD

Plan user roles

Rather than assign the global administrator role to all users who need to perform administrative tasks, an organization's approach to planning and assigning user roles should follow the principle of least privilege. This principle dictates that you should assign the minimum necessary privileges to an account required for the user associated with that account to perform tasks.

When planning user roles, determine precisely what tasks the user needs to perform, and then assign the role that allows them to perform only those tasks. For example, if a support desk technician needs to be able to reset passwords, assign that technician the password administrator role rather than a more privileged role such as security administrator or global administrator.

Manage admin roles

Azure Active Directory includes a large number of roles that provide a variety of permissions to different aspects of Azure AD and Microsoft 365 workloads. These roles, and the permissions that they grant, are listed in Table 2-3.

TABLE 2-3 Azure AD roles

Role	Description
Application administrator	Can administer enterprise applications, application registrations, and application proxy settings.
Application developer	Can create application registrations.
Authentication administrator	Can view current authentication method settings. Can set or reset non-password credentials. Can force MFA on next sign-in.
Billing administrator	Can purchase and manage subscriptions. Can manage support tickets and monitor service health.
Cloud application administrator	Can manage all aspects of enterprise applications and registrations but cannot manage application proxy.
Cloud device administrator	Can enable, disable, and remove devices in Azure AD. Can view Windows 10 BitLocker drive encryption keys through the Azure portal.
Compliance administrator	Can manage features in the Microsoft 365 compliance center, Microsoft 365 Admin Center, Azure, and Microsoft 365 Security & Compliance Center.
Conditional access administrator	Has administrative rights over Azure AD conditional access configuration.
Customer lockbox access approver	Manages customer lockbox requests. Can also enable and disable the customer lockbox feature.
Device administrator	Becomes local administrator on all computers running Windows 10 that are joined to Azure AD.
Directory reader	Role for applications that do not support consent framework. Should not be assigned to users.
Directory synchronization account	Assigned to the Azure AD Connect service and not used for user accounts.
Directory writer	A legacy role assigned to applications that do not support the consent framework. Should be assigned only to applications, not user accounts.
Dynamics 365 administrator/ CRM administrator	Provides administrative access to Dynamics 365 Online.
Exchange administrator	Provides administrative access to Exchange Online.
Global administrator/ company administrator	Provides administrative access to all Azure AD features, including services that use Azure AD identities, such as: ■ Microsoft 365 Security & Compliance Center ■ Microsoft 365 compliance center ■ Exchange Online ■ SharePoint Online ■ Skype for Business Online The account used to sign up for the tenancy becomes the global administrator. Global administrators can reset the passwords of any user, including other global administrators.

Role	Description
Guest inviter	Can manage Azure AD B2B guest user invitations.
Information protection administrator	Can manage all aspects of Azure Information Protection, including configuring labels, managing protection templates, and activating protection.
Intune administrator	Has full administrative rights to Microsoft Intune.
License administrator	Can manage license assignments on users and groups. Cannot purchase or manage subscriptions.
Message center reader	Can monitor notifications and Microsoft advisories in the Microsoft 365 message center.
Password administrator/ helpdesk administrator	Can perform the following tasks for all users except those who have administrative roles: ■ Change passwords ■ Invalidate refresh tokens ■ Manage service requests ■ Monitor service health
Power BI administrator	Has administrator permissions over Power BI.
Privileged role administrator	Can manage all aspects of Azure AD Privileged Identity Management (PIM). Can manage role assignments in Azure AD.
Reports reader	Can view reporting data in the Microsoft 365 Reports dashboard.
Security administrator	Has administrator-level access to manage security features in the Microsoft 365 Security & Compliance Center, Azure AD Identity Protection, and Azure Information Protection.
Security reader	Has read-only access to Microsoft 365–related security features.
Service support administrator	Can open and view support requests for Microsoft 365–related services.
SharePoint administrator	Has global administrator permissions for SharePoint Online workloads.
Skype for Business/Lync administrator	Has global administrator permissions for Skype for Business workloads.
Teams administrator	Can administer all elements of Microsoft Teams.
Teams communications administrator	Can manage Teams workloads related to voice and telephony, including telephone number assignment and voice and meeting policies.
Teams communications support engineer	Can troubleshoot communication issues within Teams and Skype for Business. Can view details of call records for all participants in a conversation.
Teams communications support specialist	Can troubleshoot communication issues within Teams and Skype for Business. Can only view user details in the call for a specific user.
User account administrator	Can create and manage user accounts. Can create and manage groups. Can manage user views and support tickets and monitor service health.

MORE INFO   **AZURE AD ADMINISTRATOR ROLES**

You can learn more about Azure AD administrator roles at *https://docs.microsoft.com/en-us/azure/active-directory/roles/permissions-reference*.

Allocate roles for workloads

Several Azure AD roles, such as Exchange administrator, Intune administrator, and SharePoint administrator, are specific to certain Microsoft 365 workloads. These roles often provide complete administrative rights for those workloads, but they provide no administrative permissions beyond those workloads. In organizations where staff are responsible for one or more Microsoft 365 workloads but not responsible for tasks such as user management or other workloads, ensure that you follow the principle of least privilege and assign roles only at the workload level.

Manage role allocations by using Azure AD

To assign a user to a specific role within Azure AD, perform the following steps:

1. In the **Azure Active Directory admin center**, select **Roles and administrators**.
2. Select the role to which you want to add a user. This will open the role's properties page.
3. On the role's properties page, select **Add member**. Figure 2-50 shows adding the user Adele Vance to the security administrator role.

FIGURE 2-50 Members of the security administrator role

You can also use the following Azure PowerShell cmdlets to manage role membership:

- `Add-AzureADDirectoryRoleMember`   Add a user to an Azure AD Directory role.
- `Remove-AzureADDirectoryRoleMember`   Remove a user from an Azure AD Directory role.

MORE INFO   **VIEW AND ASSIGN AZURE AD ADMINISTRATOR ROLES**

You can learn more about viewing and assigning administrator roles at *https://docs.microsoft.com/en-us/azure/active-directory/roles/manage-roles-portal*.

Configure RBAC within Azure AD

Azure role-based access control (RBAC) allows you to configure fine-grained access control to Azure resources, such as virtual machines and storage accounts. When you configure RBAC, you assign a role and a scope, with the scope being the resource you want to have managed.

Azure RBAC includes more than 70 roles. A full listing of the details of all 70 are beyond the scope of this text. However, there are four fundamental roles of which those responsible for managing Microsoft 365 should be aware that can be assigned to specific Azure subscriptions, resource groups, or resources. These roles are as follows:

- **Owner** Users who hold this role have full access to all resources within the scope of the assignment and can delegate access to others.
- **Contributor** Users who hold this role can create and manage resources within the scope of the assignment but cannot grant access to others.
- **Reader** Users who hold this role can view resources within the scope of the assignment but can't perform other tasks and cannot grant access to others.
- **User access administrator** Users who hold this role can manage user access to Azure resources within the scope of the assignment.

> **MORE INFO   AZURE RBAC**
>
> You can learn more about Azure RBAC at *https://docs.microsoft.com/en-us/azure/role-based-access-control/rbac-and-directory-admin-roles*.

Delegate admin rights

To view which users are assigned a specific role, perform the following steps:

1. In the **Azure Active Directory admin center**, select **Roles and administrators** under **Manage**, as shown in Figure 2-51.

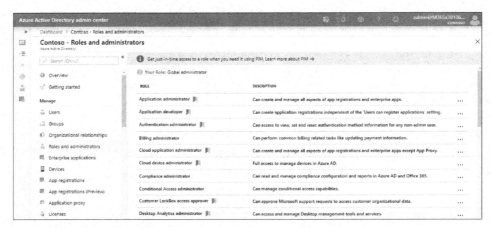

FIGURE 2-51 Roles and administrators

2. Select the role whose membership you want to see. Figure 2-52 shows members of the password administrator role.

FIGURE 2-52 Members of the password administrator role

You can use the following Azure PowerShell cmdlets to view roles and role membership:

- `Get-AzureADDirectoryRole` View a list of Azure AD directory roles.
- `Get-AzureADDirectoryRoleMember` View the users assigned membership in an Azure AD directory role.

> **MORE INFO**   **DELEGATING ADMINISTRATOR RIGHTS**
>
> You can learn more about delegating administrator rights at *https://docs.microsoft.com/en-us/azure/active-directory/roles/security-planning*.

Configure administrative accounts

Azure AD Privileged Identity Management (PIM) allows you to make role assignment temporary and contingent on approval, rather than permanent, as is the case when you manually add a member to the role. PIM requires Azure AD P2 and must be enabled before you can configure it. To configure an Azure AD administrative role for use with PIM, perform the following steps:

1. In the **Azure Active Directory admin center**, select **Roles and administrators** under **Manage**.
2. Select the role to which you want to add a user. This will open the role's properties page.
3. On the role's properties page, select **Manage in PIM**. The role's page will open, and any members assigned permanently to the role will be listed with a status of permanent, as shown in Figure 2-53.

FIGURE 2-53 Members of the security administrator role

4. Select the user you want to convert from permanent to eligible. An eligible user can request access to the role but will not have its associated rights and privileges until that access is granted. On the user's properties page, select **Make eligible**.

You can edit the conditions under which an eligible user can be granted the rights and privileges associated with a role by performing the following steps:

1. On the **Privileged Identity Management** blade, select **Azure AD roles**.

2. Under **Manage**, shown in Figure 2-54, select **Settings**.

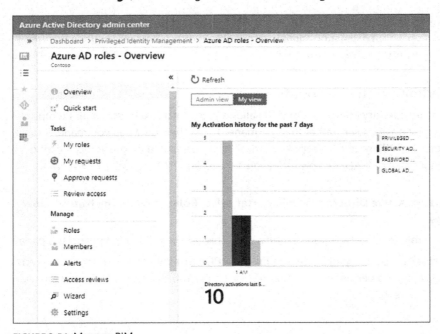

FIGURE 2-54 Manage PIM

3. Select **Roles** and select the role you want to configure. Figure 2-55 shows the PIM settings for the security administrator role where role activation can occur for an hour at most but where MFA and approval are not required.

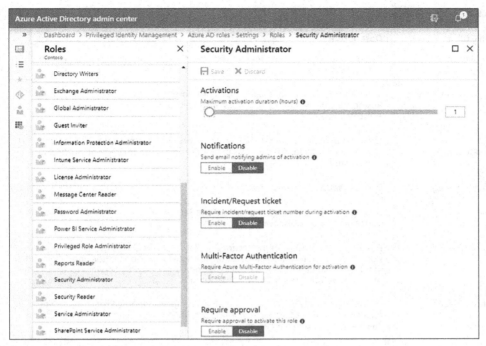

FIGURE 2-55 Manage PIM

Users can activate roles for which they are eligible from the Privileged Identity Management area of the Azure Active Directory Admin Center. Administrators with the appropriate permissions can also use the Privileged Identity Management area of the Azure Active Directory Admin Center to approve requests that require approval and to review role activations.

> **MORE INFO** **PRIVILEGED IDENTITY MANAGEMENT**
>
> You can learn more about PIM at *https://docs.microsoft.com/en-us/azure/active-directory/ privileged-identity-management/pim-configure*.

Plan security and compliance roles for Microsoft 365

The Microsoft 365 Security & Compliance Center includes default role groups that are appropriate for the most commonly performed security and compliance tasks. To assign users permission to perform these tasks, add them to the appropriate role group in the Microsoft 365 Security & Compliance Center. Table 2-4 lists Microsoft 365 security and compliance role groups.

TABLE 2-4 Security and compliance role groups

Role Group	Description
Compliance administrator	Can manage device-management settings, data loss–prevention settings, and data-preservation reports.
eDiscovery manager	Can perform searches and place holds on SharePoint Online sites, OneDrive for Business locations, and Exchange Online mailboxes. Can create and manage eDiscovery cases.
Organization management	Can control permissions for accessing the Security & Compliance Center. Can also manage settings for data loss prevention, device management, reports, and preservation.
Records management	Can manage and dispose of record content.
Reviewer	Can view the list of eDiscovery cases in the Security & Compliance Center. Cannot create or manage eDiscovery cases.
Security administrator	Has all the permissions of the security reader role, plus administrative permissions for Azure Information Protection, Identity Protection Center, and Privileged Identity Management, and the ability to monitor Office 365 Service Health and the Microsoft 365 Security & Compliance Center.
Security reader	Provides read-only access to security features of the Identity Protection Center, Privileged Identity Management, Microsoft 365 Service Health, and the Microsoft 365 Security & Compliance Center.
Service assurance user	Provides reports and documentation that explain Microsoft's security practices for customer data stored in Microsoft 365.
Supervisory review	Can create and manage policies that mediate which communications are subject to review.

> **MORE INFO SECURITY AND COMPLIANCE ROLES**
>
> You can learn more about security and compliance roles at *https://docs.microsoft.com/en-us/office365/securitycompliance/permissions-in-the-security-and-compliance-center*.

> **EXAM TIP**
>
> Remember the functionality of the various security and compliance roles that can be assigned to users.

Thought experiment

In this thought experiment, demonstrate your skills and knowledge of the topics covered in this chapter. You can find answers to this thought experiment in the next section.

You are in the process of consulting for Adatum about their planned synchronization solution that will allow them to replicate user account, group account, and mail-enabled contacts from their on-premises Active Directory environment to an Azure Active Directory instance that supports an Office 365 tenancy. The Adatum environment consists of three forests with 21 separate domains.

A preliminary assessment using the IdFix tool has found that it is necessary to make bulk changes to certain attributes used with user accounts before synchronization between the on-premises environment and the Azure Active Directory instance can commence. Before full-scale deployment of synchronization, it will also be necessary to have robust recovery procedures in place in case one or more accounts is deleted. Finally, all accounts at Adatum are in geography-based OUs. Attributes such as Department denote the departments with which users are associated.

With this in mind, answer the following questions:

1. How many instances of Azure AD Connect are necessary to sync the Adatum environment to a single Azure AD instance?

2. What tool, besides Microsoft PowerShell, could you use to bulk-modify the attributes of selected user accounts at Adatum?

3. How can you ensure that members of the Research department don't have their accounts synchronized to the Azure Active Directory instance that supports the Office 365 tenancy?

4. What feature can you enable on the on-premises Active Directory instance that will enable you to recover an accidentally deleted account without having to re-create it with a new GUID?

5. How long are objects deleted from the Azure Active Directory instance used to support Office 365 recoverable?

Thought experiment answers

This section contains the solutions to the thought experiment. Each answer explains why the answer choice is correct.

1. You need only a single instance of Azure AD Connect to synchronize from three separate Active Directory forests.

2. ADModify.NET can be used to bulk-modify the attributes of selected user accounts at Adatum.

3. You can configure Azure AD Connect to only replicate specific OUs. You can also use tools such as the Synchronization Rules Editor if more complicated synchronization rules are necessary.

4. Enabling the Active Directory Recycle Bin allows you to recover an accidentally deleted account without having to re-create it with a new GUID.

5. Objects are recoverable from the Azure Active Directory Recycle Bin for 30 days.

Chapter summary

- When determining an appropriate identity strategy, figure out which identities need to be replicated to the cloud, how often that replication should occur, and which aspects of those identities must be replicated.

- A hybrid approach is necessary when the on-premises Active Directory instance is still in operation.

- Azure AD Connect can be installed on a local member server and will allow synchronization of identities and password hashes to Azure AD.

- Before deploying Azure AD Connect, the on-premises directory should be cleaned up to remove any current settings that may block successful synchronization. Tools such as IdFix and ADModify.NET can be used to perform this task.

- If your on-premises directory uses a nonroutable domain, you will need to update on-premises accounts with a UPN suffix that is routable and configured to work with Microsoft 365. This will usually be a registered domain name associated with the tenancy.

- Password Sync with Azure AD Connect synchronizes hashes of passwords from the on-premises environment to Azure AD. It can be configured for password writeback if self-service reset is enabled.

- Pass-through authentication validates the user's password against an on-premises AD instance. This requires an agent be installed on an on-premises domain controller.

- Active Directory Federation is appropriate for environments with more sophisticated identity requirements than those catered to by Azure AD Connect Password Sync or pass-through authentication.

- The health of Azure AD Connect can be monitored through the Azure Active Directory Admin Center.

- Synchronization can be forced using the Synchronization Service Manager or through PowerShell.

- Azure AD identities can be managed through the Azure Active Directory Admin Center, the Microsoft 365 Admin Center, or Azure PowerShell.

- Self-service password resets allow users to reset their passwords after answering questions related to their identity.

- Azure AD supports two types of groups: Office 365 groups and security groups. Office 365 groups have access to additional O365 resources such as a shared mailbox and calendar. Membership can be directly assigned or dynamically configured through a query of Azure AD attributes.

- Users must be assigned licenses to use Microsoft 365 resources. This task can be performed through the Microsoft 365 Admin Center or Azure Active Directory Admin Center.

- You can delegate administrative privileges by assigning roles. You should follow the principle of least privilege and only assign users the minimum necessary administrative permissions required to perform their duties.

CHAPTER 3

Manage access and authentication

As services move to the cloud, identity becomes more and more important as a security control plane. So, when managing your company's security posture, rather than worrying about firewall configuration or which services are running on a server, you should be increasingly concerned about your organization's security practices regarding identities. This includes the following:

- Ensuring that Microsoft 365 credentials are being used in a secure manner
- Detecting and remediating risky sign-in activity
- Configuring multifactor authentication where appropriate
- Establishing relationships with partner organizations' identity providers where appropriate

In this chapter, you'll learn how to view auditing data and security reports related to identity, how to configure multifactor authentication (MFA), how to configure access to applications for users, and how to integrate those applications into Azure Active Directory. You'll also learn what steps you can take to enable people within your organization to share content with people outside the organization—lone individuals or people in partner organizations.

Skills covered in this chapter:

- Skill 3.1: Manage authentication
- Skill 3.2: Plan and implement secure access
- Skill 3.3: Configure application access

Skill 3.1: Manage authentication

This skill section deals with managing authentication for Microsoft 365 and Office 365 workloads. To master this skill, you'll need to understand the process of designing an authentication method; configuring, managing, and implementing authentication; and monitoring authentication.

This section covers the following topics:

- Design an authentication method
- Configure authentication
- Implement an authentication method
- Manage authentication
- Monitor authentication

Design an authentication method

When designing an authentication method for Microsoft 365, you must make several decisions about basic and modern authentication before getting into whether you want to implement multifactor authentication. The differences between basic and modern authentication are as follows:

- **Basic authentication**   When a client performs basic authentication, it transmits Base64-encoded credentials from the client to the server. These credentials are protected from interception within a Transport Layer Security (TLS)-encrypted session. TLS is the successor protocol to Secure Sockets Layer (SSL). Basic authentication is also termed *proxy authentication* when the client sends credentials to an Office 365–related service in Microsoft 365, and the service proxies those credentials to an identity provider on behalf of the client. Depending on the organization's configuration, the identity provider can be Azure Active Directory or an on-premises Active Directory instance if pass-through Active Directory Federation Services is configured.

- **Modern authentication**   Instead of just user name- and password-based authentication, modern authentication supports technologies such as multifactor authentication, smart card authentication, certificate-based authentication, and SAML-based third-party identity providers.

Legacy authentication, used by Office 2013 client apps by default, supports both basic authentication as well as the Microsoft Online Services Sign-In assistant. Office 2013 passed from mainstream support in October 2018. The Microsoft Online Services Sign-In Assistant is special software that enables authentication to a variety of Microsoft Online services without requiring end users to regularly reenter their credentials. You can configure Office 2013 client apps to support modern authentication by editing the registry keys listed in Table 3-1 and shown in Figure 3-1.

TABLE 3-1 Modern Authentication Registry Keys

Registry Key	Type	Value
HKCU\SOFTWARE\Microsoft\Office\15.0\Common\Identity\EnableADAL	REG_DWORD	1
HKCU\SOFTWARE\Microsoft\Office\15.0\Common\Identity\Version	REG_DWORD	1

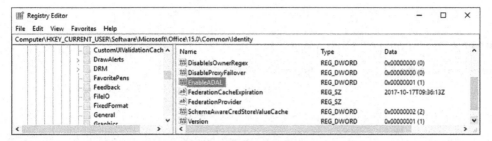

FIGURE 3-1 Office 2013 registry keys that enable use of modern authentication

Office 2016 client apps support modern authentication by default. Although it's possible to configure Office 2016 client apps so that modern authentication is disabled and only basic authentication is used, this approach is not recommended because it will substantially decrease security.

MORE INFO   **UNDERSTANDING MODERN AUTHENTICATION FOR OFFICE CLIENT APPS**

You can learn more about basic and modern authentication and how it affects Office client apps at *https://docs.microsoft.com/en-us/microsoft-365/enterprise/ modern-auth-for-office-2013-and-2016*.

Another important aspect of designing authentication is deciding which authentication methods will be supported if you want to implement self-service password reset or Azure multifactor authentication, as shown in Figure 3-2.

FIGURE 3-2 Multiple methods of verifying identity during authentication

Table 3.2 lists the authentication methods and where they can be used.

TABLE 3-2 Authentication methods and usage

Authentication Method	Where It Can Be Used
Password	Multifactor authentication and self-service password reset
Security questions	Self-service password reset only
Email address	Self-service password reset only
Microsoft Authenticator app	Multifactor authentication and self-service password reset
OATH hardware token	Multifactor authentication and self-service password reset
Mobile phone	Multifactor authentication and self-service password reset
Voice call	Multifactor authentication and self-service password reset
App password	Multifactor authentication in some cases

These authentication methods have the following properties:

- **Password** The password assigned to an Azure AD account is an authentication method. Although you can perform password-less authentication, you cannot disable the password as an authentication method.

- **Security questions** These are available only with Azure AD self-service password reset and can be used only with accounts that have not been assigned administrative roles. Questions are stored on the user object within Azure AD and cannot be read or modified by an administrator. Security questions should be used in conjunction with some other security method. Azure AD includes the following predefined questions; in addition, you can create custom questions:

  - In what city did you meet your first spouse/partner?
  - In what city did your parents meet?
  - In what city does your nearest sibling live?
  - In what city was your father born?
  - In what city was your first job?
  - In what city was your mother born?
  - What city were you in on New Year's 2000?
  - What is the last name of your favorite teacher in high school?
  - What is the name of a college you applied to but didn't attend?
  - What is the name of the place in which you held your first wedding reception?
  - What is your father's middle name?
  - What is your favorite food?

- What is your maternal grandmother's first and last name?
- What is your mother's middle name?
- What is your oldest sibling's birthday month and year? (e.g., November 1985)
- What is your oldest sibling's middle name?
- What is your paternal grandfather's first and last name?
- What is your youngest sibling's middle name?
- What school did you attend for sixth grade?
- What was the first and last name of your childhood best friend?
- What was the first and last name of your first significant other?
- What was the last name of your favorite grade school teacher?
- What was the make and model of your first car or motorcycle?
- What was the name of the first school you attended?
- What was the name of the hospital in which you were born?
- What was the name of the street of your first childhood home?
- What was the name of your childhood hero?
- What was the name of your favorite stuffed animal?
- What was the name of your first pet?
- What was your childhood nickname?
- What was your favorite sport in high school?
- What was your first job?
- What were the last four digits of your childhood telephone number?
- When you were young, what did you want to be when you grew up?
- Who is the most famous person you have ever met?

- **Email address** This is used only for Azure AD self-service password resets and should be separate from the user's Microsoft 365 Exchange Online email address.

- **Microsoft Authenticator app** This is available for Android and iOS. It either notifies the user through the mobile app and asks the user to enter the number displayed on the logon prompt into the mobile app or periodically asks the user to enter a set of changing numbers displayed on the mobile app.

- **OATH hardware tokens** Azure AD supports the use of OATH-TOTP SHA-1 tokens of both the 30- and 60-second variety. Secret keys can have a maximum of 128 characters. Once a token is acquired, it must be uploaded in comma-separated format, including the UPN, serial number, secret key, time interval, manufacturer, and model.

- **Mobile phone** The user can either enter a code sent to their mobile phone via text message into a dialog box to complete authentication or place a phone call to provide a personal authentication PIN. Phone numbers must include country code.

- **App password** A number of nonbrowser apps do not support multifactor authentication. An app password enables these users to continue to authenticate using these apps when multifactor authentication is not supported. An app password can be generated for each app, allowing each app password to be individually revoked.

> **MORE INFO** **WHAT ARE AUTHENTICATION METHODS?**
>
> You can learn more about what authentication methods are supported by Microsoft 365 and Azure AD at *https://docs.microsoft.com/en-us/azure/active-directory/authentication/ concept-authentication-methods*.

Configure authentication

Modern authentication is enabled by default for SharePoint Online, Exchange Online, and other Office 365 services available through Microsoft 365. You can verify that modern authentication is enabled by running the following PowerShell command when connected to your organization's Microsoft 365 tenancy:

```
Get-OrganizationConfig | Format-Table Name,OAuth* -Auto
```

Although not recommended, you can disable modern authentication by running the following PowerShell command when connected to your organization's Microsoft 365 tenancy:

```
Set-OrganizationConfig -OAuth2ClientProfileEnabled $false
```

To reenable modern authentication, run the following command when connected to your organization's Microsoft 365 tenancy:

```
Set-OrganizationConfig -OAuth2ClientProfileEnabled $true
```

> **MORE INFO** **ENABLE MODERN AUTHENTICATION IN EXCHANGE ONLINE**
>
> You can learn more about enabling modern authentication in Exchange Online at *https://docs.microsoft.com/en-us/exchange/clients-and-mobile-in-exchange-online/ enable-or-disable-modern-authentication-in-exchange-online*.

Another aspect of configuring authentication is configuring a password policy. Password policies determine how often users must update their password. By default, Microsoft 365 user passwords are configured to never expire, as shown in Figure 3-3. Password policies for Microsoft 365 are configured in the Microsoft 365 Admin Center.

FIGURE 3-3 Default Microsoft 365 password policy

Users who have been assigned the global administrator role can modify the password policy. After you have configured passwords to expire, you can configure the number of days before passwords expire and the number of days before a user is notified that their password will expire. Figure 3-4 shows a maximum password age of 90 days and how a user will be notified 14 days before expiration occurs. You can configure a maximum password age of up to 730 days.

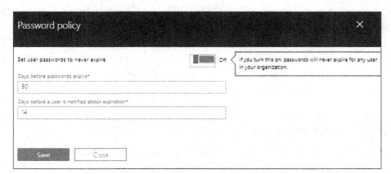

FIGURE 3-4 Configuring a Microsoft 365 password policy

> **MORE INFO PASSWORD EXPIRATION POLICIES**
> You can learn more about password expiration policies at *https://docs.microsoft.com/en-us/ microsoft-365/admin/manage/set-password-expiration-policy*.

Implement an authentication method

Microsoft 365 supports multiple authentication methods. When you enable multifactor authentication and self-service password reset, you should also enable multiple authentication methods. Doing so enables the user to fall back to a different authentication method if their chosen authentication method is not available. For example, if a user cannot get access to their mailbox and needs to perform a self-service password reset, you can allow them to answer a number of security questions to validate their identity.

You configure the authentication methods that users can use to perform self-service password reset on the Password Reset – Authentication Methods blade in Azure Active Directory Admin Center, as shown in Figure 3-5.

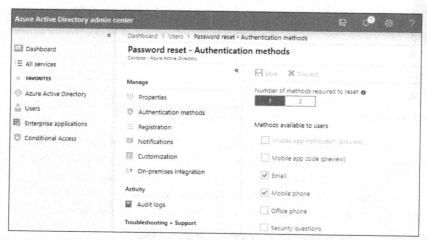

FIGURE 3-5 The Password Reset – Authentication Methods blade

Unless there is a good reason otherwise, you should enable as many authentication methods for self-service password resets as possible and require two methods to perform a reset. This strategy gives users the maximum amount of flexibility while still ensuring a high level of security.

> **MORE INFO   AUTHENTICATION METHODS**
>
> You can learn more about authentication methods at *https://docs.microsoft.com/en-us/azure/active-directory/authentication/concept-authentication-methods*.

Manage authentication

You can choose among several technologies to manage authentication in a Microsoft 365 environment:

- Azure AD Smart Lockout
- Azure AD banned passwords
- Self-service password reset
- Password-less phone sign-on
- Certificate-based Azure AD authentication

Azure AD Smart Lockout

Azure AD Smart Lockout is a technology that enables you to lock out attackers who are trying to brute-force user passwords. Based on machine learning, Smart Lockout can discern when sign-ins are coming from authentic users and treat those sign-ins differently from those that appear to come from attackers or other unknown sources.

Smart Lockout locks out an account for 60 seconds after 10 failed sign-in attempts have occurred. If there are subsequent failed sign-in attempts after the 60 seconds are up, the duration of the lockout period increases. Smart Lockout tracks only when different passwords are used, which is the pattern during a brute-force attack, so if a user enters the same incorrect password 10 times, that will only count as one bad password toward the 10 that trigger account lockout.

Azure AD Smart Lockout is enabled by default on Microsoft 365 Azure AD tenancies. You can configure a custom Smart Lockout threshold in the Authentication Methods section of the Azure AD admin center, as shown in Figure 3-6.

FIGURE 3-6 Custom Smart Lockout policy

> **MORE INFO   AZURE AD SMART LOCKOUT**
>
> You can learn more about Azure AD Smart Lockout at *https://docs.microsoft.com/en-us/azure/active-directory/authentication/howto-password-smart-lockout*.

Azure AD banned passwords

Another aspect of managing authentication is implementing a custom banned password list, as shown in Figure 3-7. Any password on the banned password list cannot be used by a user in your organization. You can implement a custom banned password list only if your organization has an Azure AD P1 or P2 license. Common character substitution within banned passwords is enabled by default.

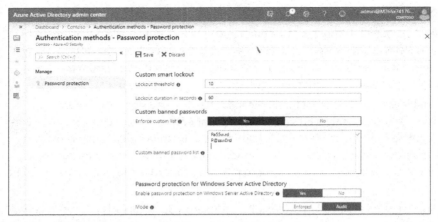

FIGURE 3-7 Custom banned passwords

There are multiple lists of commonly used passwords that you can download free from the internet and add to the Azure AD banned password list to prevent users from using them. You can also import lists of all passwords that have been exposed in data breaches to ensure that users cannot use those passwords, either.

> **MORE INFO** **AZURE AD BANNED PASSWORDS**
>
> You can learn more about Azure AD banned passwords at *https://docs.microsoft.com/en-us/ azure/active-directory/authentication/concept-password-ban-bad.*

Self-service password reset

Self-service password reset enables users to perform other forms of authentication if they forget their account's Azure AD password. As you can see in Figure 3-8, you can configure self-service password reset so that users must sign up for the service when they first authenticate and then periodically renew their information, with the default renewal period being every 180 days.

FIGURE 3-8 The Password Reset – Registration blade in the Azure AD admin center

As you learned earlier in this chapter, you can require users to provide multiple forms of authentication when performing a self-service password reset. When a user signs up for self-service password reset, they can configure the following alternate methods of authentication:

- Mobile app notification
- Mobile app code
- Email
- Mobile phone
- Office phone
- Security questions

MORE INFO   CONFIGURE SELF-SERVICE PASSWORD RESET

You can learn more about configuring self-service password reset at *https://docs.microsoft.com/en-us/azure/active-directory/authentication/tutorial-enable-sspr*.

Password-less phone sign-on

When password-less phone sign-on is enabled, users can sign into an Azure AD account and then access Microsoft 365 resources using the Microsoft Authenticator app on their mobile device. In this scenario, users need not provide a user name and password; instead, key-based authentication enables them to authenticate with the Authenticator app using a biometric or a PIN.

To enable password-less phone sign-on, users must have the latest version of the Microsoft Authenticator installed on their device. Their devices should be running iOS 8.0 or greater or Android 6.0 or greater. Users will also need to be enrolled for multifactor authentication. When these conditions have been met, an authenticator sign-in policy must be configured. You can do this when a PowerShell connection is established to the Microsoft 365 tenancy by issuing the following command:

```
New-AzureADPolicy -Type AuthenticatorAppSignInPolicy -Definition '{"Authenticator
AppSignInPolicy":{"Enabled":true}}' -isOrganizationDefault $true -DisplayName
AuthenticatorAppSignIn
```

To enable phone sign-on on the app, choose the drop-down arrow next to the account name in the app and select Enable Phone Sign-On. If an icon with a key appears next to the Microsoft 365 account name, this means that phone sign-on for the account has successfully been configured.

A drawback of using phone sign-on is that due to the way device registration functions with Azure AD, a device can only be registered against a single tenant. This means that if a user has multiple Microsoft 365 accounts, only one of those accounts can be enabled for phone sign-on.

MORE INFO   PASSWORD-LESS PHONE SIGN-ON

You can learn more about configuring password-less phone sign-on at *https://docs.microsoft.com/en-us/azure/active-directory/authentication/howto-authentication-passwordless-phone*.

Certificate-based Azure AD authentication

Certificate-based authentication enables you to eliminate the need for a user name and password combination when authenticating against Exchange Online and other Microsoft 365 services. Certificate-based authentication is supported on Windows, Android, and iOS devices, and it has the following requirements:

- Is supported only for Federated environments for browser applications or where native clients use modern authentication through the Active Directory Authentication Library (ADAL). Exchange Active Sync (EAS) for Exchange Online (EXO) is exempt from the Federation requirement and can be used with both Federated and managed accounts.
- The organization's root certificate authority (CA) and any intermediate CAs must be integrated with Azure AD.
- Each organizational CA must publish a certificate revocation list (CRL) in a location that is accessible to the internet.
- The Windows, Android, or iOS device must have access to an organizational CA that is configured to issue client certificates.
- The Windows, Android, or iOS device must have a valid certificate installed.
- Exchange ActiveSync clients require that the client certificate include the user's routable email address in the Subject Alternative Name field.

To add an organizational CA that is trusted by Azure Active Directory, you must first ensure that the CA is configured with a CRL publication location that is accessible on the internet and then export the CA certificate. After you export the CA certificate, which will include the internet-accessible location where the CRL is published, you use the New-AzureADTrustedCertificateAuthority PowerShell cmdlet to add the organizational CA's certificate to Azure Active Directory. You can view a list of trusted CAs for your organization's Azure AD instance using the Get-AzureADTrustedCertificateAuthority cmdlet.

> **MORE INFO**   **CERTIFICATE-BASED AZURE AD AUTHENTICATION**
>
> You can learn more about certificate-based Azure AD authentication at *https://docs.microsoft.com/en-us/azure/active-directory/authentication/active-directory-certificate-based-authentication-get-started*.

Monitor authentication

There are several methods through which you can monitor authentication for your organization's Microsoft 365 tenancy. Azure AD's reporting architecture includes the following elements:

- **Sign-ins**   Provides you with information about user sign-in activity and the use of managed applications
- **Audit logs**   Enables you to view information about changes that have occurred within Azure Active Directory, such as adding or removing user accounts

- **Risky sign-ins** Provides you with data about sign-in activity that has been flagged as suspicious by Microsoft's security mechanisms
- **Users flagged for risk** Provides you with a list of users that Microsoft's security mechanisms suggest might have compromised accounts

Users who have been assigned the global administrator, security administrator, security reader, or report reader Azure AD role can view data in Azure AD reports. Users without membership in these roles can view audit activities related to their account.

Each event recorded in the audit logs provides the following data:

- Data and time of the event
- Service that logged the event
- Name and category of the event logged
- Activity status (success or failure)
- Target of the action (which user, group, etc.)
- Which security principal initiated the action

Figure 3-9 shows the details of an event in the Azure AD audit log.

FIGURE 3-9 Azure AD audit log event

You can filter audit logs using the following fields:

- Service
- Category
- Activity
- Status
- Target
- Initiated by (Actor)
- Date Range

MORE INFO   **AUDIT ACTIVITY REPORTS**

You can learn more about audit activity reports at *https://docs.microsoft.com/en-us/azure/active-directory/reports-monitoring/concept-audit-logs*.

Sign-in logs

Sign-in logs provide information about user and managed application authentication activity. Figure 3-10 shows the basic sign-in log.

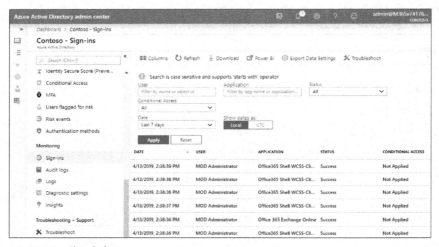

FIGURE 3-10 Sign-in log

The sign-in log enables you to answer the following questions:

- What patterns are present in a user's sign-in activities?
- How many users associated with the Microsoft 365 tenancy have signed in over the last week?
- How many sign-ins have been successful and how many have failed?

The sign-in log provides the following information by default:

- Sign-in date
- User account
- Application the user has authenticated against
- Sign-in status (success or failure)
- Risk-detection status
- Multifactor authentication status

The sign-in log can be filtered by the following fields, as shown in Figure 3-11:

- User
- Application

- Status
- Conditional Access
- Date

FIGURE 3-11 Filtering a sign-in log

MORE INFO **SIGN-IN ACTIVITY REPORTS**

You can learn more about sign-in logs at *https://docs.microsoft.com/en-us/azure/ active-directory/reports-monitoring/concept-sign-ins*.

Self-service password reset activity

You can view the self-service password reset audit log on the Password Reset – Audit Logs blade of the Azure AD admin center, as shown in Figure 3-12. These logs provide information about which user initiated the reset, when the reset was initiated, and the method used.

FIGURE 3-12 Risky sign-ins

You can use the dialog boxes and drop-down lists on this page to generate reports that enable you to determine the following information:

- How many users have registered for self-service password reset?
- Which users have registered for self-service password reset?
- What information are users providing when registering for self-service password reset?
- How many users reset their passwords using self-service password reset in the previous seven days?
- What methods are being used for authentication when performing self-service password reset?
- Is there any suspicious activity occurring during the self-service password reset process?
- Which authentication methods are generating the most problems during the self-service password reset process?

> **MORE INFO** **SELF-SERVICE PASSWORD RESET REPORTS**
>
> You can learn more about self-service password reset reports at *https://docs.microsoft.com/en-us/azure/active-directory/authentication/howto-sspr-reporting*.

 EXAM TIP

Remember the different authentication options that can be configured for self-service password reset and the requirements for organizational CAs when implementing certificate-based AD authentication.

Skill 3.2: Plan and implement secure access

This skill section deals with implementing secure access to Microsoft 365 resources. To master this skill, you'll need to understand how to design and implement conditional access, create Active Directory entitlement access packages, configure and manage Azure AD Identity Protection, implement multifactor authentication, and implement and secure access for guest and external users.

> **This section covers the following topics:**
> - Design a conditional access solution
> - Implement entitlement packages
> - Implement Azure AD Identity Protection
> - Manage conditional access
> - Implement and secure access for guest and external users

Design a conditional access solution

Azure Active Directory conditional access uses the properties of a user account, a user device, and the user's location to determine what access a user will have to organizational resources. For example, you can configure conditional access to require a user to perform multifactor authentication if they are accessing a sensitive application from an unusual location or to block a user from access if they are not using an Azure AD hybrid joined computer.

When designing a conditional access solution, take into account the following steps:

- **Engage the right stakeholders**   Rather than enabling conditional access for everyone on a whim, determine which stakeholders within your organization you should consult with when it comes to planning conditional access. The needs of the stakeholders will determine what approach you take to conditional access. For example, you might not be able to implement multifactor authentication as a part of a conditional access policy if stakeholders have concerns about requiring users to all have devices capable of responding to multifactor authentication challenges.

- **Plan communications**   When shifting to a conditional access posture, it will be necessary to explain to users why they may be required to perform multifactor authentication to access some resources and why they may be blocked from access at other times. New security procedures are far less likely to encounter resistance from end users if they are explained before they are implemented rather than justified in an apologetic email sent from the IT department after enough complaints have reached the service desk.

- **Plan a pilot**   When you've decided on the details of the conditional access policies that you want to implement, conduct a pilot where you apply those policies to a subset of users and solicit their feedback. Vocal users are the best ones to include in a pilot because they won't be shy about providing feedback. Also consider including the users who contact the service desk most often because they are the most likely group to encounter problems when conditional access policies are deployed organizationwide.

As shown in Figure 3-13, conditional access policies use assignments and access controls. *Assignments* are the conditions that determine when the policy will apply—for example, which users are included, which applications or actions are relevant, and which conditions will trigger the policy. *Access controls* specify what occurs when conditions are met. You will learn more about building conditional access policies later in this chapter.

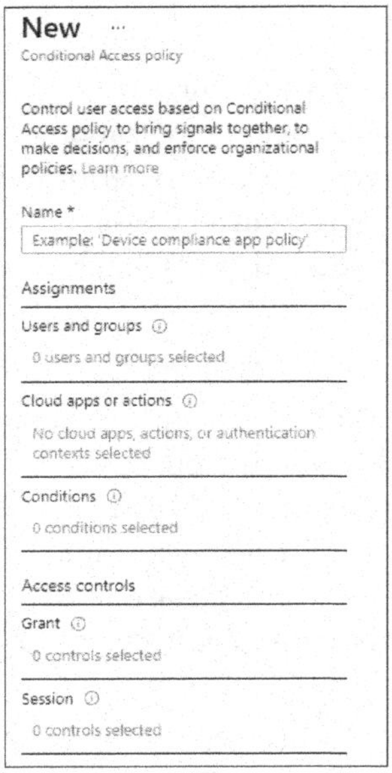

FIGURE 3-13 Conditional access policy assignments

MORE INFO **DESIGN CONDITIONAL ACCESS**

You can learn more about designing conditional access at *https://docs.microsoft.com/en-us/azure/active-directory/conditional-access/plan-conditional-access*.

Implement entitlement packages

Azure AD entitlement management enables you to automate workflows for access requests, assignments, reviews, and expirations. An entitlement access package contains resources that users can request. A user who is delegated the role of access package manager can configure policies with rules that determine which users can request access to the entitlement package, which users can approve that access, and when that access will expire.

It's also possible to give members of organizations configured through Azure AD business-to-business (B2B) relationships the ability to request access. When you enable access for a user from a directory configured in a B2B relationship with your organization's Azure AD tenancy and that access is approved, the connected organization's user will be invited to your Azure AD instance and assigned access. When that access expires, the B2B account will automatically be removed. You will learn more about Azure AD B2B later in this chapter.

Azure AD entitlement management access packages can include the following resources:

- Membership in Azure AD security groups
- Membership in Microsoft 365 groups and teams
- Assignment to Azure AD enterprise applications
- Membership in SharePoint online sites

- Microsoft 365 group-based licensing
- Role assignments to Azure resources
- Azure AD role management

To create an Azure AD entitlement management access package, perform the following steps:

1. In the Azure portal, under **Azure Active Directory**, select **Identity Governance**. Then select **Access packages**.

2. On the **Access packages** pane, shown in Figure 3-14, select **New access package**.

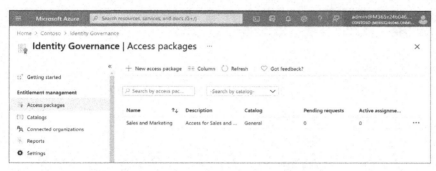

FIGURE 3-14 Access Packages

3. On the **Basics** tab, configure the following settings:
   - **Name** The name of the access package
   - **Description** A description of the access package
   - **Catalog** The catalog in which you want to store the access package

4. On the **Resource roles** tab, shown in Figure 3-15, use the **Group and Teams**, **Applications**, and **SharePoint sites** buttons to select the groups and teams, applications, and SharePoint sites that you want to include in the package. When you select one of these buttons, a pane appears that lists resources that you have permission to add to the package. After you select a resource, specify the role that you want the users who request the entitlement package to have.

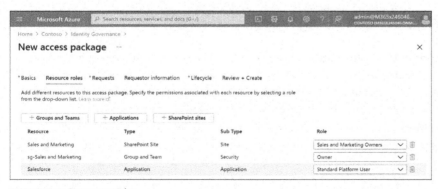

FIGURE 3-15 Resource roles

5. On the **Requests** tab, create a policy to specify which users can request the access package and what approval settings apply. You can create multiple request policies for different groups of users within a single access package.

6. Choose whether you want to require approval, whether the requestor should provide justification, and how many stages of approval are required. Figure 3-16 shows that a user's manager must provide approval for a request within 14 days and give a justification for that approval. (You can also configure a fallback approval option if the designated approver does not respond in time.)

FIGURE 3-16 Approval

7. On the **Requestor information** tab, specify the information that the requestor must present when requesting access to the access package. This information will be reviewed by the approver during the approval process. You can configure the answer to be short text or long text, or have the requestor select from a set of answers.

8. On the **Lifecycle** tab, shown in Figure 3-17, specify the amount of time that will pass before access package assignments expire. You can choose for the expiration to occur

on a specific date, a number of days after the access package request has been granted, or never. You can also choose to enable the user to request an extension and whether or not that extension requires approval.

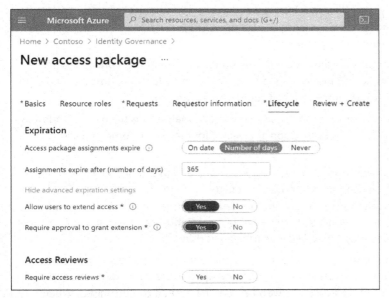

FIGURE 3-17 Lifecycle tab options

9. On the **Review + Create** tab, review the settings configured for the new access package. Then select **Create** to create the package.

> *MORE INFO* **AZURE AD ENTITLEMENT MANAGEMENT**
>
> You can learn more about Azure AD entitlement management at *https://docs.microsoft.com/ en-us/azure/active-directory/governance/entitlement-management-overview.*

Implement Azure AD Identity Protection

Azure AD Identity Protection looks at the properties of a user's sign-in activity and assesses the likelihood that the identity is compromised based on an analysis of risk factors drawn from Microsoft's security graph. The Microsoft security graph is a collection of security telemetry collected, collated, and analyzed across Microsoft's properties, including Azure, Microsoft 365, Xbox, and other services. Because these properties are regularly subject to attack from those with nefarious intent, Microsoft has been able to map the origin point of a substantive amount of malicious activity to specific IP address ranges and locations—for example, the IP addresses of compromised hosts that are used as the launching point for brute-force password or distributed denial-of-service attacks.

Risk factors included in an Azure AD Identity Protection assessment include the following:

- Is the sign-in occurring from an anonymous IP address? Is the IP address used for the sign-in unusual or is it one from which sign-ins often occur? For example, if sign-ins for a specific identity typically occur from a well-known ISP's subnets but sign-in attempts are now occurring from an anonymous IP address range not tied to a known internet provider, it could indicate a problem.

- Has the sign-in occurred from a location suspiciously different from previous sign-in activity? For example, if Rooslan signs in at 10 a.m. from Melbourne, Australia and signs in at 1 p.m. from Stockholm, Sweden, it could indicate an issue.

- Has the sign-in occurred from an IP address linked to malware? Is the host's IP address known to the Microsoft security graph as a vector for malware or other malicious activity?

- Does the sign-in have unusual properties? An example of this might be a sign-in from an unusual location compared to previous activity. Though not always an indicator of compromise, if a Microsoft 365 account that usually signs in from Sydney, Australia during Australian business hours suddenly signs in from Gaborone, Botswana at 2 a.m. local time, the sign-in activity would likely be flagged as risky.

- Are the user account's credentials included in password breach data? Many people use their Microsoft 365 credentials when signing up for third-party websites, and the account databases of some of these websites may have been compromised. When Microsoft's security research team becomes aware that Microsoft 365 credentials are present in password breach data, it increases likelihood that a sign-in using those credentials is risky.

- Has the user account been subject to a password spray attack? If multiple sign-in attempts occur over a short period using constantly changing passwords, it might indicate that a malicious actor is attempting a password spray attack, increasing the likelihood that the sign-in is designated as risky.

Azure AD Identity Protection uses three risk categories: low, medium, and high. If an identity or activity is classified as high risk, this can be reasonably interpreted to mean that Microsoft has a high degree of confidence that the identity has been compromised.

MORE INFO **AZURE AD IDENTITY PROTECTION**

You can learn more about Azure AD Identity Protection at *https://docs.microsoft.com/en-us/azure/active-directory/identity-protection/overview-identity-protection*.

Risk policies

Azure AD Identity Protection includes two types of risk policies that you can configure and apply to users in your organization:

- **User risk policies**   These apply when Microsoft detects risk conditions associated with a user account, such as a user's credentials being found in a user account database breach from a third-party site. When a user risk policy triggers, administrators can specify that the user must perform a self-service password reset and perform Azure AD multifactor authentication when doing so.

- **Sign-in risk policies**   These trigger when there is something unusual about the properties of the sign-in, such as it being from a suspicious or unusual location. When a sign-in risk policy triggers, an administrator can require that the user perform multifactor authentication to verify that they are the individual associated with the account who is attempting the sign-in.

When configuring policies, you can select exclusions for specific users. You can also configure exclusions for emergency access accounts. An emergency access account is one that is only used if there are problems with existing privileged accounts used for administrative tasks. You should ensure that each Azure AD tenancy does have an emergency access account, but the only time the account should be used is when you test it during a disaster drill or you have no other options for accessing your Azure AD tenant as an administrator. You should update the credentials of an emergency access account whenever a member of staff who has had access to the account in the past leaves your organization.

You can configure risk policies through conditional access and Azure AD Identity Protection. Microsoft recommends that you configure through conditional access. Doing so gives you the opportunity to configure multiple policies for user and sign-in risk, whereas Identity Protection enables you to configure only a single policy. Conditional access policies also enable you to account for device health, applications used, and other factors. Configuring conditional access risk policies is covered later in this chapter.

To configure a user risk policy through Identity Protection, perform the following steps:

1. In the **Azure AD Administration Portal**, select **Security**. Then select **Identity Protection**.
2. On the **Identity Protection** page, select **User risk policy**.
3. On the **User risk policy** page, shown in Figure 3-18, select the users or groups to which the policy will apply, which groups will be excluded, the risk level that triggers the policy, and what happens if the policy is triggered. The policy can be set to block access, enable access, or enable access with a password change.

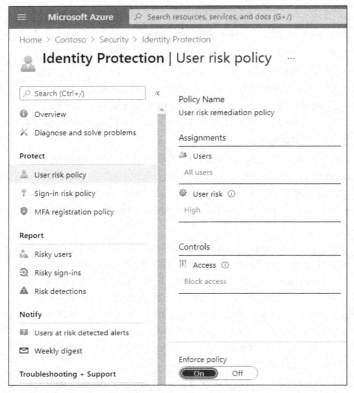

FIGURE 3-18 Configuring a user risk policy

To configure a sign-in risk policy through Identity Protection, perform the following steps:

1. In the **Azure AD Administration Portal**, select **Security**. Then select **Identity Protection**.

2. On the **Identity Protection** page, select **Sign-in risk policy**.

3. On the **Sign-in risk policy** page, specify which users the policy applies to, the risk level that triggers the policy, and the access level to which the user is restricted when the policy is triggered. With a sign-in risk policy configured through Identity Protection, you can block access, enable access, and enable access with multifactor authentication.

> **MORE INFO   RISK POLICIES**
>
> You can learn more about risk policies at *https://docs.microsoft.com/en-us/azure/active-directory/identity-protection/howto-identity-protection-configure-risk-policies*.

Investigating risky activity

Microsoft 365 and Azure AD administrators can review activity deemed risky and identities considered to be at risk by examining risk-related reports in the Identity Protection section of the Azure AD blade of the Azure Administrative Portal. Figure 3-19 shows the risky users report, but there are other reports, too.

FIGURE 3-19 The risky users report

These reports provide the following information:

- **Risky users** This report relays which users are at risk, which users have had risks remediated, which users have had risk warnings dismissed by administrators, details on risk detections, risky sign-in history, and risk history.

- **Risky sign-ins** This report includes which sign-ins are risky, confirmed compromised, confirmed safe, dismissed by administrators, or remediated. It also includes risk levels associated with sign-ins, detection types triggered, conditional access policies applied, multifactor authentication details, device information, application information, and location information.

- **Risk detections** This report includes information about each risk detection, the detection type, any risks that were detected at the same time, the location where the risky sign-in occurred, and any additional details that might be found in Microsoft Cloud App Security.

> **MORE INFO**   **INVESTIGATING RISK**
>
> You can learn more about investigating risk in Azure AD Identity Protection at *https://docs.microsoft.com/en-us/azure/active-directory/identity-protection/howto-identity-protection-investigate-risk*.

Risky sign-ins

A risky sign-in is one that Microsoft's security mechanisms have flagged as suspicious. Microsoft processes millions of sign-ins every day through services such as Azure AD, Xbox Live, and Outlook.com. Telemetry is used from these sign-ins to determine the characteristics of what constitutes a normal sign-in and which sign-ins are suspicious and should be flagged for further investigation. Flagged sign-ins appear in the risky sign-ins report, shown in Figure 3-20.

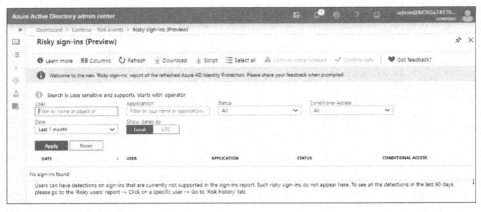

FIGURE 3-20 Risky sign-ins

Although a risky sign-ins report is available for all editions of Azure AD, the amount of detail provided by the report varies between the Free, Basic, P1, and P2 editions. The report in the Free and Basic editions provides a list of risky sign-ins with the following details:

- **User**   The user with whom the risky sign-in is associated
- **IP**   The IP address from which the sign-in occurred
- **Location**   The location that Microsoft's security intelligence data indicates is associated with the IP address
- **Sign-in time**   When the sign-in occurred
- **Status**   The status of the sign-in

When viewing entries in the risky sign-ins report, you can choose from the following actions:

- **Resolve**   Marks the event as resolved
- **Mark as false positive**   Marks the event as something that should not be classified as a risky sign-in
- **Ignore**   Marks the risk factors as ones that should be ignored in the future
- **Reactivate**   Reactivates a risky sign-in that was previously assigned another status

Risky sign-ins reports received by organizations licensed at the Azure AD P1 and P2 levels will receive the same information as those licensed at the Basic and Free levels, plus more information about the risk event type. They will also have the ability to create a user risk remediation policy, a detailed timeline on the risk event, and a list of other users for which the same risk event type has been detected.

Risk events

Azure AD Identity Protection detects the following types of suspicious activities and assigns them to the following risk-event categories:

- **Users with leaked credentials**   Microsoft examines credential data breaches for user name and password pairs associated with Azure AD tenancies. When a user name and password pair associated with an Azure AD tenancy is found, these credentials are checked; if there is a match, Azure AD Identity Protection generates a leaked credentials risk event.

- **Sign-ins from anonymous IP addresses**   Microsoft security researchers have identified which IP addresses are used by anonymous proxy services. Although it's not unusual for some users to route their traffic through anonymous VPN services, it's also a technique used by attackers attempting to compromise an account. Figure 3-21 shows sign-ins in this category.

- **Impossible travel to atypical locations**   This risk category is assigned when a user signs in from multiple locations that are so geographically disparate that travel between them would be impossible in the period between the sign-in times—for example, if a user were to sign in from Sydney, Australia and then two hours later sign in from Copenhagen, Denmark.

- **Sign-ins from infected devices**   This risk category is assigned when a user signs in from an address that Microsoft security researchers have flagged as regularly communicating with a bot server.

- **Sign-ins from unfamiliar locations**   This risk category is assigned when a user signs in from a location that is unusual given their past sign-in activity. For example, if a user typically signs in from locations around Melbourne, Australia and then signs in from Stockholm, Sweden, Azure AD Identity Protection will generate this risk event.

- **Sign-ins from IP addresses with suspicious activity**   This risk category is assigned when a user signs in from an IP address or IP address range from which there have been a substantial number of failed sign-in attempts across multiple accounts in a short period of time. Essentially, the machine learning algorithm that assigns this category is attempting to detect credential-guessing brute-force attacks before they are successful.

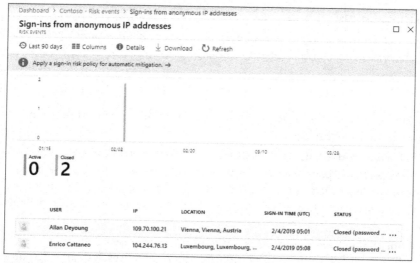

FIGURE 3-21 Risky sign-ins from anonymous IP addresses

After Azure AD Identity Protection assigns a risk category, it calculates a risk level. The severity of the risk level enables you to understand the degree of confidence Microsoft has that the identity may have been compromised and how seriously you should take the alert. The severity levels are as follows:

- **High** There is high severity and high confidence in the diagnosis. An identity related to an event that is assigned this severity level is almost certainly compromised. User accounts involved should be remediated immediately.

- **Medium** With this diagnosis, there is either high severity and lower confidence or low severity and higher confidence. Microsoft recommends that identities related to an event assigned this severity level should be proactively remediated even if you are uncertain whether the account has been compromised.

- **Low** This diagnosis involves low severity and low confidence. This is an indicator that Microsoft has flagged activity involving the activity to be suspicious. An example of this might be a sign-in from an unfamiliar location in the same region of the world—for example, if a user who has, up until now, only signed in from Sydney and Melbourne in Australia suddenly signs in from Auckland, New Zealand.

Users flagged for risk

The users flagged for risk report, accessible from the Security section of the Azure AD admin center, as shown in Figure 3-22, provides a list of users whose accounts have risk events associated with them. Depending on which edition of Azure AD you use, you'll either get a simple list of users who are flagged for risk (Basic and Free) or detailed information about underlying risk events and why each specific user was flagged (P1 and P2).

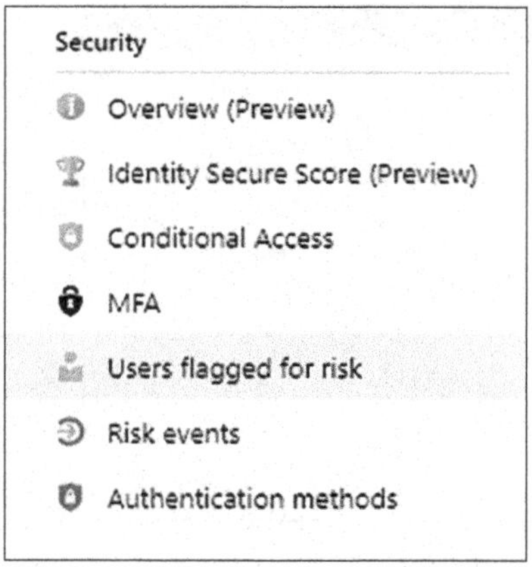

Security
- ⓘ Overview (Preview)
- 🏆 Identity Secure Score (Preview)
- 🛡 Conditional Access
- 🔒 MFA
- 👥 Users flagged for risk
- 🔄 Risk events
- 🛡 Authentication methods

FIGURE 3-22 Accessing the Users Flagged For Risk report

Manage conditional access

After you've planned your conditional access policies, you should create and test those policies. You can create policies using the Conditional Access area of the Azure portal. This area of the portal also hosts the What If tool, which enables you to simulate the results of those policies given a set of conditions. Even after you have created and tested policies using the What If tool, it's a good idea to use the reporting-only mode for a short period of time to verify that the policies are functioning as expected.

> **MORE INFO   MANAGE CONDITIONAL ACCESS POLICIES**
>
> You can learn more about managing conditional access policies at *https://docs.microsoft.com/en-us/azure/active-directory/conditional-access/concept-conditional-access-policies*.

Configure conditional access policies

To configure a user risk–based policy in the Conditional Access area of the Azure portal, perform the following steps:

1. In the **Azure Active Directory** section of the **Azure portal**, select **Security**. Then select **Conditional Access**.
2. In the left pane of the **Conditional Access** page, select **Policies**.
3. On the **Policies** page, shown in Figure 3-23, select **New policy**.

FIGURE 3-23 Conditional access policies

4. Type a name for the policy.

5. Under **Assignments**, select which users and groups the policy will apply to. Use the **Exclusions** section to exclude emergency access accounts.

6. Under **Cloud Apps or Actions**, select the cloud apps to which the conditional access policy will apply.

7. Under **Conditions**, select **User risk**. Then specify the risk level that will trigger the policy, as shown in Figure 3-24.

FIGURE 3-24 Specifying the user risk level in a conditional access policy

8. In the **Access Controls** section, choose whether to block or enable access, and the conditions under which the access should be granted.

   As shown in Figure 3-25, you can grant access but require multifactor authentication, a compliant device, a hybrid Azure AD joined device, an approved client app, an app protection policy, and/or a password change. You can require any, some, or all of these options.

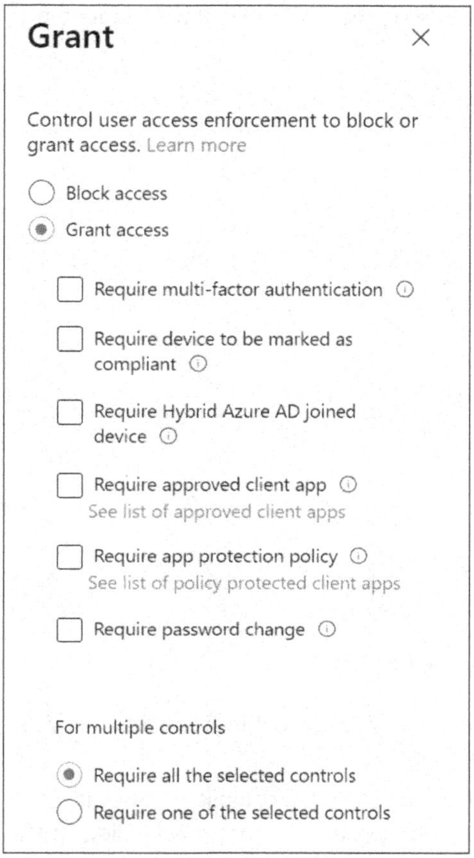

FIGURE 3-25 Grant access conditions

9. In the **Enable Policy** section, choose between **Report-only**, **On**, and **Off**. Then select **Create** to create the policy.

To configure a sign-in risk–based policy in the Conditional Access area of the Azure portal, perform the following steps:

1. In the **Azure Active Directory** section of the **Azure portal**, select **Security**. Then select **Conditional Access**.

2. In the left pane of the **Conditional Access** page, select **Policies**.

3. On the **Policies** page, select **New policy**.

4. Type a name for the policy.

5. Under **Assignments**, select which users and groups the policy will apply to. Use the **Exclusions** section to exclude emergency access accounts.

6. Under **Cloud Apps or Actions**, select the cloud apps to which the conditional access policy will apply.

7. Under **Conditions**, select **Sign-in Risk**. Then specify the risk level that will trigger the policy, as shown in Figure 3-26.

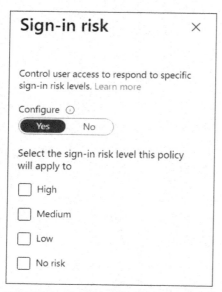

FIGURE 3-26 Specifying the sign-in risk level in a conditional access policy

8. In the **Access Controls** section, choose whether to block or enable access, and the conditions under which the access should be granted.

    You can grant access but require multifactor authentication, a compliant device, a hybrid Azure AD joined device, an approved client app, an app protection policy, and/or a password change. You can require any, some, or all of these options.

9. In the **Enable Policy** section, choose between **Report-only**, **On**, and **Off**. Then select **Create** to create the policy.

What If tool

You can use the conditional access What If tool to determine how conditional access policies will function without having to implement the policies on a pilot group of users. To run the What If tool, perform the following steps:

1. In the **Azure Active Directory** section of the **Azure portal**, select **Security**. Then select **Conditional Access**.

2. In the left pane of the **Conditional Access** page, select **Policies**.

3. On the **Policies** page, shown in Figure 3-27, select **What if**.

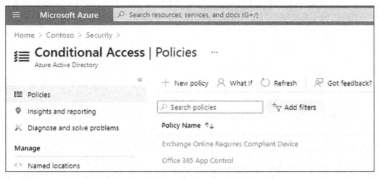

FIGURE 3-27 The What If tool on the Policies page

4. In the **What If** pane, shown in Figure 3-28, configure the following settings. Then select **What If** to view the simulated results of applying the policy.

- **User**   Select a user for which to run the What If tool. You can select only one user at a time.

- **Cloud apps, actions, or authentication context**   By default, all cloud apps are selected, but you can choose a specific cloud app when attempting to ascertain how conditional access policies will mediate access.

- **IP address**   This enables you to specify a public IPv4 address to simulate location conditions.

- **Country**   Instead of specifying a specific public IPv4 address, you can specify a country.

- **Device platform**   This enables you to specify which device platform is being used. Options include Android, iOS, Windows Phone, Windows, and macOS.

- **Client apps**   The default settings will evaluate for browser, mobile apps, and desktop clients, but you can limit it to any or all of these options.

- **Device state**   This enables you to specify whether the device is hybrid AD joined or marked as compliant.

- **Sign-in risk**   Here, you can specify the sign-in risk level you want to evaluate.

- **User risk**   This enables you to specify the user risk level you want to evaluate.

FIGURE 3-28 Configuring the What If tool

After selecting What If, you'll be informed which policies do and do not apply to the user. For all the policies that do apply to the user, the set of relevant controls are listed. For all the policies that do not apply, there is a list of reasons why the conditions of that policy were not triggered.

> **MORE INFO** **WHAT IF TOOL**
>
> You can learn more about the conditional access What If tool at *https://docs.microsoft.com/ en-us/azure/active-directory/conditional-access/what-if-tool.*

Design an MFA solution

When implementing multifactor authentication with Microsoft 365, you must decide which MFA capabilities will be included. MFA requires that more than one authentication method be used when signing into a resource integrated with Microsoft 365. Usually, this involves the user providing their user name and password credentials and one of the following:

- **A code generated by an authenticator app** This can be Microsoft Authenticator or a third-party app such as Google Authenticator.

- **A response provided to the Microsoft Authenticator app** When this method is used, Azure AD provides an on-screen code to the authenticating user that must also be selected on an application that is registered with Azure AD.

- **A phone call to a number registered with Azure AD** The user must provide a preconfigured PIN, which they will be instructed to enter by the automated service that performs the phone call. Microsoft provides a default greeting during authentication phone calls, so you don't have to record one for your organization.

- **An SMS message sent to a mobile phone number registered with Azure AD** The user provides the code sent in the message as a second factor during authentication.

When designing your solution, you'll need to have a way of ensuring that users have access to the appropriate MFA technology. This may require you to come up with a method of ensuring that all users in your organization already have the Microsoft Authenticator app installed on their mobile device before you enable MFA on their accounts.

MORE INFO **PLAN FOR MULTIFACTOR AUTHENTICATION**

You can learn more about designing a multifactor authentication solution for Microsoft 365 deployments at *https://docs.microsoft.com/en-us/azure/active-directory/authentication/howto-mfa-getstarted.*

Configure MFA for apps and users

MFA is not enabled by default on Microsoft 365 tenancies. Before you can configure accounts to use MFA, you'll need to enable MFA on the tenancy. To enable MFA on a Microsoft 365 Azure AD tenancy and configure MFA for specific users, perform the following steps:

1. In **Azure AD admin center**, navigate to **Users**, and select **All users**.

2. Select **More**. Then select **Multi-Factor Authentication**, as shown in Figure 3-29.

FIGURE 3-29 Setting up Azure MFA

Azure AD will enable MFA for the tenancy and you'll be provided with a list of user accounts in your Microsoft 365 tenancy, similar to the one shown in Figure 3-30.

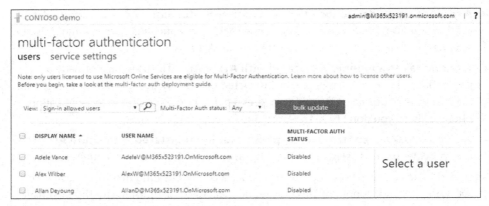

FIGURE 3-30 The Multi-Factor Authentication page

3. Select the check box next to each user account in the list for which you want to set up MFA (see Figure 3-31) and select **Enable**.

FIGURE 3-31 Setting up users for MFA

4. In the **About enabling multi-factor auth** dialog box, shown in Figure 3-32, select **enable multi-factor auth**.

FIGURE 3-32 Enabling MFA

The next time the selected users sign in, they will see a dialog box similar to the one shown in Figure 3-33, asking them to provide additional information to enroll in MFA.

FIGURE 3-33 More information required

When users see this dialog box, they should do the following:

1. Select **Next**.

2. In the **Additional security verification** pane, choose between providing a mobile phone number or an office phone number, or configuring a mobile app. As shown in Figure 3-34, **Mobile app** is selected for this example. Then select **Set up**.

FIGURE 3-34 Contact preferences

3. When you specify one of these options, you are presented with a QR code. Within the app you can add a new account by scanning the QR code.

4. After you have configured the application, you will be required to confirm that configuration has completed successfully by approving a sign-in through the app, as shown in Figure 3-35.

FIGURE 3-35 Verifying on the app

5. When prompted, the user should provide additional security information in the form of a phone number, as shown in Figure 3-36.

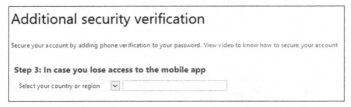

FIGURE 3-36 Providing additional security verification information

As an administrator, you can configure the following MFA service settings (see Figure 3-37):

- **App passwords**   Allow or prevent users from using app passwords for nonbrowser apps that do not support MFA.
- **Trusted ips [IP Addresses]**   Configure a list of trusted IP addresses where MFA will be skipped when Federation is configured between the on-premises environment and the Microsoft 365 Azure AD tenancy.
- **Verification options**   Specify which verification options are available to users. Choices include phone call, text message, app-based verification, and hardware token.
- **Remember multi-factor authentication**   Specify whether Azure AD should "remember" whether MFA is set up for a user for a specific period of time (the default is 14 days) on a device so that it need not be performed each time the user signs in.

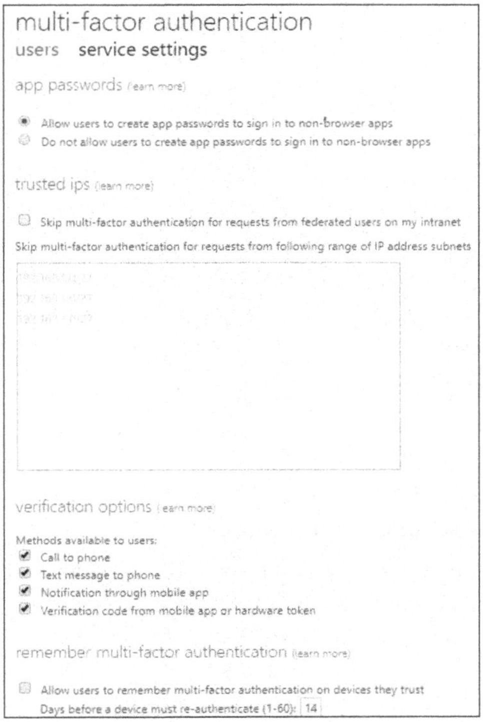

FIGURE 3-37 MFA service settings

> **MORE INFO** **SET UP MULTIFACTOR AUTHENTICATION**
>
> You can learn more about setting up multifactor authentication at *https://docs.microsoft.com/ en-us/azure/active-directory/authentication/howto-mfa-mfasettings*.

Administer MFA users

After MFA is configured for users, there may be times when you want to force users to re-register (for example, to provide updated contact methods) or revoke the user's remembered MFA sessions (to require the user to perform MFA the next time they sign in). To do so, perform the following steps:

1. With an account that has been assigned the global administrator role, open the **Azure AD admin center** and navigate to the **All users** page. (See Figure 3-38.)

FIGURE 3-38 Selecting the user to manage MFA

2. Select the user for whom you want to manage MFA.

3. On the user's properties page, select **Authentication methods**.

4. On the **Authentication methods** page, select the button for the action you want to perform. (See Figure 3-39.)

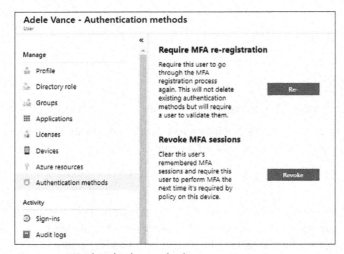

FIGURE 3-39 Authentication methods

If you want to manage MFA settings for multiple users at once—requiring them to provide contact methods again, deleting all existing app passwords they've generated, or restoring MFA on all remembered devices—perform the following steps:

1. From the **All users** page (see Figure 3-40), select the **Multi-Factor Authentication button.**

FIGURE 3-40 The All Users page

2. On the **multi-factor authentication – users** page (see Figure 3-41), select the users whose MFA settings you want to reset. Then select **Manage user settings**.

FIGURE 3-41 The Multi-Factor Authentication – Users page

3. On the **Manage user settings** page (see Figure 3-42), select the check box for each task you want to perform: require users to provide contact methods again, delete all existing app passwords, and/or restore multifactor authentication on remembered devices. Then select **Save**.

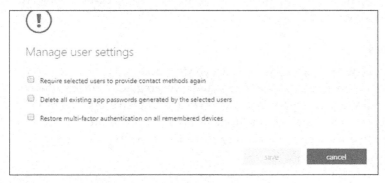

FIGURE 3-42 Managing user settings

Account lockout

MFA account lockout settings enable you to configure the conditions under which MFA lockout will occur. On the page shown in Figure 3-43, you can configure the following account lockout settings:

- The number of MFA denials that will trigger the account lockout process
- How long before the account lockout counter is reset
- The number of minutes until the account will be unblocked

FIGURE 3-43 Account lockout settings

For example, if the account lockout counter is reset after 10 minutes, and the number of MFA denials to trigger account lockout is set to 5, then five denials in 10 minutes will trigger lockout, but five denials over, say, 30 minutes will not, because the account lockout counter will have been reset during that period.

Block/unblock users

The Block/Unblock Users page (see Figure 3-44) enables you to block specific users of an on-premises MFA server from being able to receive MFA requests. Any requests sent to a user on the list of blocked users will automatically be denied. Users on the blocked users list remain blocked for 90 days, after which they are removed from the blocked users list. To unblock a blocked user, select the Unblock link in the user's entry on the Block/Unblock Users page.

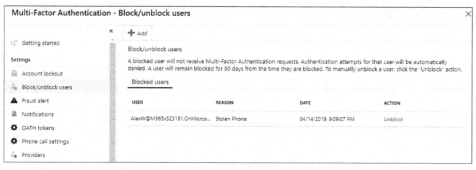

FIGURE 3-44 Blocked users list

Fraud alert

Fraud alert settings (see Figure 3-45) enable you to configure whether users can report fraudu-lent verification requests. A fraudulent verification request might occur when an attacker has access to a user's password but not to an alternative MFA method. A user becomes aware of this by receiving an MFA prompt, either through their app, an SMS, or a phone call when they haven't attempted to authenticate against a Microsoft 365 workload. When a user reports fraud—which indicates that their password is likely compromised—you can choose to have their account automatically blocked for 90 days.

FIGURE 3-45 Fraud alert

OATH tokens

The OATH Tokens page (see Figure 3-46) enables you to upload a specially formatted CSV file that contains the details and keys of the OATH tokens that you want to use for MFA.

FIGURE 3-46 The OATH Tokens page

The specially formatted CSV file should include a header row that is formatted as follows:

`"upn, serial number, secret key, time interval, manufacturer, model"`

Each file is associated with a specific user. If a user has multiple OATH tokens, these should be included in the file associated with their account.

Phone call settings

Phone call settings enable you to configure the caller ID number that is displayed when the user is contacted for MFA authentication. This number must be a U.S. number. You can also use the Phone Call Settings page (see Figure 3-47) to configure custom voice messages. The voice messages must be in WAV or MP3 format, no larger than 5 MB, and shorter than 20 seconds.

FIGURE 3-47 Phone call settings

> **MORE INFO   MANAGE MFA SETTINGS**
>
> You can learn more about managing MFA settings at *https://docs.microsoft.com/en-us/azure/ active-directory/authentication/howto-mfa-mfasettings*.

Report MFA utilization

Azure provides a number of reports that you can use to understand how MFA is being used in your organization. These reports include the following:

- **Blocked user history**   Provides a history of requests to block or unblock users.
- **Usage and fraud alerts**   Provides a history of fraud alerts submitted by users. Also provides information on overall MFA usage.
- **Usage for on-premises components**   Provides information about use of MFA through the Network Policy Server extension, Active Directory Federation Services, and on-premises MFA server.
- **Bypassed user history**   Provides information on requests to bypass MFA by a specific user.
- **Server status**   Provides status data of MFA servers associated with your organization's Microsoft 365 tenancy.

> **MORE INFO**   **AZURE MFA REPORTS**
>
> You can learn more about Azure MFA reports at *https://docs.microsoft.com/en-us/azure/active-directory/authentication/howto-mfa-reporting*.

Implement and secure access for guest and external users

This objective deals with the creation of B2B and guest accounts, as well as ways to allow external access to resources hosted in a Microsoft 365 tenancy. You perform these actions when you want to enable people in a partner organization or external users such as temporary contractors to interact with resources hosted in Microsoft 365 services such as SharePoint Online. To master this objective, you'll need to understand how to create B2B accounts, how to create guest accounts, and the factors you will need to take into consideration when designing a solution to allow external users to access Microsoft 365 resources.

Create B2B accounts

Business-to-business (B2B) accounts are a special type of guest user account that resides within Azure Active Directory to which you can assign privileges. B2B accounts are generally used when you want to allow one or more users from a partner organization to access resources hosted within your organization's Microsoft 365 tenancy. For example, if users in Contoso's partner organization, Tailwind Traders, need to interact with and publish content to a Contoso SharePoint Online site, one method of providing the necessary access is to create a set of B2B accounts.

B2B accounts have the following properties:

- They are stored in a separate Azure AD tenancy from your organization, but they are represented as a guest user in your organization's tenancy. The B2B user signs in using their organization's Azure AD account to access resources in your organization's tenancy.

- They are stored in your organization's on-premises Active Directory and then synced using Azure AD Connect and a guest user type. This is different from the usual type of synchronization, where user accounts are synced from an on-premises directory, but the Azure AD accounts are traditional Azure AD accounts and are not assigned the guest user type.

Azure Active Directory accounts use the user type to display information about the account's relationship to the organization's tenancy. The two following values are supported:

- **Member** If the user type is member, the user is considered to belong to the host organization. This is appropriate for full-time employees, some types of contractors, or anyone else on the organizational payroll or within the organizational structure. Figure 3-48 shows a user account with the user type set to Member.

FIGURE 3-48 Account with the user type set to member

- **Guest** The guest user type indicates that the user is not directly associated with the organization. The guest user type applies to B2B and more generally to guest accounts. It is used when the account is based in another organization's directory or associated with another identity provider, such as a social network identity.

The account's user type does not determine how the user signs in; it is merely an indication of the user's relationship to the organization that controls the Azure AD tenancy. It can also be used to implement policies that depend on the value of this attribute. It is the source attribute property that indicates how the user authenticates. This property can have the following values:

- **Invited user** A guest or B2B user who has been invited but has yet to accept their invitation.

- **External Active Directory** An account that resides in a directory managed by a partner organization. When the user authenticates, they do so against the partner organization's Azure AD instance.

- **Microsoft account** A guest account that authenticates using a Microsoft account, such as an Outlook.com or Hotmail.com account.

- **Windows Server Active Directory** A user who is signed in from an on-premises instance of Active Directory that is managed by the same organization that controls the tenancy. This usually involves the deployment of Azure AD Connect. In the case of a B2B user, though, the user type attribute is set to guest.

- **Azure Active Directory** A user who is signed in using an Azure AD account that is managed by the organization. In the case of a B2B user, the user type attribute is set to guest.

When you create the first type of B2B account, an invitation is sent to the user to whom you want to grant B2B access. The process of creating and sending this invitation also creates an account within your organization's Azure AD directory. This account will not have any credentials associated with it because authentication will be performed by the B2B user's identity provider. Figure 3-49 shows the screen used to send an invitation to a user.

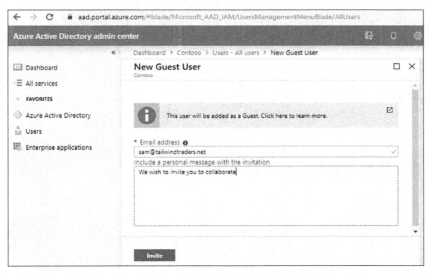

FIGURE 3-49 Creating a guest B2B user in the Azure AD Admin Center

Until the invitation is accepted, the source property of an invited B2B guest user account will be set to Invited User, as shown in Figure 3-50. You can also resend the invitation if the target user does not receive or respond to it.

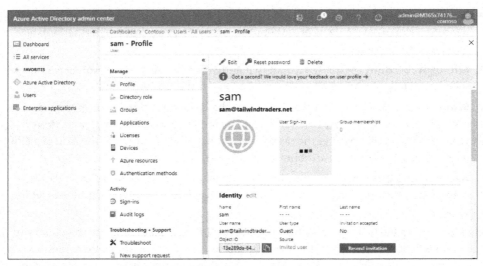

FIGURE 3-50 Source attribute set to Invited User

When the user accepts the invitation, the source attribute will be updated to External Azure Active Directory, as shown in Figure 3-51. If the user's account is synchronized from an on-premises Active Directory instance but the user type is set to guest, the source property will be listed as Windows Server Active Directory.

FIGURE 3-51 Source attribute set to External Azure Active Directory

---

MORE INFO   **AZURE AD B2B COLLABORATION**

You can learn more about Azure AD B2B collaboration users at *https://docs.microsoft.com/ en-us/azure/active-directory/external-identities/user-properties*.

Create guest accounts

A B2B account is a guest account. Although the exam objectives suggest a substantial difference exists between these two types of accounts, it is perhaps more accurate to say that a guest account might be considered a type of B2B account where the account is a Microsoft account or a social account. For example, a guest account might have an @outlook.com email address, or it might be a social media account such as a Facebook account. The main difference between the two is that, in general, a B2B account implies a business-to-business relationship, whereas a guest account implies a business-to-individual relationship.

You create a guest account in exactly the same way as a B2B account, as outlined in the preceding section. You send an invitation, an account is created, the user accepts the invitation, and then the individual uses the account to access Microsoft 365 resources to which they have been granted permissions.

You can view a list of all users in an Azure AD instance that have guest accounts by selecting Guest Users Only from the Show drop-down list on the All Users page, as shown in Figure 3-52.

FIGURE 3-52 Viewing guest accounts

Guest users are blocked from performing certain tasks, including enumerating users, groups, and other Azure AD resources. You can remove the guest user default limitations by performing the following steps:

1. On the **Azure Active Directory** blade, under **Manage**, select **User settings**.
2. On the **User settings** blade, select **Manage External Collaboration Settings**.
3. On the **External collaboration settings** page, select **No** under **Guest users l permissions are limited**, as shown in Figure 3-53.

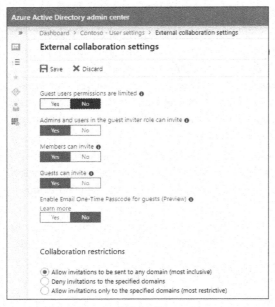

FIGURE 3-53 External collaboration settings

> **MORE INFO** **ADDING GUEST USERS**
>
> You can learn more about this topic at *https://docs.microsoft.com/en-us/azure/active-directory/external-identities/b2b-quickstart-add-guest-users-portal*.

Design solutions for external access

When designing a solution to enable external access to Microsoft 365 resources, you should understand that Microsoft 365 external sharing and Azure AD B2B collaboration are almost the same thing. Except for OneDrive and SharePoint Online, all external sharing uses the Azure AD B2B collaboration invitation APIs.

OneDrive and SharePoint Online have a separate invitation manager, and their functionality differs slightly from Microsoft 365 external sharing and Azure AD B2B collaboration. For example, unlike Azure AD B2B, OneDrive and SharePoint Online will only add a user to the Azure AD instance after the user has redeemed their invitation. In contrast, Azure AD B2B adds the user to the directory during invitation creation. This means you can perform actions such as granting access to an Azure AD B2B guest user before they have accepted their invitation because they will be present in the directory—something that is not possible with invitations sent through OneDrive and SharePoint Online.

You manage external sharing for SharePoint Online using the Sharing page of the Share-Point Admin Center. To configure SharePoint so that only Azure AD B2C sharing is enabled, select Allow Sharing Only With The External Users That Already Exist In Your Organization's Directory, as shown in Figure 3-54.

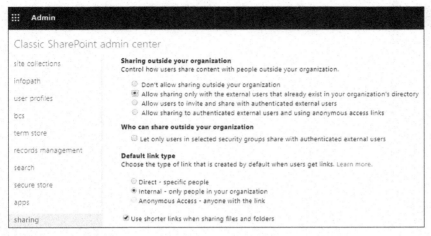

FIGURE 3-54 SharePoint Online Sharing options

> **MORE INFO   B2B AND MICROSOFT 365 EXTERNAL SHARING**
>
> You can learn more about external sharing and Azure AD B2B collaboration at *https://docs. microsoft.com/en-us/azure/active-directory/external-identities/o365-external-user*.

You can use the External Collaboration Settings page (see Figure 3-55), accessible from the Azure AD User Settings blade, to configure the following collaboration settings:

- **Guest users permissions are limited**   Enabled by default, this option enables you to configure guest users so that they have the same permissions as standard users.

- **Admins and users in the guest inviter role can invite**   Users who hold the administrator and guest inviter roles can send invitations.

- **Members can invite**   Users who are not administrators and who have not been assigned the guest inviter roles can send invitations.

- **Guests can invite**   Users with guest status can invite other users as B2B users or guests.

- **Enable Email One-Time Passcode for guests**   This is a one-time passcode for guests who do not have an Azure AD or Microsoft account and for which Google Federation has not been configured. Guests who use one-time passcodes remain authenticated for 24 hours.

- **Allow invitations to be sent to any domain**   The default setting. This enables guest and B2B invitations to be sent to any domain.

- **Deny invitations to specified domains**   This enables you to create a block list of domains to which guest and B2B invitations cannot be sent.

- **Allow invitations only to the specified domains**   Use this option to allow guest and B2B invitations only to specific domains. Invitations to domains not on the allowed list are blocked.

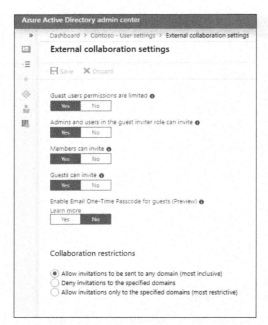

FIGURE 3-55 Collaboration settings

MORE INFO **ALLOW OR BLOCK B2B USERS FROM SPECIFIC ORGANIZATIONS**

You can learn more about allowing or blocking invitations to users from specific organizations at *https://docs.microsoft.com/en-us/azure/active-directory/external-identities/allow-deny-list*.

EXAM TIP

You can configure an allow list of specific domains to which invitations can be sent, and you can configure a block list where you only block invitations to specific domains.

Skill 3.3: Configure application access

When an application is registered with Azure AD, users can use single sign-on (SSO) to access that application in the same manner they use SSO once and access Microsoft 365 workloads such as Exchange Online and SharePoint Online. Application registration enables users to access software-as-a-service (SaaS) applications from third-party vendors, applications deployed in the organization's on-premises environment, and line-of-business applications. When an application is registered with Azure AD, you can secure access to that application by implementing multifactor authentication and conditional access policies.

Configure application registration in Azure AD

You can register an application with Azure AD from the enterprise application gallery. You can then register an application that you are developing, configure an on-premises application, or add a third-party application that is not present in the gallery, as shown in Figure 3-56. Registering an application enables users who have accounts in your organization's Azure AD tenancy to sign in and use that application with their Microsoft 365 credentials rather than having to use a separate set of credentials registered with the application.

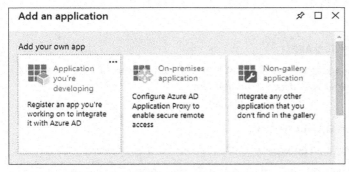

FIGURE 3-56 Adding an application

> **MORE INFO** **APPLICATION MANAGEMENT WITH AZURE AD**
>
> You can learn more about application management with Azure AD at *https://docs.microsoft.com/en-us/azure/active-directory/manage-apps/what-is-application-management.*

Plan application integration

Before integrating applications with Azure AD, you must know what the authentication requirements are for each application. Azure AD supports signing certificates with applications that use WS-Federation, SAML 2.0, Open ID Connect Protocols, and password-based SSO.

You must also think about how you might want to provide SSO access to applications hosted on your organization's internal network. You can do this by deploying Azure AD App Proxy. When you do, a special connector is installed on a host on your internal network, allowing users both inside and outside the network to authenticate against and access the application.

MORE INFO   **PLANNING APPLICATION INTEGRATION**

You can learn more about planning application integration at *https://docs.microsoft.com/ en-us/azure/active-directory/manage-apps/plan-an-application-integration*.

Manage access to apps

How you assign access to applications depends on the edition of Azure AD that your organization has licensed. If your organization uses a free edition of Azure AD, you'll only be able to assign access to applications on a per-user basis. If your organization uses a paid edition of Azure AD, then you'll be able to perform group-based assignment. When you do, a user's ability to access an application will depend on whether that user is a member of the group at the time they attempt to access the application.

The groups used to assign access to applications can be any form of Azure AD group, including attribute-based dynamic groups, on-premises Active Directory groups, and self-service managed groups. Nested group membership is not presently supported when it comes to assigning access to applications through Azure AD.

MORE INFO   **MANAGE ACCESS TO APPS**

You can learn more about managing access to apps at *https://docs.microsoft.com/en-us/azure/ active-directory/manage-apps/what-is-access-management*.

Assign users access to an application

To assign a user or group access to an enterprise application, perform the following steps:

1. In the **Azure AD admin center**, select **Azure Active Directory**.

2. Under the **Manage** section, shown in Figure 3-57, select **Enterprise applications**.

FIGURE 3-57   Azure AD Manage section

3. On the **Enterprise Applications** blade, ensure that **All applications** is selected, as shown in Figure 3-58. Then select the application to enable user access.

FIGURE 3-58 All applications

4. On the **Overview** page for the application, select **Users and groups**. (See Figure 3-59.)

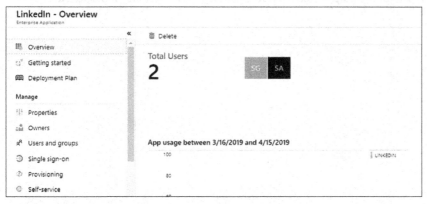

FIGURE 3-59 Application overview

5. On the application's **Users and groups** page (see Figure 3-60), select **Add user**. (Note that you use this same button to add a group assignment if Azure AD is licensed at the appropriate level.)

FIGURE 3-60 Users and Groups

6. On the **Add Assignment** page, shown in Figure 3-61, search for the user or group for which you want to grant application access.

FIGURE 3-61 Adding users and groups

7. Select the user or group you want to add, as shown in Figure 3-62, and select **Select**.

FIGURE 3-62 Select group assignment

8. Select **Assign**.
9. Verify the assignment by reviewing the newly updated list of users and groups, as shown in Figure 3-63.

FIGURE 3-63 Enterprise application users and groups

MORE INFO   ASSIGN USERS AND GROUPS ACCESS

You can learn more about this topic at *https://docs.microsoft.com/en-us/azure/active-directory/manage-apps/assign-user-or-group-access-portal*.

Configure Azure AD Application Proxy

The Azure AD Application Proxy enables users on the internet to access web applications hosted on your organization's secure internal network as well as in the cloud through an external URL or internal application portal. You can use the Azure AD Application Proxy to enable single sign-on access to teams, SharePoint, Remote Desktop, and line-of-business applications.

Azure AD Application Proxy has the following benefits:

- Applications need not be updated to work with Application Proxy.
- On-premises applications can leverage Azure AD's authorization controls and security analytics. Features such as multifactor authentication and conditional access policies can be applied to on-premises applications.
- Azure AD Application Proxy does not require inbound ports to be opened on your organization's perimeter firewall.
- Application Proxy does not require the deployment of additional appliances on the on-premises internal or perimeter network.

The architecture of the Azure AD Application Proxy has the Azure AD Application Proxy service running in the cloud with the Azure AD Application Proxy connector running on an on-premises server. In this configuration, Azure AD, the Azure AD Application Proxy service, and the Azure AD Application Proxy connector manage the secure transmission of a user's sign-on token from Azure AD to the web application the user wishes to access.

Azure AD Application Proxy supports single sign-on and works with the following applications:

- Web applications that use Integrated Windows Authentication for authentication
- Web applications that use header-based or form-based access
- Client apps integrated with Active Directory Authentication Library
- Applications hosted behind Remote Desktop Gateway

Azure AD Application Proxy functions in the following manner:

1. The user accesses the application through a URL or an end-user portal, which redirects the user to an Azure AD authentication page.
2. The user successfully authenticates.
3. Azure AD transmits a token to the user's device.
4. The device forwards the token to the Azure AD Application Proxy service.
5. The Azure AD Application Proxy service extracts the user principal name (UPN) and security principal name (SPN) from the token.

6. The Azure AD Application Proxy service forwards the request to the Azure AD Application Proxy connector.

7. If single sign-on has been configured, the Azure AD Application Proxy connector performs all additional authentication tasks on behalf of the user.

8. The Azure AD Application Proxy connector forwards the request to the on-premises application.

9. The response from the application is routed through the Azure AD Application Proxy connector and the Azure AD Application Proxy service to the user.

> **MORE INFO** **ACCESS ON-PREMISES APPLICATIONS WITH AZURE AD APPLICATION PROXY**
>
> You can learn more about remote access to on-premises applications through Azure Active Directory Application Proxy at *https://docs.microsoft.com/en-us/azure/active-directory/app-proxy/application-proxy*.

The Azure AD Application Proxy connector is an agent that you install on an on-premises server running the Windows Server 2012 R2, Windows Server 2016, Windows Server 2019, or Windows Server 2022 operating systems. Computers that host the Azure AD Application Proxy connectors must be able to send outbound requests to the internet on TCP port 443 and also must be able to communicate with the on-premises servers hosting the application that will be accessed by remote clients. As mentioned, it is not necessary to open inbound ports to the Azure AD Application Proxy connector for the service to function.

If your organization wants to support SSO to applications that use Integrated Windows Authentication (IWA), the Azure AD Application Proxy connector must be installed on a Windows Server computer that is domain joined or in a domain or forest that has a trust relationship with the computer that hosts the application. If SSO to applications that use IWA is not necessary, the Azure AD Application Proxy connector can be installed on a computer that is not domain joined.

Although it is possible to deploy only one Azure AD Application Proxy connector on your organization's protected internal network, Microsoft recommends that you deploy multiple Azure AD Application Proxy connectors to ensure that the service is redundant and remains available when the Azure AD Application Proxy connector agent automatically updates.

Windows Server must have TLS 1.2 enabled before you install the Azure AD Application Proxy connector. You can ensure that TLS 1.2 is enabled by setting the following registry keys and restarting the server:

```
[HKEY_LOCAL_MACHINE\SYSTEM\CurrentControlSet\Control\SecurityProviders\SCHANNEL\
Protocols\TLS 1.2]
[HKEY_LOCAL_MACHINE\SYSTEM\CurrentControlSet\Control\SecurityProviders\SCHANNEL\
Protocols\TLS 1.2\Client] "DisabledByDefault"=dword:00000000 "Enabled"=dword:00000001
[HKEY_LOCAL_MACHINE\SYSTEM\CurrentControlSet\Control\SecurityProviders\SCHANNEL\
Protocols\TLS 1.2\Server] "DisabledByDefault"=dword:00000000 "Enabled"=dword:00000001
[HKEY_LOCAL_MACHINE\SOFTWARE\Microsoft\.NETFramework\v4.0.30319]
"SchUseStrongCrypto"=dword:00000001
```

Azure AD Application Proxy connectors are stateless and do not store any data on the host Windows Server computer. Azure AD Application Proxy connectors regularly poll the Azure AD Application Proxy service to determine if updates are available. Updates to the connector are automatically downloaded and applied without requiring administrator intervention.

You can use connector groups to assign specific Azure AD Application Proxy connectors to specific on-premises applications. You can group a number of these connectors together and then assign each application that you want to make available to the group. Connector groups are especially useful when applications are hosted in different regions. For example, imagine you have one on-premises web application hosted in Sydney, Australia and another hosted in Copenhagen, Denmark. You could create one connector group for the Azure AD Application Proxy connectors in the Denmark location and assign it to the application hosted in Denmark. You could then create another connector group for the Azure AD Application Proxy connectors in the Australian location and assign it to the application hosted in Australia.

> **MORE INFO   AZURE AD APPLICATION PROXY CONNECTORS**
>
> You can learn more about Azure AD Application proxy connectors at *https://docs.microsoft.com/en-us/azure/active-directory/app-proxy/application-proxy-connectors*.

> **MORE INFO   WORKING WITH ON-PREMISES PROXY SERVERS**
>
> You can learn more about working with on-premises proxy servers at *https://docs.microsoft.com/en-us/azure/active-directory/app-proxy/application-proxy-configure-connectors-with-proxy-servers*.

Publish enterprise apps in Azure AD

Azure includes a gallery that hosts thousands of applications configured for easy integration with Azure AD. To add an application from the gallery to the Azure AD tenant associated with your organization's Microsoft 365 tenancy, you must sign into the Azure portal with an account that is assigned global administrator privileges. The following procedure details how to add an enterprise application from the gallery:

1. In the **Azure AD admin center**, select **Azure Active Directory**. Then, under **Manage**, select **Enterprise applications**. (See Figure 3-64.)

FIGURE 3-64 The Azure AD Manage section

2. On the **Enterprise applications** blade, ensure that **All applications** is selected in the pane on the left (see Figure 3-65) and then select **New application**.

FIGURE 3-65 Selecting all applications

3. On the **Add an application** page, shown in Figure 3-66, type the name of the application that you want to add. You can also use this page to add an application you are developing, an on-premises application, or a non-gallery application.

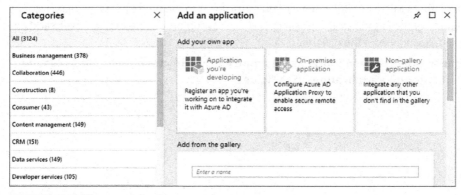

FIGURE 3-66 Adding an application

4. In the search results pane, select the application you want to add. If the application hasn't already been added to your Azure AD tenancy, you'll have the option to select **Add** to add it. (See Figure 3-67.)

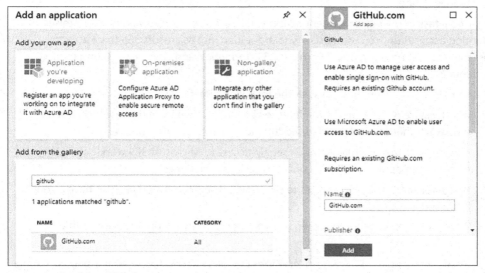

FIGURE 3-67 Adding GitHub

5. An application-specific **Getting Started** page opens. Fill out the form on this page to configure the application for your organization.

> **MORE INFO** **ADD AN APPLICATION TO YOUR AZURE AD TENANCY**
>
> You can learn more about adding applications to your Azure AD tenancy at *https://docs. microsoft.com/en-us/azure/active-directory/manage-apps/add-application-portal*.

EXAM TIP

Remember what the requirements are for Azure AD Application Proxy connectors.

Thought experiment

In this thought experiment, demonstrate your skills and knowledge of the topics covered in this chapter. You can find answers to this thought experiment in the next section.

You are the Microsoft 365 administrator for Tailwind Traders. You are currently in the process of configuring authentication and authorization. You have access to a list of the 100 passwords most commonly seen in data breaches. You want to make sure users in your organization do not use any of these passwords. You also want to empower users who forget their password to resolve the problem themselves.

After several account compromise events in the past, you want to get an idea of which users are most likely to have compromised accounts. Similarly, if users receive 2FA notifications on their Microsoft Authenticator app, they should have a way of reporting this event so that your team can investigate.

Your final task in managing authentication and authorization involves an on-premises accounting application. You want users who are signed into Microsoft 365 to be able to access this application using their Microsoft 365 credentials and without requiring them to reauthenticate.

With this information in mind, answer the following questions:

1. Which Azure AD authentication feature can you use to ensure that users do not use passwords that are on the list of the 100 most commonly used passwords?

2. How can you ensure that users can regain access to Microsoft 365 workloads if they forget their password without contacting the service desk?

3. Which report should you consult to determine whether a user is likely to have a compromised account?

4. Which MFA feature should you enable so that users can report suspicious MFA notifications?

5. What do you need to deploy on-premises to enable access to the accounting app using Azure AD single sign-on?

Thought experiment answers

This section contains the solution to the thought experiment. Each answer explains why the answer choice is correct.

1. Populate and enable the Azure AD custom banned passwords list with the passwords on the 100 most commonly used list.

2. Configure self-service password reset. This feature must be enabled, and the user or group should be included in the scope of the feature.

3. Consult the users flagged for risk report to determine which users are likely to have compromised accounts.

4. Enable the fraud alert option to allow users to notify you if they receive notifications for authorization on their Microsoft Authenticator app when they haven't attempted authentication.

5. Deploy the Azure AD Application Proxy connector on-premises to enable access to the on-premises accounting app using Azure AD single sign-on.

Chapter summary

- Modern authentication supports technologies such as multifactor authentication, smart card authentication, certificate-based authentication, and SAML-based third-party identity providers.

- Microsoft 365 supports a variety of authentication methods for self-service password reset and MFA, including passwords, security questions, email addresses, the Microsoft Authenticator app, OATH hardware tokens, SMS, voice calls, and app passwords.

- When configuring self-service password reset, enable multiple authentication methods and require two separate authentication methods to be used before allowing password reset.

- Smart Lockout is a technology that enables you to lock out attackers who are trying to brute-force user passwords.

- Any password on the Azure custom banned list cannot be used by a user in your organization.

- Certificate-based authentication is supported for Federated environments where an organizational CA is trusted by Azure AD and the CRL is published in an internet-accessible location.

- Azure AD's reporting architecture enables you to monitor sign-ins, risky sign-ins, users flagged for risk, and Azure administrator activity.

- Multifactor authentication methods include phone calls, text messages, notification through mobile app, or verification code from mobile app or hardware token.

- Applications must be registered with Azure AD before users can access them through Azure AD single sign-on.

- Azure AD Application Proxy enables users on the internet to access web applications hosted on your organization's secure internal network as well as in the cloud through an external URL or internal application portal.

- The Azure AD Application Proxy service runs in the cloud with the Azure AD Application Proxy connector running on an on-premises server.

- A business-to-business (B2B) account is a special type of guest user account that resides within Azure Active Directory and to which you can assign privileges.

- Authentication for guest accounts occurs through a trusted provider, after which the user gains access to resources they have been assigned permissions to within Azure AD.

CHAPTER 4

Plan Office 365 workloads and applications

Before they existed in the cloud, many Microsoft 365 workloads were hosted on-premises in organizational data centers. Some customers still have some Microsoft 365 workload servers deployed on-premises, whereas other workloads are in the cloud. Some even exist in a hybrid state, with servers on-premises working in conjunction with servers in the cloud.

Similarly, deployment of Microsoft 365 applications has changed. Whereas you might have deployed previous versions of Office, such as Office 2007, from a DVD-ROM drive or network share, today you're likely to deploy Microsoft 365 applications either directly from Microsoft 365 or through other automated tools. In this chapter you'll learn how to plan for Microsoft 365 workload deployments and how to deploy the applications that interact with those workloads.

Skills covered in this chapter:

- Skill 4.1: Plan for Microsoft 365 Apps deployment
- Skill 4.2: Plan for messaging deployments
- Skill 4.3: Plan for Microsoft SharePoint Online and OneDrive for Business
- Skill 4.4: Plan for Microsoft Teams Infrastructure
- Skill 4.5: Plan Microsoft Power Platform integration

Skill 4.1: Plan for Microsoft 365 Apps deployment

This skill section deals with planning for Microsoft 365 apps deployment. In this section you'll learn how to plan connectivity for apps, how to manage those apps, how to plan for users who interact with the apps through a browser, how to assess readiness for apps, manage app compatibility, manage app updates, and manage app telemetry and reporting.

This section covers the following topics:

- Plan for Microsoft connectivity
- Manage Microsoft 365 Apps
- Plan for Office online
- Assess readiness using Microsoft analytics
- Plan Microsoft 365 App compatibility
- Manage Office 365 software downloads
- Plan for Microsoft apps updates
- Plan Microsoft telemetry and reporting

Plan for Microsoft connectivity

Microsoft 365 Apps for enterprise, previously called Office 365 ProPlus, is similar to other versions of Office that you deploy to users and that they run locally on their desktop computers or laptops. Network connectivity requirements for Microsoft 365 Apps for enterprise depend on how you have determined you want to install updates. If you want to manage the update deployment from a location on your organization's internal network, then client computers will only need to be able to access the location on the network that hosts the updates. The majority of Microsoft 365 Apps for enterprise deployments are more likely to use the default option of obtaining updates from Microsoft over the internet. To obtain Microsoft 365 Apps for enterprise updates over the internet, client computers will require access to the Office content delivery networks (CDNs).

> **MORE INFO   MICROSOFT 365 APPS**
>
> You can learn more about Microsoft 365 content delivery networks at *https://docs.microsoft.com/en-us/microsoft-365/enterprise/content-delivery-networks*.

   The Office CDNs are used not only for the deployment of Microsoft 365 Apps for enterprise updates, but also to improve the performance of SharePoint Online pages by hosting cached versions of static assets in locations more proximate to the organization's users. Access to the Office 365 CDNs is over the HTTP/2 protocol. This maximizes compression and improves download speeds when clients access content that the CDNs host. Office 365 CDNs are hosted with Akamai. To ensure the best performance and minimize latency, ensure that traffic from Microsoft 365 Apps for enterprise clients to the Office CDNs is not routed through proxies and instead can pass directly from the client to the Office CDN. Microsoft 365 Apps for enterprise also requires internet connectivity for activation and reactivation.

MORE INFO   **OFFICE 365 CONTENT DELIVERY NETWORKS**

You can learn more about Office 365 content delivery networks at *https://docs.microsoft.com/
en-us/microsoft-365/enterprise/content-delivery-networks*.

Manage Microsoft 365 Apps

Microsoft has made Word, Excel, Outlook, PowerPoint, Teams, OneDrive, and OneNote
Microsoft 365 apps available for the iOS and Android mobile platforms. You can choose among
several ways to install the apps on these devices.

The first is to navigate to the Microsoft 365 portal using the mobile device on which you want
to install each application. Simply select Get Office Apps to open a page on Microsoft's website
that provides a link to the app's page in the appropriate vendor's app store. Figure 4-1 shows the
Apple App Store page that opens when the Excel link on the Microsoft 365 portal is selected.
The application can then be downloaded from the App Store and installed on the device.

FIGURE 4-1 Excel app in the Apple App Store

These applications can also be installed directly from each mobile device operating system vendor's app store. To use all the available features of each app, such as accessing documents in OneDrive for Business that are associated with your organization's Microsoft 365 subscription, it will be necessary to sign in to the app using your Microsoft 365 user account credentials. Premium features include the following:

- The ability to track changes, change page orientation, insert chart elements, and add WordArt and picture effects in the Word app
- Use Pivot Tables and add and modify chart elements in the Excel app
- Use Presenter view with speaker notes, perform audio and video edits, and use picture styles in the PowerPoint app
- Take advantage of technical support options from Microsoft

Select the Sign In option for an app to connect the app to a Microsoft 365 subscription. (See Figure 4-2.)

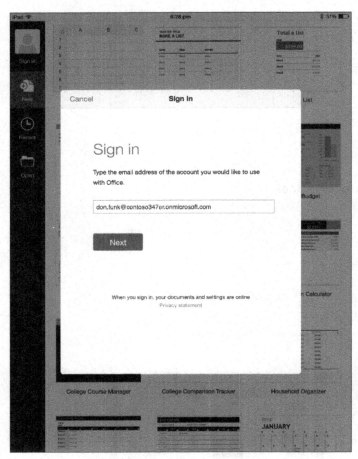

FIGURE 4-2 Sign in to Microsoft 365

Plan for Office online

Office Online allows you to access the basic functionality of a variety of Microsoft Office applications through a supported web browser. You can open Word Online, Excel Online, PowerPoint Online, and OneNote Online directly from the Microsoft 365 portal, as shown in Figure 4-3.

FIGURE 4-3 Office Online

People with Microsoft 365 User Accounts will be able to access documents stored in organizational locations such as OneDrive for Business and SharePoint Online. Documents will also be able to be opened directly from the Outlook Web App. Figure 4-4 shows the interface of the Word Online Office Web App.

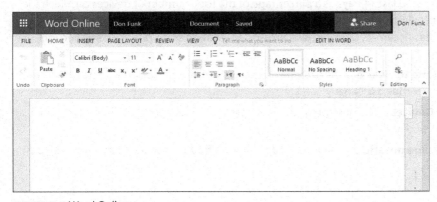

FIGURE 4-4 Word Online

Assess readiness using Microsoft analytics

Organizations upgrading to Windows 10 or Windows 11 should perform a compatibility assessment to determine whether existing applications that are currently being used could have problems once the upgrade is complete. One tool you can use to assess readiness is Desktop Analytics, included in Configuration Manager (formerly System Center Configuration Manager), which is now a part of Microsoft 365's Endpoint Manager solution. Desktop Analytics will assess the environment and categorize readiness in the following manner:

- **Low**   The application is likely to work after the upgrade is completed.
- **Medium**   The application may have some impaired functionality after the upgrade is completed. It may be possible to remediate these impairments.
- **High**   The application is unlikely to function after the upgrade is completed.
- **Unknown**   The application was not assessed, and a functionality determination cannot be made.

Desktop Analytics uses the Microsoft app compatibility database to identify known issues. This means that although Desktop Analytics is useful for assessing the compatibility of publicly available applications, it will be unable to provide an accurate assessment of the compatibility of custom applications that may have been written by your organization's developers or that your organization commissioned software developers to create for you.

Desktop Analytics also allows you to view the health status of applications in your environment to determine if the deployment of a software update has affected application functionality. Desktop Analytics will provide you with the following app health status information:

- **% Devices with crashes**   The number of devices where a specific application has crashed in the last 14 days as a percentage of the total number of devices on which the app is installed. Data can be segmented into crashes that occurred before and after update has occurred. Data can also provide an average crash rate across all versions of the app.
- **Mean time to failure**   The average elapsed time between application crashes on each device over the past 14 days.
- **Active Devices**   The number of devices where a user launched a specific app within the past 14 days.
- **Total usage duration**   The total usage duration for the specified app during the past 14 days.

MORE INFO   ASSESS READINESS USING ANALYTICS

You can learn more about assessing readiness using Microsoft analytics at *https://docs. microsoft.com/en-us/mem/configmgr/desktop-analytics/compat-assessment*.

Plan Microsoft 365 App compatibility

Many organizations that use Office products have Visual Basic for Applications (VBA) macros and add-ins that are critical for their workflow but that might not be compatible with the current version of Microsoft 365 Apps. You can use the Readiness Toolkit for Office Add-ins and VBA to determine whether there are compatibility issues within your organization's VBA macros and add-ins before upgrading to the current version of Microsoft 365 Apps. The Readiness Report Creator checks VBA macros and add-ins in Word, Excel, PowerPoint, Outlook, Access, Project, Visio, and Publisher files for all versions of Office from 2003 on.

The Readiness Report Creator has the following limitations:

- It is unable to scan password-protected files.
- It cannot scan files saved in a SharePoint document library, in OneDrive, or in another cloud-based storage location.
- It can return only 1,046,575 results, with each issue found equal to a single result and multiple issues possible per file.

The Readiness Report Creator can create a basic or an advanced report. Advanced reports provide the following information about compatibility issues:

- Remediation advice on how to resolve compatibility issues with VBA macros.
- Readiness status for Office add-ins, including whether updated and compatible versions of add-ins are available from a provider.

MORE INFO   MICROSOFT 365 APP COMPATIBILITY

You can learn more about Microsoft 365 app compatibility at *https://docs.microsoft.com/ en-us/deployoffice/readiness-tools*.

Manage Office 365 software downloads

Depending on your organization's policies, you might want to allow users to install software directly from the Microsoft 365 portal, to restrict this ability entirely, or to allow users to install some applications but restrict them from installing others. Microsoft 365 Apps for enterprise is the version of Microsoft Office that is available to appropriately licensed users in a Microsoft 365 tenancy. Microsoft 365 Apps for enterprise includes the following software products:

- Access
- Excel
- InfoPath

- OneNote
- Outlook
- PowerPoint
- Publisher
- Word

Depending on the Microsoft 365 subscription associated with a tenancy, Project, Visio, and other applications might also be available.

To configure which Office software users can install from the portal, configure Apps & Devices in the My Account section of the Microsoft 365 Admin Center. You can also configure whether users can install Office through the Office Installation Options panel in the Org settings.

Although you can make Office 365 software available to users through the Microsoft 365 portal, this doesn't mean that users will automatically be able to successfully install this software. When allowing users to self-provision software from the Microsoft 365 portal, keep the following points in mind:

- To successfully run Office 365, users will need an Office 365 license.
- For users to be able to install the software they downloaded from the Microsoft 365 portal, they will need to have local administrator privileges on their computer. This means that self-provisioning of software through the Microsoft 365 portal is a suitable strategy in bring your own device (BYOD) scenarios where the user is the owner of the computer and is responsible for its configuration. Self-provisioning of software is less of a concern for most environments where each user is assigned a computer with a standard operating environment (SOE), because users in these environments rarely have local administrator credentials.
- If you do not make Office software available to users, they will see a message that informs them that Office installations have been disabled when they navigate to the Software page in the Microsoft 365 portal.
- Microsoft 365 Apps for enterprise is only supported on the following operating systems:
  - Windows 7
  - Windows 8
  - Windows 8.1
  - Windows 10
  - Windows 11
  - Windows Server 2008 R2
  - Windows Server 2012
  - Windows Server 2012 R2
  - Windows Server 2016
  - Windows Server 2019
  - Windows Server 2022

By default, if a user installs Microsoft 365 Apps for enterprise from the Microsoft 365 portal, all programs included with Microsoft 365 Apps for enterprise (Access, Excel, InfoPath, OneNote, Outlook, PowerPoint, Publisher, and Word) will also install. Administrators can configure deployments so that only some, rather than all, of these programs will install. You can configure which programs are excluded from Microsoft 365 Apps for enterprise by using the Office Deployment Tool. You will learn more about configuring the Office Deployment Tool later in this chapter.

Manual deployment

The typical method of deploying Microsoft 365 Apps for enterprise on a computer is for a user to access the installation files from the Microsoft 365 portal. You can install Microsoft 365 Apps for enterprise on a computer by performing the following steps:

1. Sign in to the computer with a user account that is a member of the local administrators group.

2. Open a web browser and sign in to the Microsoft 365 portal at **https://portal.office.com**.

3. Select **Install Office** if you want to install using the default, or select **Other Install Options** and select **Apps & devices**. (See Figure 4-5.)

4. Use the **Version** drop-down list to select between the 32-bit and the 64-bit options and select **Install** to download the Microsoft 365 Apps for enterprise installer click-to-run setup file.

5. Choose whether you want to save or run the installation file. It's often sensible to save the file and then run it, because doing so simplifies the process of running the installer again should something interrupt the installation process.

FIGURE 4-5 Install Office on your PC

6. After the installer has finished downloading, double-click it to initiate installation.

7. Verify that the **User Account Control** dialog box lists Microsoft Office as the program name (see Figure 4-6) and select **Yes**. The installation process will commence.

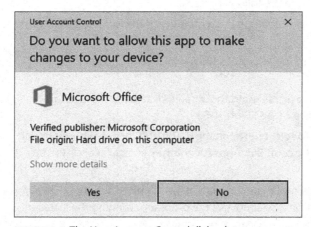

FIGURE 4-6 The User Account Control dialog box

8. On the **You're all set!** page (see Figure 4-7), select **Close**.

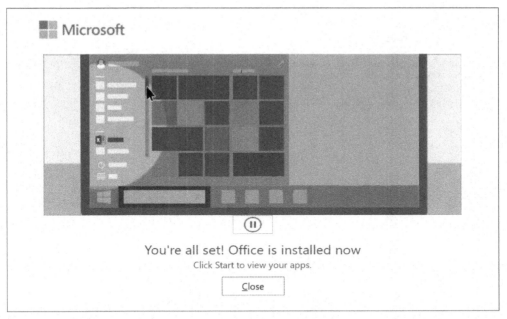

You're all set! Office is installed now
Click Start to view your apps.

Close

FIGURE 4-7 Office is installed

9. Open one of the Office applications.

   The first time you run one of these applications, you'll be presented with the Welcome to Office screen and asked to sign in to activate Office with your account.

10. Select **Continue** to use the account you used to download Office from the Microsoft 365 portal or select **Change Account** to use a different account.

11. After you authenticate your account, you'll be asked whether you want Windows to remember your account and whether you want the organization to manage the device, as shown in Figure 4-8. Select **OK** and then **Done** to continue.

12. When prompted, select **Yes** to accept the license agreement.

13. Select **Yes** to confirm you have read the information provided about privacy settings.

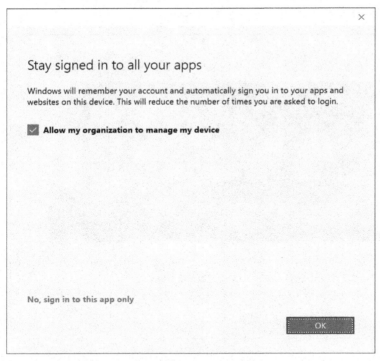

FIGURE 4-8 Organization management permission page

After you've dealt with all these dialog boxes, you can get down to using the Office app to perform some productive work that is not related to endlessly answering dialog box queries.

> *MORE INFO*   **MANUALLY INSTALLING MICROSOFT 365 APPS FOR ENTERPRISE**
>
> You can learn more about installing Microsoft 365 Apps for enterprise at *https://support. microsoft.com/en-us/office/download-and-install-or-reinstall-microsoft-365-or-office-2019-on-a-pc-or-mac-4414eaaf-0478-48be-9c42-23adc4716658*.

Central deployment

With special preparation, Microsoft 365 Apps for enterprise can be downloaded to a local shared folder and then deployed centrally. To use this central deployment method, the IT department must use the Office Deployment Tool to download the Microsoft 365 Apps for enterprise software from Microsoft servers on the internet.

Although it is possible to deploy Microsoft 365 Apps for enterprise centrally, successful installation of Microsoft 365 Apps for enterprise requires the ability for the software to activate against Microsoft Office 365 servers on the internet. You can't use a volume licensing activation solution, such as a Key Management Service (KMS) server, to activate Microsoft 365 Apps for enterprise even when you are deploying it centrally.

Office Deployment Tool

The Office Deployment Tool allows IT departments to perform the following tasks:

- **Generate a click-to-run for Office 365 installation source** This allows administrators to create a local installation source for Office 365 rather than requiring that the files be downloaded for each client from the internet.

- **Generate a click-to-run for Office 365 clients** This allows administrators to configure how Microsoft 365 Apps for enterprise will be installed—for example, blocking the installation of PowerPoint.

- **Creating an App-V package** This allows administrators to configure Microsoft 365 Apps for enterprise to work with application virtualization.

To install the Office Deployment Tool, perform the following steps:

1. On the computer on which you want to deploy the Office Deployment Tool, open a web browser and navigate to the following address: *https://www.microsoft.com/en-us/download/details.aspx?id=49117*.

2. On the **Office Deployment Tool** webpage shown in Figure 4-9, select **Download**.

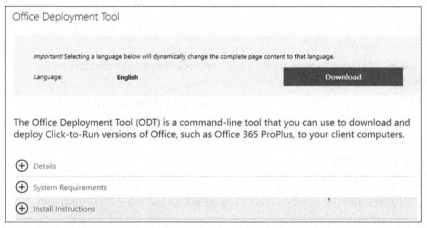

FIGURE 4-9 The Office Deployment Tool for click-to-run versions of Office

3. Save the installer file to a location on the computer.

4. After the file is downloaded, double-click it to start the deployment tool setup.

5. In the **User Account Control** dialog box, select **Yes**.

6. On the **Microsoft Software License Terms** page, select the **Click Here to Accept the Microsoft Software License Terms** option and select **Continue**.

7. On the **Browse for Folder** page, select the folder in which to store the files associated with the tool. Although these files can be extracted anywhere, you will need to interact with the tool frequently, so you should create a folder in the root folder of a volume. Four files will be extracted, as shown in Figure 4-10.

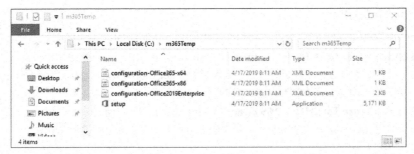

FIGURE 4-10 Deployment Tool folder

The Office Deployment Tool is a command-line utility that provides administrators with four general options:

- **/download** mode   Allows administrators to download the click-to-run installation source for Microsoft 365 Apps for enterprise, as well as language pack files to a central on-premises location
- **/configure** mode   Allows for the configuration and installation of click-to-run Office products and language packs
- **/packager** mode   Allows for the creation of an App-V package from downloaded click-to-run installation files
- **/customize** mode   Allows you to apply new application settings to computers that already have Microsoft 365 Apps for enterprise installed

The Office Deployment Tool must be run from an elevated command prompt in the /configure and /packager modes. To run the Office Deployment tool in /download mode against a configuration file stored in the c:\ClickToRun folder, use the following syntax:

```
Setup.exe /download c:\ClickToRun\configuration.xml
```

To run the Office Deployment Tool in /configure mode, when the tool is hosted on the share \\SYD-Deploy\O365 and the configuration file is stored on the share \\SYD-Deploy\Configs, run this command:

```
\\SYD-Deploy\O365\Setup.exe /configure \\SYD-Deploy\Configs\Configuration.xml
```

Configuration.xml

The deployment tool ships with three sample Configuration.xml files: Configuration-Office365-x64.xml, Configuration-Office365-x86.xml and Configuration-Office2019Enterprise.xml. You use these files to perform the following tasks:

- Add or remove Office products from an installation
- Add or remove languages from the installation
- Specify display options, such as whether the installation occurs silently
- Configure logging options, such as how much information will be recorded in the log
- Specify how software updates will work with click-to-run

Figure 4-11 shows one of the sample Configuration.xml files available with the Office Deployment Tool.

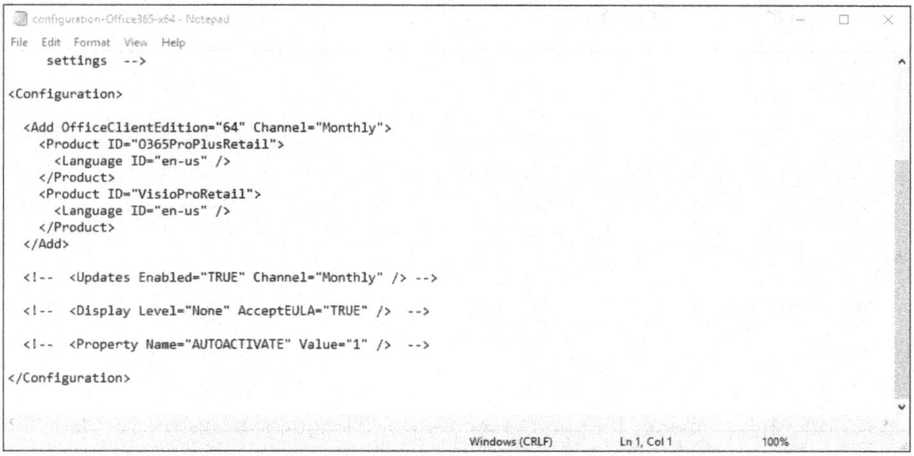

```
configuration-Office365-x64 - Notepad                          —    □    ×
File  Edit  Format  View  Help
      settings  -->
<Configuration>

<Add OfficeClientEdition="64" Channel="Monthly">
  <Product ID="O365ProPlusRetail">
    <Language ID="en-us" />
  </Product>
  <Product ID="VisioProRetail">
    <Language ID="en-us" />
  </Product>
</Add>

<!-- <Updates Enabled="TRUE" Channel="Monthly" /> -->

<!-- <Display Level="None" AcceptEULA="TRUE" /> -->

<!-- <Property Name="AUTOACTIVATE" Value="1" /> -->

</Configuration>

                              Windows (CRLF)       Ln 1, Col 1           100%
```

FIGURE 4-11 The Office365 x64 Configuration.xml

Important attributes include:

- SourcePath   When you run the tool in /download mode, the SourcePath attribute determines the location where the click-to-run files will be stored. When you run the tool in /configure mode, the SourcePath attribute determines the installation source.

- OfficeClientEdition   This value is required and must be set to either 32 or 64. This determines whether the x86 or x64 version of Office applications are retrieved or installed.

- Version   If this element is not set, the most recent version of files will be downloaded or installed. If a version is set, then that version of the files will be downloaded or installed.

- Display   This element allows you to specify what information the user sees during deployment. The options are:

  - Level=None   The user sees no UI, completion screen, error dialog boxes, or first run UI.

  - Level=FULL   The user sees the normal click-to-run user interface, application splash screen, and error dialog boxes.

  - AcceptEULA=True   The user does not see the Microsoft Software License Terms dialog box.

  - AcceptEULA=False   The user will see the Microsoft Software License Terms dialog box.

- ExcludeApp   You use this element to exclude applications from being installed. Valid values of this attribute are as follows:

  - Access

  - Excel

- `Groove` (used for OneDrive for Business)

- `InfoPath`

- `Lync` (used for Skype for Business)

- `OneNote`

- `OneDrive`

- `Outlook`

- `PowerPoint`

- `Project`

- `Publisher`

- `SharePointDesigner`

- `Visio`

- `Word`

- `Language ID` This element allows you to specify which language packs are installed—for example, `en-us` for US English. You can have multiple `Language-ID` elements, one for each language you install.

- `Logging` This element allows you to disable logging, enable logging, and specify the path where the log file is to be written.

- `Product ID` This element allows you to specify which products to install. The available options are:

  - `O365ProPlusRetail` Microsoft 365 Apps for enterprise

  - `VisioProRetail` Visio Pro

  - `ProjectProRetail` Project Professional

  - `SPDRetail` SharePoint Designer

- `Remove` If this element is set to `ALL=TRUE`, then all click-to-run products are removed.

- `Updates` This element allows you to configure how updates are managed and includes the following options:

  - `Enabled` When set to `TRUE`, the click-to-run update system will check for updates.

  - `UpdatePath` If this element is not set, updates will be retrieved from Microsoft servers on the internet. If the element is set to a network, local, or HTTP path, then updates will be sourced from the specified path.

  - `TargetVersion` Allows you to apply updates to a specific Office build version. If not specified, the most recent version is updated.

  - `Deadline` Specifies the deadline by which updates must be applied. You can use `Deadline` with `Target Version` to force Office applications to be updated to a specific version by a specific date. The `Deadline` setting will only apply to a single set of updates. To ensure that Office applications are always up to date, it is necessary to revise the `Deadline` setting when new updates are available.

MORE INFO **CONFIGURATION.XML**

You can learn more about the format of Configuration.xml at *https://docs.microsoft.com/ en-us/deployoffice/office-deployment-tool-configuration-options*.

Click-to-run vs. MSI

Click-to-run and MSI are two different formats through which Office applications can be distributed to users. Click-to-run offers the following features:

- **Streaming installation**   Allows an application to be run before installation has completed. When the installation of an application is streamed, the first part of the application installed provides the minimum functionality necessary to get the application running. This allows the user to begin working with the application while installation completes.

- **Slipstreamed Servicing**   Updates are included in the installation. Rather than installing Office in a traditional manner and then running a Windows Update check to locate and install any relevant updates, relevant updates are already included within the click-to-run installation files. Slipstreamed Servicing means that end users have the most secure and up-to-date version of the application immediately, rather than having to wait for the post-deployment update cycle to complete.

- **User-based licensing**   The Microsoft 365 Apps for enterprise license is associated with the Microsoft 365 user account, not the computer that the user is signed on to. Depending on the type of license associated with the user and the tenancy, the user can install Microsoft 365 Apps for enterprise on up to five different computers as well as tablets and phones. It is possible to remove licenses from computers that have had Microsoft 365 Apps for enterprise installed on them at an earlier point in time.

- **Retail activation**   Microsoft 365 Apps for enterprise is activated using retail rather than volume license methods. Activation occurs over the internet. This means that the computer must connect to the internet every 30 days; otherwise, Office apps will enter reduced-functionality mode.

- **SKU-level application suites**   Unless an administrator configures an appropriate configuration file, Microsoft 365 Apps for enterprise installs all products in the suite. The products installed will depend on the specifics of the Office 365 subscription, but are usually Access, Excel, InfoPath, OneNote, Outlook, PowerPoint, Publisher, and Word. These products will be installed for all users in the tenancy. It is not possible to choose to install the PowerPoint program for some users but not others when all users are using the same click-to-run installation file and configuration file. It is possible to have separate sets of applications deployed to users, but this requires separate configuration files for each set of applications.

MSI files are a method through which applications are packaged. MSI files allow organizational IT departments to automate the deployment of applications, such as Office, using tools such as Microsoft Endpoint Configuration Manager. MSI files are appropriate for organizations that have a managed desktop environment and are less suitable for the types of BYOD scenarios in which click-to-run products, such as Microsoft 365 Apps for enterprise, are suitable. MSI files offer the following features:

- **Classic installation**   MSI files can be installed by double-clicking on the installer file and can be deployed using group policies, Microsoft Endpoint Configuration Manager, or third-party application deployment products. The application is not available to the user until the installation of the application is complete. This differs from the click-to-run method's streaming technology, which allows a user to begin using an application with a reduced set of features before the installation of the application completes.

- **Layered servicing**   MSI files represent the application at the time that it was packaged as an MSI file. This means that after deployment, it will be necessary for the IT department to apply any required software updates to the application. Depending on the age of the MSI file and the number of software updates that have been released since the application was first packaged, it can take quite some time for the application to be updated to the current patch level after the application is deployed. This substantially increases the amount of time between an application being deployed and the user being able to use the application to perform their job tasks. IT departments can update MSI files with the latest updates and patches, but this is a complex, usually manual, process that requires deploying the application to a reference computer, updating the application, and then performing a technique known as a *capture* to create the new updated MSI file. With click-to-run technology, application updates are slipstreamed into the application by Microsoft, meaning the application is current with updates as soon as it is deployed.

- **Volume licensing**   The versions of Office that you can deploy from an MSI file, including Office 2016 and Office 2019, have editions that support volume licensing. Volume licensing gives you the option of using a volume license key. Volume licensing is not something that is automatically supported by the MSI format and depends on the properties of the deployed software. Volume licensing is only available to organizations that have volume-licensing agreements with Microsoft.

- **Volume activation**   Like volume licensing, volume activation is not a property of an MSI file, but a feature that is supported by some versions of Office that use this packaging format. Volume activation allows large numbers of products to be activated either through the use of a special activation key each time the installation is performed or through technologies such as a Key Management Service (KMS) server on the organization's internal network. Volume activation is available only to organizations that have volume-licensing agreements.

- **Selective application installation**   Rather than deploying all products in the Office suite, the MSI-based deployment method makes it simple for organizations to deploy individual products in the suite. For example, it is possible to choose to deploy Word and Excel to some users and PowerPoint to others.

- **Scenario limitations** Unlike click-to-run Microsoft 365 Apps for enterprise, which uses retail activation, the volume-licensed versions of Office 2016 and Office 2019 can be used on Remote Desktop Services servers and can be deployed on networks that do not have internet connectivity.

While there are differences between the click-to-run Microsoft 365 Apps for enterprise and MSI-based Office 2019, there are also certain similarities:

- Both can be configured through group policies.
- Both provide telemetry visible through the Telemetry Dashboard.
- Extensions designed for the Office 2019 version of a product will work with the Office 365 version of that product.

> **MORE INFO CLICK-TO-RUN VERSUS MSI**
>
> You can learn more about click-to-run versus MSI at *http://blogs.technet.com/b/office_resource_kit/archive/2013/03/05/the-new-office-garage-series-who-moved-my-msi.aspx.*

Plan for Microsoft apps updates

Microsoft provides new features and updates to Office programs on a regular basis. Depending on your organization, you can choose between an update channel that provides new features as they become available and an update channel that provides new features less frequently. The following update channels are available:

- **Current Channel** Provides users with the most recent features as soon as they become available.
- **Monthly Enterprise** Provides users with new features on a monthly basis.
- **Semi-Annual Enterprise Channel** New features are deployed every six months, in January and July.

You choose which update channel to use by doing one of the following:

- Editing the configuration.xml file for the Office Deployment Tool
- Configuring the Update Channel group policy setting under Computer Configuration\Administrative Templates\Microsoft Office 2016 (Machine)\Updates when the Office 2016 group policy template files are installed
- Configuring the Update Channel group policy setting under Computer Configuration\Administrative Templates\Microsoft Office 2019 (Machine)\Updates when the Office 2019 group policy template files are installed

You can also configure release channel settings in the Microsoft 365 Admin Center in the Office Installation Options panel in the Org settings. (See Figure 4-12.)

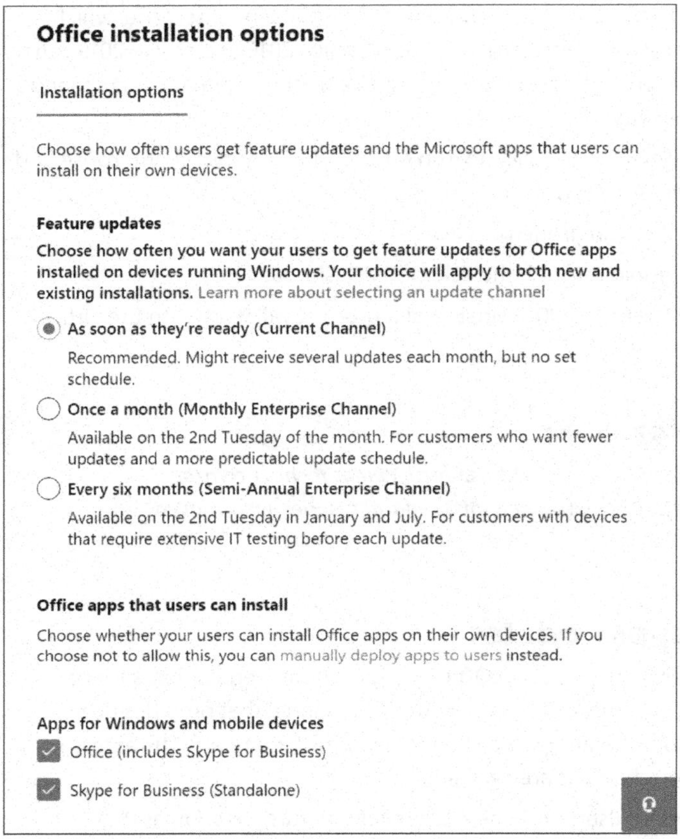

Office installation options

Installation options
_____

Choose how often users get feature updates and the Microsoft apps that users can install on their own devices.

Feature updates
Choose how often you want your users to get feature updates for Office apps installed on devices running Windows. Your choice will apply to both new and existing installations. Learn more about selecting an update channel

(●) As soon as they're ready (Current Channel)

    Recommended. Might receive several updates each month, but no set schedule.

(○) Once a month (Monthly Enterprise Channel)

    Available on the 2nd Tuesday of the month. For customers who want fewer updates and a more predictable update schedule.

(○) Every six months (Semi-Annual Enterprise Channel)

    Available on the 2nd Tuesday in January and July. For customers with devices that require extensive IT testing before each update.

Office apps that users can install
Choose whether your users can install Office apps on their own devices. If you choose not to allow this, you can manually deploy apps to users instead.

Apps for Windows and mobile devices
☑ Office (includes Skype for Business)

☑ Skype for Business (Standalone)

FIGURE 4-12 Feature update settings

> ***MORE INFO*** **MICROSOFT 365 APPS UPDATE CHANNELS**
> You can learn more about update channels at *https://docs.microsoft.com/en-us/deployoffice/overview-update-channels*.

Plan Microsoft telemetry and reporting

Office Telemetry is a compatibility-monitoring framework. You can use it to assess Office compatibility issues. Office Telemetry provides similar functionality to the following Office 2010 compatibility tools:

- Office Migration Planning Manager
- Office Code Compatibility Inspector
- Office Environment Assessment Tool

Office Telemetry works with Office 2019, Office 2016, Office 2013, and the versions of Office apps that ship with Microsoft 365 apps. This functionality is built into the applications. Some Office Telemetry features are available for earlier versions of Office if the Office Telemetry Agent is installed on each computer running the previous version of Office.

Deploy Telemetry Dashboard

The Telemetry Dashboard allows you to view information collected by the Telemetry Processor, a special server that you deploy on the network to collect telemetry information. The Telemetry Dashboard is a specially configured Excel worksheet that connects to a database hosted on a supported SQL instance. You can start the Telemetry Dashboard in the following manner:

- On computers running Windows Server 2012 or Windows Server 2012 R2, open the **Search** box from the **Start** menu and type **Telemetry Dashboard**.

- On computers running Windows 10, Windows 11, Windows Server 2022, Windows Server 2019, or Windows Server 2016, select the **Start** menu and type **Telemetry Dashboard**, as shown in Figure 4-13.

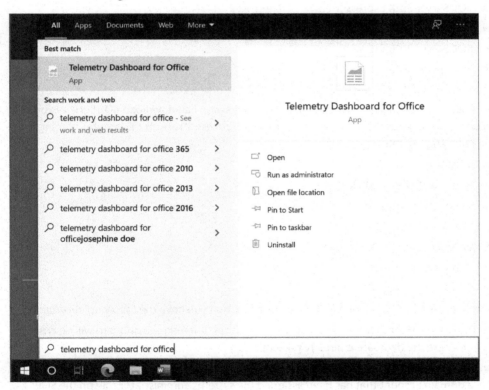

FIGURE 4-13 Search for Telemetry Dashboard

You must have Excel installed to open the Telemetry Dashboard. To use the Telemetry Dashboard, you must configure a computer to function as the Telemetry Processor and a computer to host the SQL Server database used by the Telemetry Dashboard. The computer that functions as the Telemetry Processor and the computer that hosts the SQL Server database used by the Telemetry Dashboard can be the same computer.

You can use the following versions of SQL server to host the back-end database for the Telemetry Dashboard:

- SQL Server 2005
- SQL Server 2005 Express Edition
- SQL Server 2008
- SQL Server 2008 Express Edition
- SQL Server 2008 R2
- SQL Server 2008 R2 Express Edition
- SQL Server 2012
- SQL Server 2012 Express
- SQL Server 2014
- SQL Server 2014 Express
- SQL Server 2016
- SQL Server 2016 Express
- SQL Server 2019
- SQL Server 2019 Express

The Telemetry Dashboard contains links from which you can download SQL Server Express. Microsoft recommends that you host the Telemetry Processor role on a computer running one of the following operating systems:

- Windows Server 2008
- Windows Server 2008 R2
- Windows Server 2012
- Windows Server 2012 R2
- Windows Server 2016
- Windows Server 2019
- Windows Server 2022

Before deploying the Telemetry Processor, ensure that you have the following information:

- The name of the SQL Server instance on which the Telemetry Dashboard will be created or where the database is already present.
- Permission to create and configure the database on the SQL Server. This needs to be a domain account that has been assigned the systems administrator role on the SQL Server instance.
- Permission to create a shared folder or the UNC path of an existing folder.
- 11 GB or more of free hard drive space on the computer that hosts the Telemetry Processor role.

To deploy the Telemetry Processor, perform the following steps:

1. Open the Telemetry Dashboard spreadsheet and select the **Getting Started** worksheet in the workbook.

2. Select the **Install Telemetry Processor** down arrow. (See Figure 4-14.)

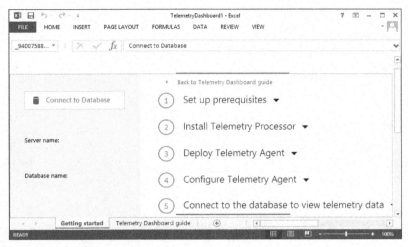

FIGURE 4-14 Getting started

3. Under **Install Telemetry Processor**, select either the **x86** or the **x64** link, as shown in Figure 4-15.

   For deployment of the Telemetry Processor on Windows Server 2012 and later, select the **x64** option. While the x86 version will run, Windows Server 2012 requires an x64 processor and the x64 version of the Telemetry Processor will be able to use more resources than the x86 version.

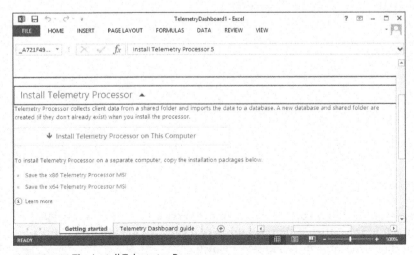

FIGURE 4-15 The Install Telemetry Processor page

4. Save the file to a location where you will be able to retrieve it. For example, Figure 4-16 shows the file osmdp64.msi being saved to the desktop.

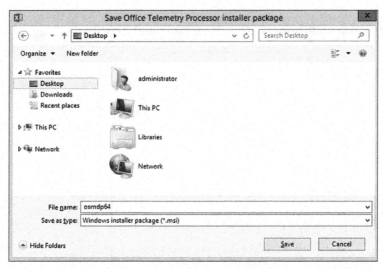

FIGURE 4-16 The Save Office Telemetry Processor Installer Package dialog box

5. After the file has saved, double-click it to run the Telemetry Processor installer.

6. On the **Welcome to the Microsoft Office Telemetry Processor** page of the Setup Wizard, shown in Figure 4-17, select **Next**.

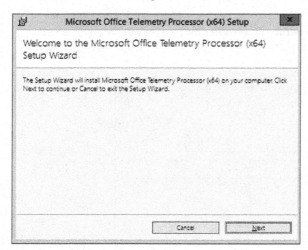

FIGURE 4-17 Welcome page

7. On the **Completed the Microsoft Office Telemetry Processor Setup Wizard** page, ensure that the **Run the Office Telemetry Processor settings wizard now** check box is selected, as shown in Figure 4-18, and select **Finish**.

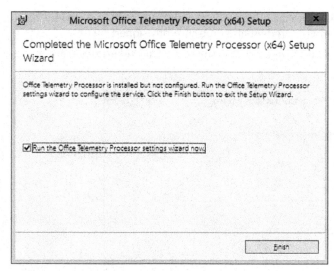

FIGURE 4-18 Installation complete; now run setup

8. On the **Getting Started** page of the **Office Telemetry Processor settings wizard**, shown in Figure 4-19, review the information and then select **Next**.

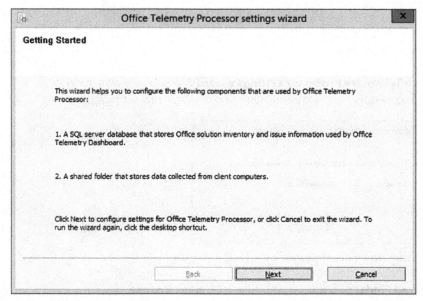

FIGURE 4-19 Setup requirements

9. On the **Database Settings** page, select the database server and select **Connect**. The connection will be made using the credentials of the currently signed-on user.

10. Select a database—Figure 4-20 shows a database named **OfficeTelemetry**—and select **Create**. Then select **Next**.

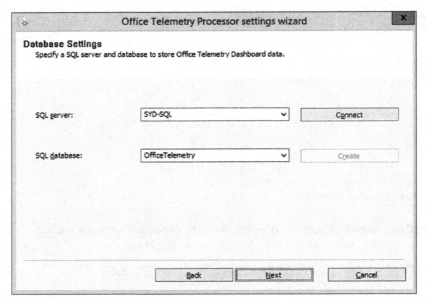

FIGURE 4-20 Database Settings page

11. In the **Office Telemetry Processor settings wizard** dialog box, shown in Figure 4-21, select **Yes** to configure database permissions and database role settings.

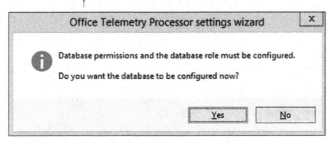

FIGURE 4-21 Database permissions configuration

12. On the **Shared Folder** page, shown in Figure 4-22, select **Browse**.

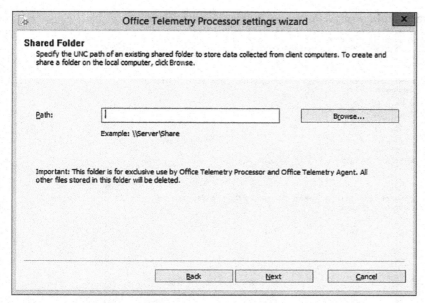

FIGURE 4-22 Shared Folder page

13. Create and select a shared folder, as shown in Figure 4-23. If you are going to use an existing folder, ensure that it is empty.

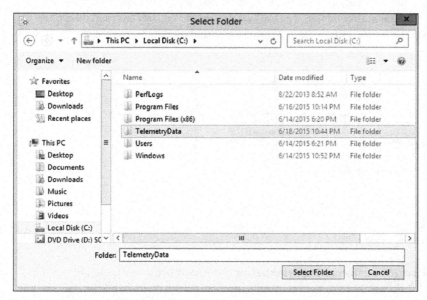

FIGURE 4-23 Select Folder dialog box

14. On the **Shared Folder** page, shown in Figure 4-24, select **Next**.

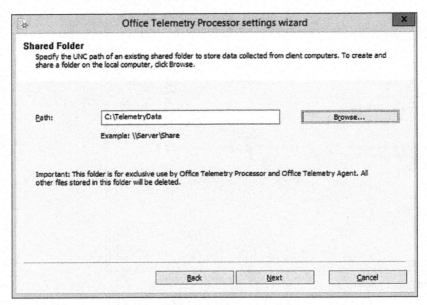

FIGURE 4-24 The Shared Folder page with a folder selected

15. Review the information in the information dialog box, shown in Figure 4-25. Here, it informs you that authenticated users will be granted the ability to create files and write data in the folder without being able to browse the contents of that folder. Then select **Yes**.

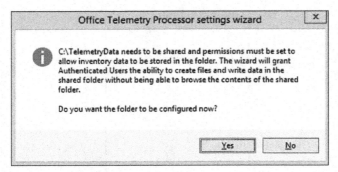

FIGURE 4-25 Permissions warning

16. On the **Microsoft Customer Experience Improvement Program** page, shown in Figure 4-26, indicate whether you want to participate in the Customer Experience Improvement Program, and select **Next**.

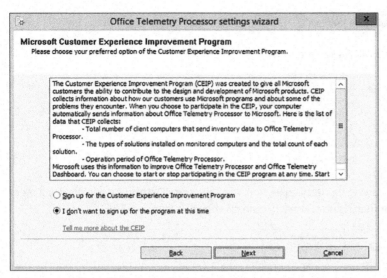

FIGURE 4-26 Microsoft Customer Experience Improvement Program page

17. On the **Configuration Successful** page, select **Finish**.

18. After the Telemetry Processor is deployed, return to the Getting Started worksheet in the Telemetry Dashboard workbook. Then, under section 5, **Connect to the database to view telemetry data**, select **Connect to Database**. (See Figure 4-27.)

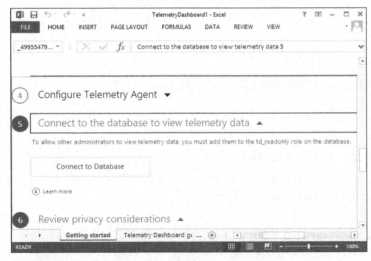

FIGURE 4-27 The Connect to Database button

19. The **Data connection settings** dialog box, shown in Figure 4-28, should be automatically populated with the name of the SQL instance and of the database. Select **Connect**.

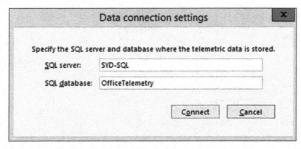

FIGURE 4-28 Data Connection Settings dialog box

Until you have configured telemetry collection, the Telemetry Dashboard will display a message informing you that there is no telemetry data, as shown in Figure 4-29.

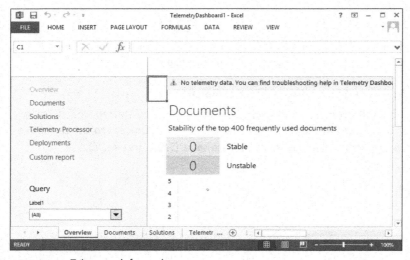

FIGURE 4-29 Telemetry information

> **MORE INFO**   **DEPLOY TELEMETRY DASHBOARD**
>
> You can learn more about deploying the Telemetry Dashboard at *https://docs.microsoft.com/ en-us/DeployOffice/compat/deploy-telemetry-dashboard*.

Enable telemetry through Group Policy

Before you can enable telemetry through group policy, you must install the Microsoft 365 Apps for enterprise, Office 2019, and Office 2016 Group Policy administrative template. You can download the administrative template from the Microsoft website at *https://www.microsoft. com/en-us/download/details.aspx?id=49030*.

You'll need to download the file to a domain controller and then run it. When running the file downloaded from the internet, you will be asked to agree to the license terms. When you have agreed to the license terms, select **Continue**.

You will be asked to choose a temporary directory in which to extract the template files. After you have extracted the files, you will need to do the following:

- Copy the Office16.admx file to the C:\Windows\PolicyDefinitions folder. Even though the file is named Office16.admx, it will work for Office 2019 and Microsoft Apps for enterprise.

- Copy the language-appropriate Office16.adml file to the C:\Windows\PolicyDefinitions\ Language folder. For example, if using EN-US for US English, copy the Office16.adml file from the EN-US folder where you extracted the templates to the C:\Windows\ PolicyDefinitions\en-US folder.

When the ADMX and ADML files are copied to the appropriate folders, you'll be able to edit the policies located in the User Configuration\Policies\Administrative Templates\Microsoft Office 2016\Telemetry Dashboard node. (See Figure 4-30.)

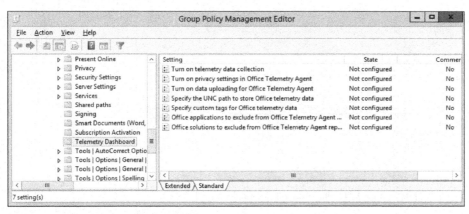

FIGURE 4-30 Telemetry Dashboard policies

TURN ON TELEMETRY DATA COLLECTION

The Turn On Telemetry Data Collection policy (see Figure 4-31) must be enabled for telemetry data collection to be enabled. If this policy is not enabled, Office telemetry data collection will not occur.

TURN ON DATA UPLOADING FOR OFFICE TELEMETRY AGENT

When you enable the Turn On Data Uploading for Office Telemetry Agent policy, as shown in Figure 4-32, Office telemetry data is uploaded to a shared folder specified in another policy. If you don't enable this policy, Office telemetry data is stored on the client and cannot be accessed at a central location through the Telemetry Dashboard.

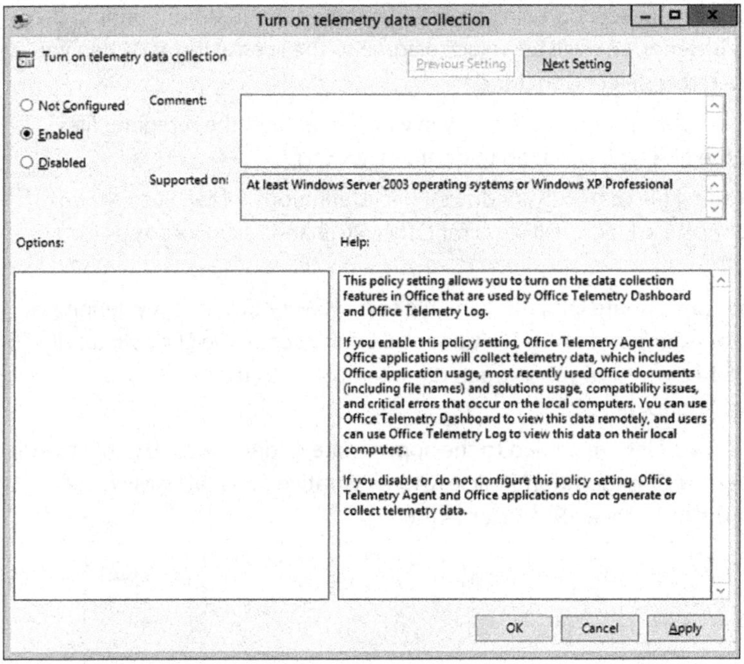

FIGURE 4-31 The Turn On Telemetry Data Collection policy

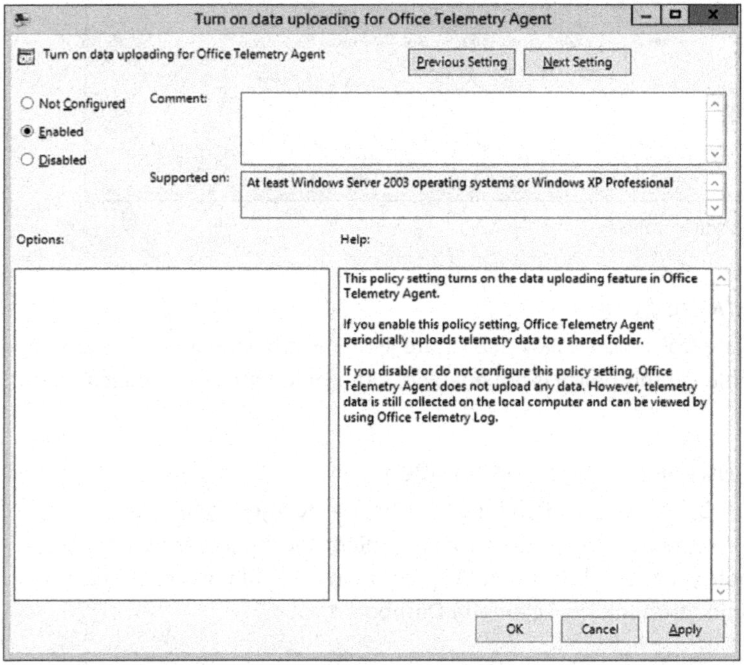

FIGURE 4-32 The Turn on Data Uploading for Office Telemetry Agent policy

SPECIFY THE UNC PATH TO STORE OFFICE TELEMETRY DATA

If you have configured telemetry data to be uploaded to a shared folder using the Turn On Data Uploading for Office Telemetry Agent policy, you'll need to configure the Specify the UNC Path to Store Office Telemetry Data policy, shown in Figure 4-33, to specify the address to which the data will be uploaded.

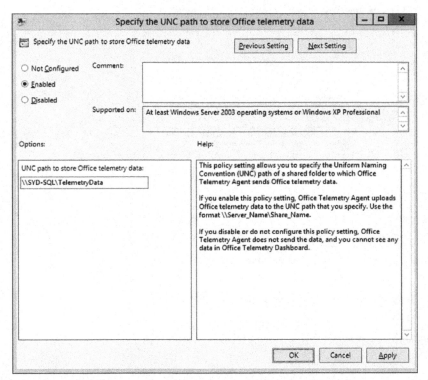

FIGURE 4-33 The Specify the UNC Path to Store Office Telemetry Data policy

SPECIFY CUSTOM TAGS FOR OFFICE TELEMETRY DATA

The Specify Custom Tags for Office Telemetry Data policy allows you to apply tags to telemetry data forwarded to the shared folder used by the Telemetry Processor. You can specify up to four separate tags, as shown in Figure 4-34.

TURN ON PRIVACY SETTINGS IN OFFICE TELEMETRY AGENT

Enabling the Turn On Privacy Settings in Office Telemetry Agent policy, shown in Figure 4-35, obfuscates the file name, file path, and title of Office documents before telemetry data uploads into the shared folder. If this policy is not enabled, the file name, path, and title of documents remain visible.

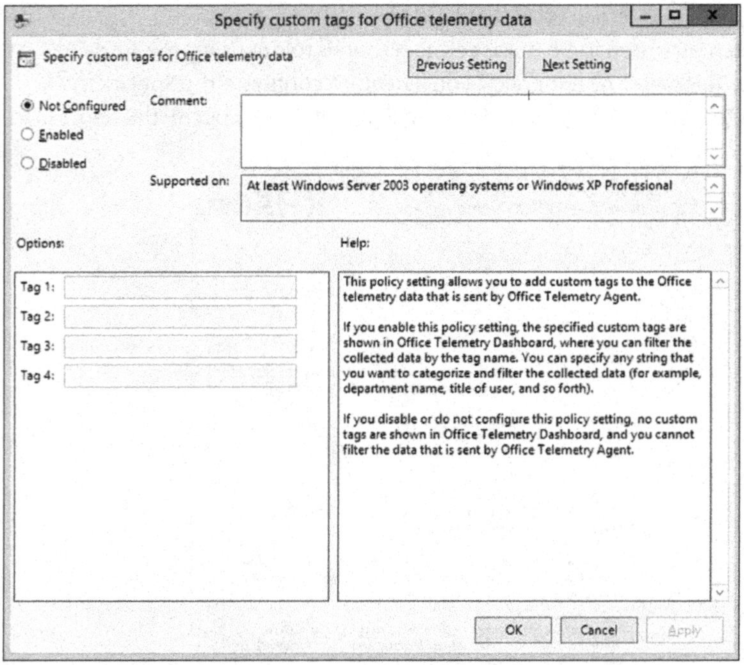

FIGURE 4-34 The Specify Custom Tags For Office Telemetry Data policy

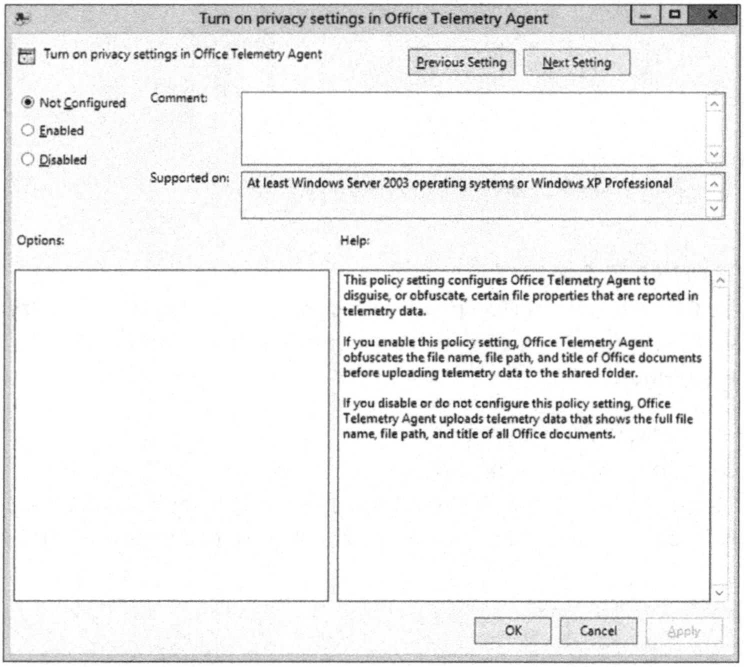

FIGURE 4-35 The Turn On Privacy Settings in Office Telemetry Agent policy

OFFICE APPLICATIONS TO EXCLUDE FROM OFFICE TELEMETRY AGENT REPORTING

You can use the Office Applications to Exclude from Office Telemetry Agent Reporting policy to exclude telemetry data from specific applications from being forwarded to the shared folder used by the Telemetry Processor. Figure 4-36 shows a configuration that excludes telemetry from Publisher and Visio from being sent to the Telemetry Processor.

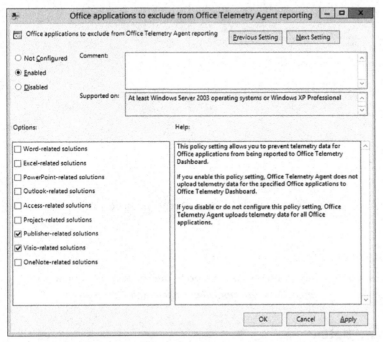

FIGURE 4-36 The Office Applications to Exclude from Office Telemetry Agent Reporting policy

OFFICE SOLUTIONS TO EXCLUDE FROM TELEMETRY AGENT REPORTING

Configuring the Office Solutions to Exclude from Telemetry Agent Reporting policy allows you to stop telemetry data from the following Office solution categories from being forwarded to the Telemetry Processor:

- Office document files
- Office template files
- COM add-ins
- Application-specific add-ins
- Apps for Office

Figure 4-37 shows this policy configured so that telemetry from Office template files and COM add-ins won't be forwarded to the Telemetry Processor.

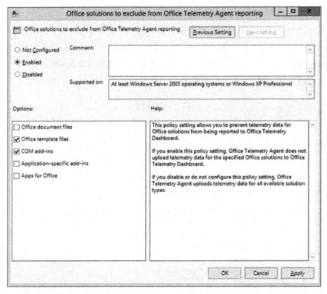

FIGURE 4-37 The Office Solutions to Exclude from Office Telemetry Agent Reporting policy

---

MORE INFO **TELEMETRY AGENT POLICIES**

You can learn more about configuring group policies related to the Telemetry Agent at *https://docs.microsoft.com/en-us/DeployOffice/compat/deploy-telemetry-dashboard*.

Telemetry Dashboard details

When connected to the telemetry database, the Telemetry Dashboard includes the following worksheets:

- **Overview** Provides information about how documents and solutions are functioning on monitored computers. This worksheet provides a high-level view of solution and document stability.

- **Documents** Provides a list of documents collected by Telemetry Agent scans and telemetry documents. This worksheet provides information about the most frequently used documents in your organization.

  - **Document Details** Available through the Documents worksheet. This worksheet shows which users have accessed a document.

  - **Document Issues** Available through the Documents worksheet. This worksheet contains information about unique events related to a specific document, such as if the document was open during an application crash.

  - **Document Sessions** Available through the Documents worksheet. This worksheet shows information about sessions during which issues occurred, including data, user name, computer name, and domain information.

- **Solutions** Provides information about solutions collected by Telemetry Log and Telemetry Agent scans. Solutions include COM add-ins, application-specific add-ins, and apps for Office.
  - **Solution Details** Available through the Solutions worksheet. This worksheet shows which users are using a solution.
  - **Solution Issues** Available through the Solutions worksheet. This worksheet shows details of unique events related to a solution.
  - **Solution Sessions** Available through the Solutions worksheet. This worksheet shows session information about events related to a solution, such as when it occurred, the user, and the computer on which the event occurred.
- **Telemetry Processor** Provides information about the health of the Office Telemetry infrastructure. This worksheet is shown in Figure 4-38.

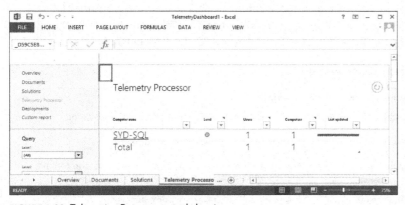

FIGURE 4-38 Telemetry Processor worksheet

- **Agents** Provides information about the users who have computers forwarding data to the Telemetry Processor.
- **Deployments** Provides information about the number of Office clients deployed in the organization.
- **Custom Report** Creates relationships based on data in the database in a pivot table.

MORE INFO **TELEMETRY DASHBOARD DETAILS**

You can learn more about the Telemetry Dashboard at *https://support.office.com/en-us/ article/Best-practices-for-Office-Telemetry-570c7fb3-d7a5-49cd-8cbf-7300ea656328*.

Configure the Telemetry Agent through the registry

In some scenarios, you will want to enable the collection of telemetry data from computers that are not members of an Active Directory domain and hence are not subject to group policies. In this scenario, you can create and import registry settings that will configure the Telemetry Agent. You do this by using a text file with the .reg extension and then importing it into the registry. The following example shows the settings required to configure a computer to upload its data to the shared folder \\SYD-SQL\TelemetryData.

```
[HKEY_CURRENT_USER\Software\Policies\Microsoft\Office\15.0\osm]
"CommonFileShare"="\\\\SYD-SQL\\TelemetryData"
"Tag1"="<TAG1>"
"Tag2"="<TAG2>"
"Tag3"="<TAG3>"
"Tag4"="<TAG4>"
"AgentInitWait"=dword:00000258
"Enablelogging"=dword:00000001
"EnableUpload"=dword:00000001
"EnableFileObfuscation"=dword:00000000
"AgentRandomDelay"=dword:000000F0
```

Report user issues

The Office Telemetry Log is a local log file that is automatically installed when you install Office 2019, Office 2016, or Microsoft 365 Apps for enterprise. The Office Telemetry Log tracks the solution types listed in Table 4-1 for Office 2019, 2016, and Microsoft 365 Apps for enterprise applications.

TABLE 4-1 Office Telemetry Log properties

Solution type	Applications	Description
Task pane apps	Excel, Word, Project	Apps located in the task pane of the client application
Content apps	Excel	Apps integrated into an Office document
Mail apps	Outlook	Apps that appear in Outlook, often when a message contains specific words or phrases
Active documents	Word, PowerPoint, Excel	■ Office binary files (DOC, PPT, PPS, XLS) ■ Office OpenXML files (DOCX, PPTX, PPSX, XLSX) ■ Macro-enabled files with Visual Basic for Applications (VBA) code (DOCM, DOTM, PPTM, POTM, XLSM, XLTM) ■ Files with ActiveX controls ■ Files with external data connections
COM add-ins	Word, PowerPoint, Excel, Outlook	COM add-ins, including Office development tools in Visual Studio application-level add-ins
Excel automation add-ins	Excel	Excel-supported automation add-ins built on COM add-ins
Excel XLS RTD add-ins	Excel	Excel worksheets that use the RealTimeData worksheet function
Word WLL add-ins	Word	WLL add-ins are word-specific add-ins built with compilers that support the creation of DLLs
Application add-ins	Word, PowerPoint, Excel	Application-specific files that contain VBA code (DOTM, XLA, XLAM, PPA, PPAM)
Templates	Word, PowerPoint, Excel	Application-specific templates (DOT, DOTX, XLT, XLTX, POT, POTX)

A file or solution must be either loaded or opened within the local Office application before information about it will be present in the Telemetry Log. To open the Telemetry Log, type **Telemetry Log for Office** in the Start menu and select the result. This opens Excel with the Telemetry Log Events worksheet displayed. This worksheet shows event information and is the primary view of the log you would use if attempting to diagnose user issues using the Telemetry Log.

The System Info worksheet provides information about the computer on which the Telemetry Log is being run, including user name, computer name, system type, Windows edition, time zone, Telemetry Log version, and Office edition.

MORE INFO **OFFICE TELEMETRY LOG**

You can learn more about the Office Telemetry Log at *https://docs.microsoft.com/en-us/office/client-developer/shared/troubleshooting-office-files-and-custom-solutions-with-the-telemetry-log*.

EXAM TIP

Remember which policies must be enabled to allow telemetry data to be forwarded to the Telemetry Processor.

Skill 4.2: Plan for messaging deployments

This skill section deals with migrating on-premises Exchange server deployments to Exchange Online. In this section, you'll learn how to plan a migration strategy, plan a messaging deployment, identify hybrid requirements, plan for connectivity, plan for mail routing, and plan email domains.

This section covers the following topics:

- Plan migration strategy
- Plan messaging deployment
- Identify hybrid requirements
- Plan for connectivity
- Plan for mail routing
- Plan email domains

Plan migration strategy

How you migrate Exchange mailboxes from an on-premises deployment to Exchange Online will depend on the nature of your existing deployment. The approach you use with Exchange 2007 may be different to your approach if you have Exchange 2019 (especially given that it's out of support) but will depend on the number of mailboxes that must be moved. Table 4-2 lists the differences between the various methods you can use to migrate from an on-premises messaging environment to Exchange Online.

TABLE 4-2 Migration type comparison

On-premises Messaging Environment	Number of Mailboxes	Will User Accounts Be Managed On-premises?	Migration Method
Exchange 2007–Exchange 2019	Less than 2,000	No	Cutover migration
Exchange 2007	Less than 2,000	No	Staged migration
Exchange 2007	More than 2,000	Yes	Staged migration or remote move migration in hybrid deployment
Exchange 2010–Exchange 2019	More than 2,000	Yes	Remote move migration in hybrid deployment
Exchange 2010 or later with no ongoing directory synchronization	No maximum	No	Minimal hybrid/express migration
Non-Exchange on-premises messaging system	No maximum	Yes	IMAP migration

> **MORE INFO   CHOOSING A MIGRATION PATH**
>
> You can learn more about choosing a migration path at *https://docs.microsoft.com/en-us/ exchange/mailbox-migration/decide-on-a-migration-path*.

Remote move migration method

You use a remote move (also known as a *batch*) migration when you have an existing Exchange hybrid deployment, where an on-premises Exchange deployment coexists with an Exchange Online deployment. You must use a hybrid deployment and the remote move migration method when you need to migrate more than 2,000 Exchange Server 2010, Exchange Server 2013, Exchange Server 2016, or Exchange Server 2019 mailboxes to Exchange Online.

With a hybrid deployment, you get the following advantages:

- User accounts are managed through your on-premises tools.
- Directory synchronization connects your on-premises Exchange organization with Exchange Online.

- Users can use single sign-on to access their mailbox whether the mailbox is hosted in the on-premises Exchange organization or Exchange Online.
- Email is routed securely between the on-premises Exchange deployment and Exchange Online.
- Free/busy calendar sharing is available for users with mailboxes hosted in the on-premises Exchange organization and mailboxes hosted in Exchange Online.

Before performing a remote move migration, you must ensure that the following prerequisites are met:

- A hybrid deployment has already been configured between your on-premises Exchange organization and Exchange Online.
- You need the appropriate permissions assigned. For mailbox moves in a hybrid deployment, this means you must have an account that has the organization management or recipient management role.
- You must have deployed the Mailbox Replication Proxy Service (MRSProxy) on all on-premises Exchange 2013 or Exchange 2016 Client Access servers.

Once these prerequisites have been met, you can move mailboxes from your on-premises Exchange deployment to Exchange Online by performing the following steps:

1. **Create migration endpoint**   Migration endpoints host connection settings for an on-premises Exchange server running the MRSProxy service.

2. **Enable MRSProxy service**   The MRSProxy service is hosted on on-premises Client Access servers. This service can be enabled using Exchange Administration Console by selecting the Client Access server, editing the properties of the EWS virtual directory, and ensuring that the MRS Proxy Enabled check box is selected.

3. **Move mailboxes**   You can move mailboxes using the Office 365 tab in EAC on the on-premises Exchange server by creating a new migration batch in Exchange Admin Console or by using Windows PowerShell. When moving mailboxes, you move some, not all, mailboxes at a time in groups, which are termed *batches*.

4. **Remove completed migration batches**   After the migration of a batch is complete, you remove the batch using the Exchange Administration Center or Windows PowerShell.

5. **Reenable offline access for Outlook Web App**   If users have been migrated from on-premises Exchange Server to Office 365, you must reset the offline access setting in their browser.

MORE INFO   **REMOTE MAILBOX MOVE MIGRATIONS**

You can learn more about remote mailbox move migrations at *https://docs.microsoft.com/en-us/exchange/hybrid-deployment/move-mailboxes*.

Staged migration method

In a staged migration, you migrate mailboxes from your on-premises Exchange deployment to Exchange Online in groups, or batches. You should perform a staged migration in the following circumstances:

- Your organization has more than 2,000 on-premises mailboxes hosted in Exchange 2007.
- Your organization intends to completely move its messaging infrastructure to Office 365.
- Your available migration period is in the timeframe of several weeks to several months.
- After migration completes, you still plan to manage user accounts with on-premises management tools and have account synchronization performed with Azure Active Directory.
- The primary domain name used for your on-premises Exchange organization must be configured as a domain associated with the tenancy in Office 365.

Staged migration involves the following general steps:

1. Create a CSV file that includes a row for every user who has an on-premises mailbox that you want to migrate. This is not every user in the organization, but just those who you will migrate in a particular batch. You can migrate a maximum of 2,000 mailboxes per batch.

2. Create a staged migration batch using Exchange Admin Center or Windows PowerShell.

3. Trigger the migration batch. When you do, Exchange Online performs these steps:
   - It verifies that directory synchronization is enabled and functioning. Directory synchronization migrates distribution groups, contacts, and mail-enabled users.
   - It verifies that a mail-enabled user exists in Office 365 for every user listed in the batch CSV file.
   - It converts the Office 365 mail-enabled user to an Exchange Online mailbox for each user in the migration batch.
   - It configures mail forwarding for the on-premises mailbox.

4. After these steps have been completed, Exchange Online sends you a status report informing you of which mailboxes have and have not migrated successfully. Successfully migrated users can start using Exchange Online mailboxes.

5. After migration is successful, convert the mailboxes of successfully migrated on-premises users to mail-enabled users in the on-premises Exchange deployment.

6. Configure a new batch of users to migrate and delete the current migration batch.

7. After all users have been migrated, assign licenses to Office 365 users, configure MX records to point to Exchange online, and create an Autodiscover record that points to Office 365.

8. Decommission the on-premises Exchange deployment.

MORE INFO **STAGED MIGRATION METHOD**

You can learn more about staged migrations at *https://docs.microsoft.com/en-us/exchange/*
mailbox-migration/perform-a-staged-migration/perform-a-staged-migration.

Cutover migration method

In a cutover migration, all mailboxes in an on-premises Exchange deployment are migrated to
Exchange Online in a single migration batch. Cutover migrations migrate global mail contacts
as well as distribution groups. Cutover migrations are suitable when:

- You intend for all mailboxes to be hosted in Microsoft 365 when the migration
completes.
- You intend to manage user accounts using Microsoft 365 tools.
- You want to perform the migration in less than a week.
- Your organization has fewer than 2,000 mailboxes.
- Your on-premises messaging solution is Exchange Server 2007 or later. (Exchange Server
2007 reached end of extended support on April 11, 2017.)
- The primary domain name used for your on-premises Exchange deployment must be
configured as domain associated with the tenancy in Microsoft 365.

You can perform a cutover migration using the Exchange Admin Center or by using
Windows PowerShell.

The cutover migration method involves the following general steps:

1. Create empty mail-enabled security groups in Microsoft 365.
2. An administrator connects Microsoft 365 to the on-premises Exchange deployment.
This is also termed creating a migration endpoint.
3. An administrator creates and starts a cutover migration batch using Exchange Admin
Center or Windows PowerShell. Batches should consist of no more than 150 users.
4. When the migration batch is triggered, Exchange Online performs the following steps:
   - It queries the on-premises Exchange deployment's address book to identify
   mailboxes, distribution groups, and contacts.
   - It provisions new Exchange Online mailboxes.
   - It creates distribution groups and contacts within Exchange Online.
   - It migrates mailbox data, including email messages, contacts, and calendar items,
   from each on-premises mailbox to the corresponding Exchange Online mailbox.
   - It forwards the administrator a report providing statistics including the number of
   successful and failed migrations. This report includes automatically generated passwords for each new Exchange Online mailbox. (Users are forced to change passwords
   the first time they sign in to Microsoft 365.)

Incremental synchronization occurs every 24 hours, updating Exchange Online with any
new items created in the on-premises mailboxes.

5. After migration issues have been resolved, change the MX records to point to Exchange Online.

6. When mail flow to Exchange Online has been successfully established, delete the cutover migration batch. This terminates synchronization between the on-premises mailboxes and Microsoft 365.

7. Perform post-migration tasks, including assigning Microsoft 365 licenses, creating an Autodiscover DNS record, and decommissioning on-premises Exchange servers.

> **MORE INFO**   **CUTOVER MIGRATION**
>
> You can learn more about cutover migrations at *https://docs.microsoft.com/en-us/exchange/mailbox-migration/cutover-migration-to-office-365*.

Minimal hybrid or Express migration

Minimal hybrid or express migration is appropriate for organizations that are running Exchange 2010 or later, have a migration timetable that is shorter than a few weeks, and that do not intend to have an ongoing directory service configuration. For example, this method is appropriate if your organization intends to retire its on-premises Active Directory Domain Services infrastructure after migration is complete.

Performing a minimal hybrid migration involves performing the following steps:

1. In the Microsoft 365 console, add the domain that you use for your on-premises Exchange organization by configuring a TXT record (or by signing into GoDaddy if your organization uses that registrar) and verify that the TXT record is properly configured.

2. Sign in to the Microsoft 365 account using global administrator credentials.

3. Start the **Exchange Hybrid Configuration Wizard** from the **Data Migration** page under **Setup** in the **Microsoft 365 admin console**.

4. Connect to the on-premises Exchange Server organization.

5. Choose the **Minimal Hybrid Configuration** option.

6. Select the option to synchronize users and passwords one at a time. You will be prompted to install Azure AD Connect with the default options. Synchronization will occur once and then be turned off.

7. Configure Microsoft 365 licenses for migrated users and then begin migrating user mailbox data.

8. Update DNS MX records to point away from the on-premises Exchange deployment to Exchange Online.

> **MORE INFO**   **MINIMAL HYBRID MIGRATION**
>
> You can learn more about minimal hybrid migrations at *https://docs.microsoft.com/en-us/exchange/mailbox-migration/use-minimal-hybrid-to-quickly-migrate*.

IMAP migration

IMAP migrations use the IMAP protocol to move the contents of on-premises user mailboxes to Exchange Online. IMAP migrations are suitable where the on-premises mail server is not running Exchange Server but is instead running an alternate mail server solution.

IMAP migration is supported for the following on-premises messaging solutions:

- Courier-IMAP
- Cyrus
- Dovecot
- UW-IMAP

IMAP migrations involve the following general steps:

1. Create Microsoft 365 user accounts and assign them Exchange Online user licenses. This provisions the user accounts with Exchange Online mailboxes. (This step must be completed by a tenant administrator.)

2. Create a CSV file that includes a row for each on-premises user who will be migrated to Exchange Online using IMAP. This CSV file needs to include the passwords used by each on-premises IMAP mailbox user. It is recommended that you reset user passwords for on-premises IMAP mailbox users to simplify this process. (This step must be completed by a tenant administrator.)

3. Create and trigger an IMAP migration batch. This can be done using the Migration dashboard, available from the Microsoft 365 console.

4. Once the migration batch is initiated, Exchange Online does the following:

    - It creates a migration request for each user in the CSV file. Each migration request includes the credentials for the user in the on-premises IMAP messaging system.

    - It copies messages from each user's IMAP mailbox to the corresponding Exchange Online mailbox until all data is migrated.

    - It provides a status email to the administrator informing them of the status of the migration. This email contains statistics about the number of mailboxes successfully migrated, how many could not be migrated, and any error reports.

    Exchange Online and the IMAP messaging system are synchronized every 24 hours to move any new messages from the on-premises environment to Exchange Online.

5. When all migration issues have been resolved, update MX records to point to Exchange Online.

6. When mail is flowing to Exchange Online, delete the migration batches.

MORE INFO **IMAP MIGRATIONS TO EXCHANGE ONLINE**

You can learn more about IMAP migrations at *https://docs.microsoft.com/en-us/exchange/mailbox-migration/migrating-imap-mailboxes/migrating-imap-mailboxes.*

Import service

Network upload allows you to import PST files into Exchange Online. This can be done either by directly uploading the files to Azure blob storage or by shipping hard drives to Microsoft and having them import data directly.

To import PST files, perform the following steps:

1. On the **Data Governance** page of the **Security & Compliance Center**, use the settings in the **Import** section to create a Shared Access Signature (SAS) key, also known as the SAS URL. This key provides the necessary permission and location to upload PST files to an Azure storage location.

2. Download and install the Azure AzCopy tool.

3. Use AzCopy with the SAS URL to upload one or more PST files. You can also do this with Azure Storage Explorer.

4. Review the list of PST files that have been successfully transferred to Microsoft 365. You can do this with Azure Storage Explorer.

5. Create a mapping file that maps uploaded PST files to Microsoft 365 mailboxes. This file must be in CSV format.

6. Create a PST import job from the **Data Governance** page of the **Security & Compliance Center**. You specify the mapping file when creating this job.

7. Run the job to import the data into the appropriate Microsoft 365 mailboxes.

> **MORE INFO**   **IMPORT SERVICE**
>
> You can learn more about the import service at *https://docs.microsoft.com/en-us/microsoft-365/compliance/use-network-upload-to-import-pst-files*.

Plan messaging deployment

Microsoft 365 supports two deployment options:

- **Cloud-only**   All user mailboxes are hosted in Microsoft's Azure data centers through Exchange Online.
- **Exchange hybrid**   Some mailboxes are hosted on-premises on an Exchange Server deployment and other mailboxes are hosted in Exchange Online.

Organizations that are doing completely new deployments of Microsoft 365 generally opt for the cloud-only deployment, because this approach minimizes the number of servers they must deploy on-premises. The exception to this rule is where regulation might require certain types of data to be stored on-premises or within a specific geographical area where no local Microsoft 365 data center is available.

Organizations with an existing Exchange infrastructure may choose a hybrid messaging deployment. In this scenario, some mailboxes and users are migrated to Exchange Online, while others—especially executives who are important enough to laugh at the notion of staying within their mailbox quota—maintain their mailboxes on-premises. Another reason for a hybrid deployment might be when a site has low or intermittent bandwidth, such as certain research stations in Antarctica where it makes much more sense economically to connect to a mailbox server on the local area network than it does to connect to one over a low-bandwidth satellite link.

> **MORE INFO PLAN MESSAGING DEPLOYMENT**
>
> You can learn more about planning messaging deployment at *https://docs.microsoft.com/ en-us/office365/servicedescriptions/exchange-online-service-description/planning-and-deployment*.

Identify hybrid requirements

Before an organization with an on premises–only Exchange deployment can shift to a hybrid deployment, it will need to meet certain prerequisites. The first is that it must have Exchange 2007 or later on-premises. The version of Exchange that you have deployed determines the type of hybrid deployment that is available (see Table 4-3).

TABLE 4-3 Hybrid deployment options

On-premises Deployment	Hybrid Deployment Options
Exchange 2007	■ Exchange 2010–based hybrid deployment ■ Exchange 2013–based hybrid deployment
Exchange 2010	■ Exchange 2010–based hybrid deployment ■ Exchange 2013–based hybrid deployment ■ Exchange 2016–based hybrid deployment
Exchange 2013	■ Exchange 2013–based hybrid deployment ■ Exchange 2016–based hybrid deployment ■ Exchange 2019–based hybrid deployment
Exchange 2016	■ Exchange 2016–based hybrid deployment ■ Exchange 2019–based hybrid deployment
Exchange 2019	■ Exchange 2019–based hybrid deployment

When selecting a hybrid deployment option, you should choose the most modern version available for your organization. For example, if your organization has Exchange 2013 deployed, your preference should be to configure an Exchange 2019–based hybrid deployment.

Hybrid deployments require that the on-premises Exchange systems have the most recent cumulative update or update rollup deployed. Generally, the release before the most recent cumulative update or update rollup will also work, but older cumulative updates or update rollups will not be supported. Cumulative updates and update rollups are generally released on a quarterly basis.

You must have specific roles deployed within the on-premises Exchange organization. Which roles are deployed depends on the hybrid deployment option you are choosing. These requirements are as follows:

- **Exchange 2010 hybrid deployment**   A minimum of one Exchange 2010 server with the Mailbox, Hub Transport, and Client Access server roles installed. You can also meet the prerequisite requirements by deploying these Exchange 2010 roles on separate servers. Autodiscover public DNS records for existing SMTP domains point at the on-premises Client Access server.

- **Exchange 2013 hybrid deployment**   A minimum of one server with the Mailbox and Client Access roles installed. The prerequisites can also be met by deploying these roles on separate servers. Autodiscover public DNS records for existing SMTP domains point at the on-premises Client Access server.

- **Exchange 2016 hybrid deployment**   A minimum of one server with the mailbox server role installed. Autodiscover public DNS records for existing SMTP domains point at the on-premises Mailbox server.

- **Exchange 2019 hybrid deployment**   A minimum of one server with the mailbox server role installed. Autodiscover public DNS records for existing SMTP domains point at the on-premises Mailbox server.

Hybrid Exchange deployments have the following additional requirements:

- Azure AD Connect is configured to synchronize the on-premises Active Directory instance with Azure Active Directory.

- Custom domains are registered with your organization's Azure AD tenancy.

- Connect the Microsoft 365 organization to the Exchange Admin Center. You must do this prior to running the Hybrid Configuration Wizard.

- You must install valid digital certificates purchased from a trusted certificate authority (CA) on the IIS instance on Exchange servers configured in the hybrid deployment. The Exchange Web Services' external URL and the Autodiscover endpoint specified in your organization's public DNS records must be listed in the Subject Alternative Name (SAN) section of these certificates.

- If your organization's Exchange deployment uses Edge Transport servers and you want to configure those servers for hybrid secure mail transport, you will need to ensure that EdgeSync is configured before running the Hybrid Configuration Wizard.

MORE INFO **HYBRID EXCHANGE DEPLOYMENT PREREQUISITES**

You can learn more about hybrid Exchange deployment prerequisites at *https://docs. microsoft.com/en-us/exchange/hybrid-deployment-prerequisites*.

Plan for connectivity

The ports, protocols, and endpoints listed in Table 4-4 must be configured to allow the appropriate connectivity in an Exchange hybrid deployment.

TABLE 4-4 Exchange hybrid ports, protocols, and endpoints

Protocol	Upper-Level Protocol	Hybrid Functionality	On-premises Endpoint
TCP 25 (SMTP)	SMTP/TLS	Hybrid mail flow	▪ Exchange 2016/2019 Mailbox/Edge Transport ▪ Exchange 2013 CAS/Edge Transport ▪ Exchange 2010 Hub/Edge Transport
TCP 443 (HTTPS)	Autodiscover	Autodiscover	▪ Exchange 2016/2019 Mailbox ▪ Exchange 2010/2013 Client Access
TCP 443 (HTTPS)	EWS	Free/busy, MailTips, message tracking	▪ Exchange 2016/2019 Mailbox ▪ Exchange 2010/2013 Client Access
TCP 443	Autodiscover, EWS	When using OAuth	▪ Exchange 2016/2019 Mailbox ▪ Exchange 2010/2013 Client Access

> **MORE INFO** **EXCHANGE HYBRID PORTS, PROTOCOLS, AND ENDPOINTS**
>
> You can learn more about Exchange hybrid ports, protocols, and endpoints at *https://docs. microsoft.com/en-us/exchange/hybrid-deployment-prerequisites#hybrid-deployment-protocols-ports-and-endpoints*.

Plan for mail routing

Organizations with hybrid messaging deployments can choose to route all incoming messages from senders on the internet through Exchange Online or to configure messages to be routed to an SMTP server that they manage hosted on a location such as a perimeter network.

Microsoft recommends that you configure MX records for email domains to point to Exchange Online Protection (EOP) in Microsoft 365. Routing all incoming mail in this manner has the benefit of having unsolicited commercial email filtered out by Microsoft before the mail passes further into your organization. If your organization chooses to have MX records configured to an SMTP server that you manage, you'll need to configure your internal mail infrastructure to route messages destined for Exchange Online mailboxes to Exchange Online.

If your organization has configured a hybrid deployment where Exchange infrastructure is hosted both on-premises and in the cloud, mail will be routed between both locations as required. This routing will occur independently of whether messages enter Exchange through Exchange Online Protection or an on-premises Edge Transport Server.

MORE INFO **TRANSPORT ROUTING**

You can learn more about transport routing at *https://docs.microsoft.com/en-us/exchange/transport-routing*.

Plan email domains

The vast majority of organizations that use Exchange Online with Microsoft 365 use a single email domain such as contoso.com or tailwindtraders.net. In these situations, setting up the domain as an accepted domain and configuring the appropriate MX record settings in the appropriate DNS zone is all you need to do when it comes to configuring email domains.

When you add a domain to Microsoft 365, it becomes an accepted domain within Exchange Online. There are two types of accepted domain:

- **Authoritative** Email will be delivered to email addresses that are configured for recipients for this domain. Email to unknown recipients is rejected. This can be used if all recipients are using Microsoft 365 or your own email servers.

- **Internal relay (non-authoritative)** Email is delivered using a mail flow connector to your on-premises mail server. You should not choose this option when all recipients for this domain use Microsoft 365.

You configure the type of accepted domain using in the Accepted Domains section of Exchange Admin Center, shown in Figure 4-39.

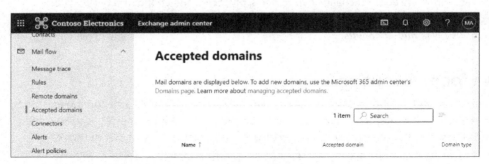

FIGURE 4-39 Accepted domains

MORE INFO **ACCEPTED DOMAINS IN EXCHANGE ONLINE**

You can learn more about accepted domains in Exchange Online at *https://docs.microsoft.com/en-us/exchange/mail-flow-best-practices/manage-accepted-domains/manage-accepted-domains*.

You can use subdomains of accepted domains for on-premises mail servers in a hybrid environment. For example, if you have configured the accepted domain tailwindtraders.net, you could configure the subdomain itopstalk.tailwindtraders.net. All email sent to the itopstalk.

tailwindtraders.net subdomain would be routed to on-premises mail servers, while all email sent to the tailwindtraders.net accepted domain would be routed to Exchange Online.

There are two ways to configure subdomains. If you have a small number of subdomains, Microsoft recommends that you configure each as an accepted domain. If you have a larger number of subdomains, you should configure matching. To configure matching, perform the following steps:

1. In **Exchange admin center**, navigate to **Accepted Domains** under **Mail Flow** and select the mail domain for which you want to configure matching.

2. In the **Details** pane, ensure that **Internal relay** is selected.

3. Enable the **Accept mail for all subdomains** check box, as shown in Figure 4-40.

M365x246046.onmicrosoft.com

Accepted domains have been added to your Exchange organization. Users in accepted domains can send and receive email.

Name

M365x246046.onmicrosoft.com

Accepted domain

M365x246046.onmicrosoft.com

This accepted domain is

⚪ Authoritative
Email is delivered to email addresses that are listed for recipients in Microsoft 365 or Office 365 for this domain. Emails for unknown recipients are rejected.

🔘 Internal relay
Recipients for this domain can be in Microsoft 365 or Office 365 or your own email servers. Email is delivered to known recipients in Office 365 or is relayed to your own email server if the recipients aren't known to Microsoft 365 or Office 365.

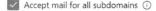 ☑ Accept mail for all subdomains ⓘ

FIGURE 4-40 Accept mail for subdomains

MORE INFO   **EMAIL SUBDOMAINS IN EXCHANGE ONLINE**

You can learn more email subdomains in Exchange Online at *https://docs.microsoft.com/en-us/exchange/mail-flow-best-practices/manage-accepted-domains/enable-mail-flow-for-subdomains.*

 EXAM TIP

Remember the different options for Exchange migration.

Skill 4.3: Plan for Microsoft SharePoint Online and OneDrive for Business

This skill section deals with SharePoint Online and OneDrive for Business. In this section, you'll learn how to plan a migration strategy, plan external share settings, determine how to configure SharePoint in a hybrid configuration, configure access, manage groups, manage SharePoint tenant and site settings, and manage OneDrive for Business.

> **This section covers the following topics:**
> - Plan migration strategy
> - Plan external share settings
> - Identify hybrid requirements
> - Manage access configurations
> - Manage Microsoft groups
> - Manage SharePoint tenant and site settings
> - Manage OneDrive for Business

Plan migration strategy

While it's possible to directly upload one file at a time to a SharePoint Online tenant, or install the OneDrive sync client and have that content automatically synchronize to either OneDrive or SharePoint Online, most organizations migrating from an on-premises SharePoint Server deployment to SharePoint Online use the SharePoint Migration Tool (SPMT).

The SPMT allows for the migration of files from on-premises SharePoint Server document libraries to SharePoint Online. You can also use the SPMT to migrate existing file shares to SharePoint Online. To allow web parts to be migrated, 24 hours before performing a migration with the SPMT you must configure the following settings in the SharePoint Admin Center:

- Allow Users to Run Custom Script on Personal Sites
- Allow Users to Run Custom Script on Self-Service Created Sites

When running the tool, you have the option of specifying a migration either from a Share-Point on-premises deployment or from a file share. When migrating a SharePoint on-premises site, you must specify the site location, credentials to access that site, and the specific document library that you want to migrate. If you are migrating an on-premises file share to Share-Point Online, you must specify the file share location, the URL of the SharePoint Online site that is the destination for the migrated files, and the document library within that site that will host the files.

After you perform a migration, you have the option to save the migration job so that it can be run at a different time. This allows you to migrate any files that were modified or created after the last migration from the source location to the destination SharePoint Online site.

Plan external share settings

External users are people outside your organization who need to collaborate with people inside your organization using content hosted on SharePoint Online, but who haven't been provisioned with an organizational Microsoft 365 or SharePoint Online license.

The use rights available to external users depend on the features available to the SharePoint Online tenancy with which they are collaborating. For example, if your organization has an E3 Enterprise Plan, and a SharePoint site uses enterprise features, the external user can use and view those enterprise features.

External users can perform the following tasks:

- Use Office Online to view and edit documents in the browser.
- Use their own version of Office to interact with content hosted in SharePoint Online (but are not eligible for licenses to the tenancy's Microsoft 365 Apps for enterprise software).
- Perform tasks on the site commensurate with their permission level. For example, adding an external user to the members group grants that user edit permissions. They can add, edit, and delete lists, list items, and documents.
- View other site content, including navigating to subsites to which they have been invited, and view site feeds.

External users are restricted from performing the following tasks:

- Creating personal sites
- Editing their profiles
- Viewing the companywide newsfeed
- Adding storage to the tenant storage pool
- Enacting searches against "everything" or accessing the Search Center
- Accessing the site mailbox
- Accessing Power BI features, including Power View, Power Pivot, Quick Explore, and Timeline Slicer
- Using eDiscovery
- Opening downloaded documents protected by Azure Rights Management (it is still possible to open these documents using Office Online)
- Accessing SharePoint Online data connection libraries
- Using Excel Services features such as calculated measures and calculated members, decoupled PivotTables and PivotCharts, field lists, field support, filter enhancements, and search filters
- Using Visio services

Enable external user sharing globally

The external sharing options configured at the SharePoint Online tenancy level override those configured at the site-collection level. You can configure the following global external sharing options, shown in Figure 4-41:

- **Anyone** Documents and folders can be shared via anonymous links. Anyone with the link can view or edit the document or upload data to the folder. This applies only at the document and folder level and does not apply at the site level.
- **New and Existing Guests** Sites, folders, and documents can be shared with users who have a Microsoft account. This includes accounts such as outlook.com accounts or users from other Microsoft 365 or Azure Active Directory instances.
- **Existing Guests** Sites, folders, and documents are sharable with external users who exist within the Azure AD instance linked to your Microsoft 365 tenancy. A user is added to the directory if they have previously accepted a sharing invitation or have been imported from a separate Office 365 or Azure Active Directory instance.
- **Only People in Your Organization** All users on all sites within the SharePoint Online tenancy are prevented from sharing sites or content with external users.

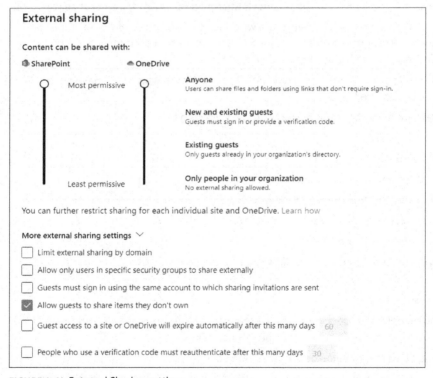

FIGURE 4-41 External Sharing settings

You can configure the following additional settings:

- **Limit external sharing by domain**   Limits sharing to specific domains or allows all domains except those explicitly blocked.
- **Only allow users in specific security groups to share externally**   Limits the ability to share with members of specific security groups.
- **Guests must sign in using the same account to which sharing invitations are sent**   Guest access must occur using the same account used for the sharing invitation. This can be used to block a sharing link from being copied and used by others.
- **Allow guests to share items they don't own**   Allows guests to share items.
- **Guess access to site or OneDrive will expire automatically after this many days**   Configures how long, in days, shared sites or OneDrive locations are accessible before they must be shared again.
- **People who use a verification code must reauthenticate after this many days**   Allows you to configure the period after which someone who has used a verification code must reauthenticate.

To configure external user sharing for the SharePoint Online tenancy, perform the following steps:

1. Sign in to the **Microsoft 365 admin center** with a user account that has SharePoint Online administrator privileges.
2. Under **Admin**, select **SharePoint**.
3. In the **SharePoint admin center**, select **Policies**. Then select **Sharing**. (See Figure 4-42.)

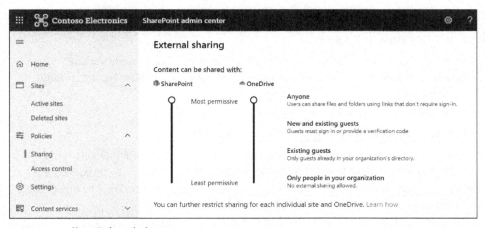

FIGURE 4-42 SharePoint admin center

4. In the **Sharing** section, choose one of the following options:
   - Anyone
   - New and Existing Guests

- Existing Guests
- Only People in Your Organization

Turning off external sharing has the following consequences:

- If you disable and then reenable external sharing, external users who have been granted access to content regain access.
- If you disable and then reenable external sharing, site collections that had sharing enabled have sharing reenabled.
- If you want to block specific site collections from having sharing reenabled, disable external sharing on a per–site collection basis before reenabling external sharing.
- When you disable external sharing on a specific site collection, any configured external user permissions for that site collection are permanently deleted.
- Turning off external sharing at the site-collection level disables guest links but does not remove them. To remove access to specific documents, you must disable anonymous guest links.
- Changes made to external access do not occur immediately and might take up to 60 minutes.

You can also use the `Set-SPOSite` PowerShell cmdlet with the `SharingCapability` parameter to configure sharing options. You can use the following options with this parameter:

- `ExternalUserSharingOnly`
- `ExternalUserAndGuestSharing`
- `ExistingExternalUserSharingOnly`
- `Disabled`

> **MORE INFO   EXTERNAL SHARING**
>
> You can learn more about external sharing at *https://support.office.com/en-us/article/ Manage-external-sharing-for-your-SharePoint-Online-environment-c8a462eb-0723-4b0b-8d0a-70feafe4be85*.

Enable external user sharing per site collection

Only SharePoint Online administrators can make changes to the SharePoint Online tenancy's external user sharing settings. Site-collection administrators are allowed to configure sharing settings on a per–site collection basis as long as external user sharing is set to one of the following options:

- Allow External Users Who Accept Sharing Invitations and Sign In As Authenticated Users
- Allow Both External Users Who Accept Sharing Invitations and Anonymous Guest Links

The sharing options at the site-collection level are similar to those available at the SharePoint Online tenancy level.

Settings configured at the SharePoint Online tenancy level determine those available at the individual site-collection level. If sharing is only allowed for external users at the SharePoint Online tenancy level, the option to allow anonymous guest links to be sent at the site-collection level will not be available. If sharing is blocked at the SharePoint Online tenancy level, then sharing will not be possible at the site-collection level. Modifications to the external sharing settings for the My Site site collection apply to any existing personal sites as well as any personal sites created in the future.

To configure sharing at the site-collection level, perform the following steps:

1. Sign in to the **Microsoft 365 admin center** with a user account that has SharePoint Online administrator privileges.

2. Under **Admin**, select **SharePoint**.

3. In the **SharePoint admin center**, under **Active Sites**, select the site collection for which you want to configure sharing, and select **Sharing**.

4. In the **Sharing** dialog box, specify the type of sharing you want to enable, and select **Save**. (See Figure 4-43.)

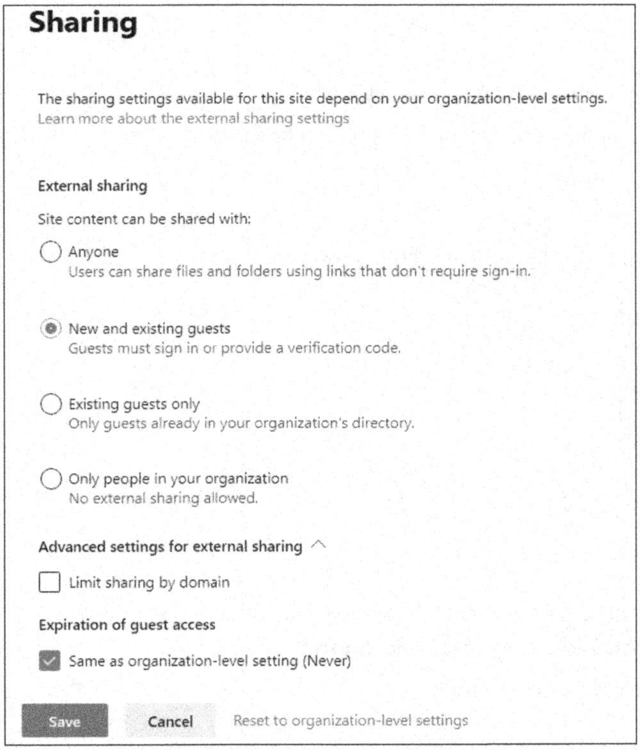

FIGURE 4-43 Sharing options

Sharing settings configured at the site-collection level determine the sharing options available at the document level. If sending anonymous links is not allowed at the site-collection level, it will not be allowed from a document hosted within a site in that collection.

> **MORE INFO** **SITE-COLLECTION SHARING**
>
> You can learn more about sharing at the site-collection level at *https://support.office.com/en-us/article/Manage-external-sharing-for-your-SharePoint-Online-environment-c8a462eb-0723-4b0b-8d0a-70feafe4be85.*

After sharing is appropriately configured at the SharePoint Online tenancy level and at the site-collection level, there are three basic methods that allow you to share content with external users:

- Share an entire site and invite users to sign in using a Microsoft account (including Microsoft 365 accounts from separate organizations, such as workplaces or schools).
- Share individual documents by inviting external users to sign in using a Microsoft account.
- Send users a guest link that allows users external to the organization access to each individual document that you want to share anonymously.

Share a site

To share a site with an external user, perform the following steps:

1. Sign in to Microsoft 365 with an account that has permission to share the site.
2. Select **SharePoint** in the list of apps.
3. Select the site that you want to share.
4. In the upper-right corner of the Site page, select **Share**, as shown in Figure 4-44.

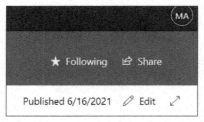

FIGURE 4-44 Share

5. In the **Share site** dialog box, provide the name of the person with whom you want to share the site, specify the permission level, and select **Share**.

   You can choose between the following levels:

   - Read
   - Edit
   - Full Control

An invitation is automatically sent to the person or people you invited. If the invitation isn't accepted within seven days, it expires. Users accepting an invitation must sign in with a Microsoft account, such as an Outlook.com or Hotmail.com account, or an Office 365 account.

You can determine which external users a SharePoint Online site collection has been shared with by performing the following steps:

1. Sign in to Microsoft 365 with an account that has permission to share the site.

2. Select **SharePoint** in the list of apps.

3. In the list of sites, select the site whose external users you want to see.

   The **Share site** dialog box lists all users with whom the site collection has been shared. (See Figure 4-45.)

FIGURE 4-45 Site permissions

Share a document

There are two ways to share a document:

- With an external user who must authenticate using a Microsoft account
- Through an anonymous guest link

To share with an external user who must authenticate using a Microsoft account, which includes the option of using a Microsoft 365 account, perform the following steps:

1. Sign in to Microsoft 365 with an account that has permission to share the site.

2. Select **SharePoint** in the list of apps.

3. In the list of sites, select the site that hosts the document that you want to share.

4. Select the **Documents** node, select the document you want to share, and select **Share**. (See Figure 4-46.)

FIGURE 4-46 Sharing a document

5. In the **Send Link** dialog box, specify what level of sharing and permission you would like to provide: **Can Edit** and/or **Can View**.

    Figure 4-47 shows the ExemplarDocument document set to be shared to Kim Akers's account and giving Kim Akers permission to edit the document.

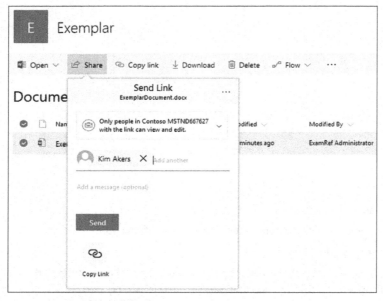

FIGURE 4-47 Send Link dialog box

6. Select **Send** to share the document.

    You can view which users and groups have access to a document by selecting the document in the **Documents** node, selecting the ellipsis (**...**) on the right side of the buttons along the top of the node, and choosing **Manage Access**. The **Manage Access** dialog box opens, displaying the permissions assigned. Figure 4-48 shows the permissions assigned to the UI UX Guidelines. docx document.

FIGURE 4-48 Permissions assigned to a document

The process of creating a shared link is similar. Sign in to Microsoft 365, locate the document you want to share, and then open the Send Link dialog box. Then select Copy Link, as shown in Figure 4-49.

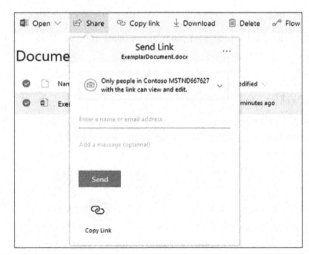

FIGURE 4-49 Copy Link

Remove external user access

You can revoke external user access to a site only after a user has accepted their invitation. You revoke access by removing the external user's permission to the site. To revoke access, perform the following steps:

1. Sign in to Microsoft 365 with an account that has permission to share the site.
2. Select **SharePoint** in the list of apps.
3. In the list of sites, select the site whose permissions you want to modify.
4. Select **Share**. Then, in the **Share** dialog box, select the ellipsis (**...**), and choose **Manage Access**.
5. Select the external user from whom you want to revoke access.

You can also use the `Remove-SPOExternalUser` PowerShell cmdlet to revoke access to a SharePoint Online from an external user.

There is no way, at the SharePoint Online tenancy level, to determine all the sites to which an external user has been granted access. You must view the settings for individual sites to determine if a specific external user has been granted access to the site. There is also no method, at the SharePoint Online tenancy level, to determine which documents have been shared externally.

EXAM TIP

Remember that the sharing settings configured at the SharePoint Online level override the settings that can be configured at the site-collection level.

Identify hybrid requirements

Beyond the basics of having a functional on-premises Active Directory instance and a con-figured Microsoft 365 tenancy, you will need to have a functional on-premises SharePoint Server farm. This SharePoint Server farm must be configured so that all services are running locally on the farm as farms that leverage Federated services and are not supported in a hybrid configuration.

You will need to configure the SharePoint primary web application on the on-premises SharePoint farm to use a certificate from a trusted public third-party CA for Transport Layer Security (TLS), also known as Secure Sockets Layer (SSL) communication. Microsoft recom-mends using the default SharePoint security token service (STS) certificate when configuring hybrid workloads. It is not necessary to have a new certificate for this service issued by a public third-party CA.

You will need to configure a reverse proxy device to support inbound connectivity for your hybrid SharePoint deployment if you want to support the following services:

- Inbound hybrid search
- Hybrid Business Connectivity Services
- Hybrid Duet Enterprise Online for Microsoft SharePoint and SAP

The certificate used for authentication and encryption between the reverse proxy device and SharePoint Online must be configured as a wildcard certificate or have an appropriate Subject Alternative Name. It must also be issued by a trusted public third-party certification authority.

> **MORE INFO   HYBRID FOR SHAREPOINT**
>
> You can learn more about Hybrid for SharePoint Server requirements at *https://docs.microsoft.com/en-us/sharepoint/hybrid/install-and-configure-sharepoint-server-hybrid*.

In a SharePoint Server hybrid configuration, you must make sure the following networking requirements are met:

- A publicly resolvable DNS record for the SharePoint primary site points at the external endpoint for the reverse proxy device, which publishes the primary site to the internet.
- The SharePoint primary site has a binding for a TLS certificate from a publicly trusted certificate authority.
- You have chosen an appropriate site collection strategy. Options include host-named site collection, path-based web application with alternate access mappings, and path-based web application without alternate access mapping.
- You have configured split DNS so that internal clients connect to the internal IP address of the SharePoint primary site and external clients connect to the external endpoint of the reverse proxy device.

> **MORE INFO   SHAREPOINT SERVER HYBRID CONNECTIVITY**
>
> You can learn more about SharePoint Server hybrid connectivity at *https://docs.microsoft.com/en-us/sharepoint/hybrid/configure-inbound-connectivity*.

Manage access configurations

SharePoint's access request feature enables users to request access to items to which they currently do not have permission. To configure whether users can request access to SharePoint content, perform the following steps:

1. Open the site in SharePoint and select the **Gear** icon to access the **Settings** options. (See Figure 4-50.)

FIGURE 4-50 Site settings

2. Select the **Site Permissions** link.

3. Under **Site Sharing**, select **Change How Members Can Share**.

4. In the **Site sharing settings** dialog box (see Figure 4-51), ensure the **Allow access requests** setting is set to **On** and specify which users will receive and respond to access requests either by specifying the owners of the site or a specific email address.

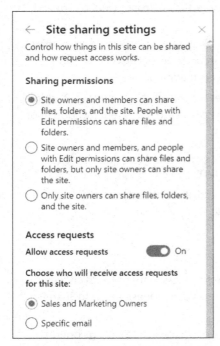

FIGURE 4-51 Site Sharing Settings dialog box

To approve or decline an access request for a SharePoint site, perform the following steps:

1. Open the site in SharePoint and select the **Gear** icon to access the **Settings** options.

2. Select **Site Contents**. Then select **Access Requests**. (This option will be available only if there are pending access requests.)

3. Under **Pending Requests**, locate the request to which you want to respond, and select the ellipsis (**...**).

4. Under **Permissions**, select the permission level you want to assign. Then select **Approve** or **Decline**.

MORE INFO **MANAGE ACCESS REQUESTS**

You can learn more about managing access configurations at *https://support.microsoft.com/ en-us/office/set-up-and-manage-access-requests-94b26e0b-2822-49d4-929a-8455698654b3.*

Manage Microsoft groups

Groups allow you to group users and then assign them privileges and access to workloads or services. Rather than directly assigning privileges and access to workloads or services to users, you can assign these rights to a group and then indirectly assign them to users by adding the user accounts to the appropriate group.

Using groups allows you to assign access and rights by adding and removing users from a group. Although it's possible to assign access and rights on a per-user basis, doing so is administratively cumbersome and makes it challenging to determine which users have a specific right. Determining rights can be much easier to do if rights are only delegated to groups. That way, if you need to determine rights, you just have to check the group membership.

You can use the Azure AD admin center in the Azure portal to manage groups. You access the Azure Active Directory Admin Center at https://aad.portal.azure.com or through the Azure portal Azure AD blade.

Azure AD supports two group types:

- Security groups
- Microsoft 365 (previously Office 365) groups

Figure 4-52 shows how to select the group type when creating the group. Microsoft 365 groups are used for collaboration between users where organizations use services such as Microsoft 365 or Office 365. Users in groups can be internal or external to the organization.

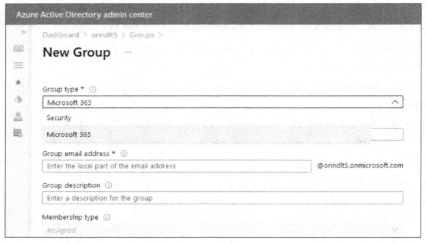

FIGURE 4-52 Creating an Azure AD group

Microsoft 365 group types can be configured as assigned or dynamic:

- **Assigned** When a group's membership is assigned, members are added and removed manually by administrators or other users who have the appropriate rights.
- **Dynamic** When the Dynamic option is selected, group membership is determined based on the results of a query against user or device attributes. For example, with Microsoft 365 groups, you can have group membership determined by user attributes such as location or manager.

You can use the following PowerShell commands from the Azure AD PowerShell module to manage Azure AD Groups:

- `Get-AzureADGroup` Provides information about Azure AD groups
- `New-AzureADGroup` Creates a new Azure AD group
- `Set-AzureADGroup` Configures the properties of an Azure AD group
- `Remove-AzureADGroup` Removes an Azure AD group
- `Add-AzureADGroupMember` Adds a user to an Azure AD group
- `Remove-AzureADGroupMember` Removes a user from an Azure AD group
- `Add-AzureADGroupOwner` Adds a user as an owner of an Azure AD group and gives the user limited group-management privileges
- `Remove-AzureADGroupOwner` Removes a user as owner of an Azure AD group

> **MORE INFO**   **AZURE AD GROUPS**
>
> You can learn more about Azure AD groups at *https://docs.microsoft.com/en-us/azure/active-directory/fundamentals/active-directory-groups-view-azure-portal.*

Azure AD allows you to add a security group as a member of another security group, which is known as a *nested group*. When you add a nested group, the member group will inherit the attributes and properties of the parent group.

Nesting groups allows you to further simplify the management of large numbers of users. For example, you might have groups for managers in Melbourne, Sydney, and Adelaide. You could add these three groups to an Australian Managers group and then assign top-level group rights and permissions to Australian Managers rather than assigning those rights to each city-level Managers group. This also provides you with flexibility should you add additional city-level managers groups, such as Brisbane and Perth, at some point in the future; you'd just add these groups to the Australian Managers group to assign the same permissions.

As of this writing, Azure AD does not support the following nesting scenarios:

- Adding an Azure AD group to a group synchronized from on-premises Active Directory
- Adding Azure AD security groups to Microsoft 365 groups
- Adding Microsoft 365 groups to groups other than other Microsoft 365 groups
- Assigning apps to nested groups
- Assigning licenses to nested groups
- Nesting distribution groups

To nest groups using the Azure portal, perform the following steps:

1. On the **Groups – All groups** page of the Azure Active Directory blade of the Azure portal (see Figure 4-53), select the group you want to nest. In this example, let's add the Melbourne group to the Australia group.

FIGURE 4-53 List of Azure AD groups

2. Select the **Group Memberships** item in the **Manage** section of the group's properties, as shown in Figure 4-54.
3. On the **Group Memberships** page, select **Add Memberships**.
4. On the **Select groups** page, select the group you want to nest this group within. In this case, we will select the **Australia** group, as shown in Figure 4-55. Then select **Select** to nest the group. A group can be nested within multiple groups.

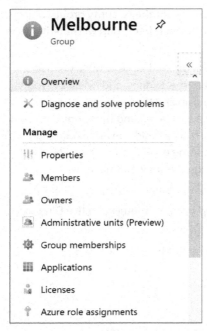

FIGURE 4-54 Options for the Melbourne group

FIGURE 4-55 Selecting a group in which to nest

To remove a group from another group, open the parent group's Group Membership page. Then remove the nested group by selecting it and selecting Remove Memberships.

> **MORE INFO** **NESTING GROUPS**
>
> You can learn more about nesting groups at *https://docs.microsoft.com/en-us/azure/ active-directory/fundamentals/active-directory-groups-membership-azure-portal*.

Manage SharePoint tenant and site settings

You can view SharePoint settings by selecting Settings in the SharePoint Admin Center, as shown in Figure 4-56. Table 4-5 lists the available options.

FIGURE 4-56 The SharePoint Settings page

TABLE 4-5 SharePoint tenancy settings

Setting	Description	Possible Values
Default Admin Center (SharePoint)	Use new or classic SharePoint admin center	■ New SharePoint admin center ■ Classic SharePoint admin center
Notifications (SharePoint)	Allow notifications about SharePoint site activity	■ Allow notifications (enable/disable)
Pages (SharePoint)	Allow users to create and comment on pages	■ Allow users to create new modern pages (enable/disable) ■ Allow commenting on modern pages (enable/disable)
Site Creation (SharePoint)	Default settings for new sites	■ Let users create sites from the SharePoint start page and OneDrive (enable/disable)

Setting	Description	Possible Values
Site Storage Limits (SharePoint)	Use automatic or manual SharePoint site storage limits	■ Automatic storage limits ■ Manual (specify limit per site)
Notifications (OneDrive)	Allow notifications about OneDrive file activity	■ Allow notifications (enable/disable)
Retention (OneDrive)	Configure OneDrive retention for deleted users	■ Value between 30–3,650 days
Storage Limit (OneDrive)	Configure OneDrive user storage limit	■ Value between 1 GB and 5 TB
Sync (OneDrive)	Manage sync settings for OneDrive and SharePoint	■ Show the Sync button on the OneDrive website (enable/disable) ■ Allow syncing only on computers joined to specific domains (enable/disable) ■ Block upload of specific file types (enable/disable)

MORE INFO **SHAREPOINT PROPERTIES**

You can learn more about SharePoint Online properties at *https://docs.microsoft.com/en-us/ sharepoint/manage-sites-in-new-admin-center*.

Manage OneDrive for Business

OneDrive for Business allows you to store, sync, and share work files. OneDrive for Business is separate from OneDrive, which was formerly known as SkyDrive. OneDrive for Business differs from OneDrive in the following ways:

- OneDrive is associated with a personal Microsoft account. People in your organization cannot access or manage OneDrive.

- OneDrive for Business is managed by an organization and is made available through a Microsoft 365 subscription. This means that Microsoft 365 administrators can access files stored in OneDrive for Business. OneDrive for Business allows Microsoft 365 users to share files with one another for the purposes of collaboration. OneDrive for Business can also be used with an on-premises SharePoint deployment.

Access OneDrive for Business

A user can access OneDrive for Business by performing the following steps:

1. Sign in to Microsoft 365 with your user account.

2. On the list of apps, select **OneDrive**.

    The OneDrive for Business site, which is a SharePoint Online personal site, opens. (See Figure 4-57.) Documents can be uploaded to this site or created and added to this location. It is also possible to create a folder hierarchy in this location.

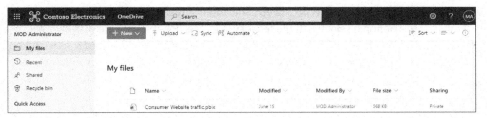

FIGURE 4-57 OneDrive for Business

Collaborate with OneDrive for Business

Collaborating with someone using OneDrive for Business is very similar to collaborating using SharePoint Online. This makes sense, considering that OneDrive for Business stores data in SharePoint Online. The main difference is that an administrator usually manages the sharing done through SharePoint Online directly, whereas the sharing done through OneDrive for Business is usually managed directly by an end user.

An end user can choose to share individual files or create and share folders. As is the case with SharePoint Online, it's possible to share with people using a Microsoft account or by sending an external link. Sharing settings are dependent on the sharing settings configured in the SharePoint Online tenancy.

- **Don't Allow Sharing Outside Your Organization**   If this option is selected at the tenancy level, users will only be able to share with other users in the tenancy. If users attempt to share with external users, they will see the message shown in Figure 4-58, explaining that sharing with external users is not possible.

FIGURE 4-58 No sharing with external users

- **Allow External Users Who Accept Sharing Invitations and Sign In As Authenticated Users**   If this option is selected at the tenancy level, sharing with external users is possible as long as those users have a Microsoft account or a Microsoft 365 account.

- **Allow Both External Users Who Accept Sharing Invitations And Anonymous Guest Links** If this option is selected at the tenancy level, it is possible to share with external users with Microsoft 365 or Microsoft accounts. It is also possible to forward links to shared documents or folders to users so they can access content without having to authenticate.

To share an individual document, perform the following steps:

1. Sign in to Microsoft 365 with your user account.

2. On the list of apps, select **OneDrive**.

3. In the OneDrive for Business site, select the document you want to share.

4. Select the **Share** button.

   If the **Allow Both External Users Who Accept Sharing Invitations and Anonymous Guest Links** option is selected at the tenancy level, users will be able to share to external users and generate links.

5. To share with an external user, enter the user's email address and determine if the user should have read-only or edit access. Then select **Send**. Figure 4-59 shows the user orin.thomas@outlook.com is granted the edit permission.

FIGURE 4-59 Sharing a document

You can view users with whom a document has been shared on the document's Share page. Note that if you've invited someone to a document and they haven't accepted the invitation, their account will not be listed on this page. Invitations remain valid for seven days.

To view users whom a document is shared with, perform the following steps:

1. Sign in to Microsoft 365 with your user account.

2. On the list of apps, select **OneDrive**.

3. In the OneDrive for Business site, select the document whose sharing properties you want to see.

4. On the toolbar, select **Share**, select the ellipsis (**...**) in the **Send Link** dialog box, and select **Manage Access**.

 The **Manage Access** page shows you whom the document has been shared with. You can choose to remove someone's permission to access a document from this page.

You can share folders from OneDrive for Business. All the content in a folder inherits the sharing settings of the parent folder. This makes sharing documents a matter of placing them in the appropriately configured folder.

To share a folder, perform the following steps:

1. Sign in to Microsoft 365 with your user account.

2. On the list of apps, select **OneDrive**.

3. In the OneDrive for Business site, select the folder you want to share. Figure 4-60 shows the Hovercraft folder selected.

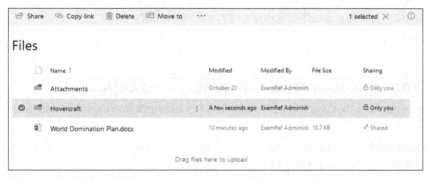

FIGURE 4-60 Sharing a folder

4. On the toolbar, select **Share**.

5. On the **Invite People** page, enter the email addresses of the people whom you want to invite to the folder and specify their permissions—**Read Only** or **Edit**.

6. Select **Send**.

You can't create links for anonymous users to folders. Anonymous links can only be created for documents.

EXAM TIP

Remember how to configure access reviews for SharePoint Online content.

Skill 4.4: Plan for Microsoft Teams Infrastructure

This skill section deals with how to plan for your organization's Microsoft Teams infrastructure. In this section, you'll learn how to plan for call quality and capacity, replace your on-premises PBX with Microsoft Teams Phone System, plan the deployment of Teams, plan Teams organizational settings, plan for external guest access, and configure Teams hybrid connectivity and coexistence.

> **This section covers the following topics:**
> - Plan for communication and call quality and capacity
> - Plan for Phone System
> - Plan Microsoft Teams deployment
> - Plan Microsoft Teams organizational settings
> - Plan for guest and external access
> - Plan for Microsoft Teams hybrid connectivity and coexistence
> - Teams cmdlets

Plan for communication and call quality and capacity

Teams includes specific tools that you can use to monitor, troubleshoot, manage, and improve call quality:

- **Call Quality Dashboard (CQD)**   Analyze trends or problems across the Teams deployment. This dashboard gives you a network-wide view of call quality.
- **Call analytics**   Analyze call and meeting quality for individual users. Provides detailed information about devices, networks, and connectivity related to specific calls and meetings for each user in Teams.
- **Quality of Service (QoS)**   Prioritize important network traffic.

You use the CQD and call analytics separately or together to diagnose call-quality problems. For example, if a user complains about the quality of their Teams calls, you can check if it's just that user or if broader problems exist with Teams across the organization.

You can use QoS to prioritize delay-sensitive network traffic such as voice and video over traffic where delays are less problematic, such as file copy operations or software update deployments. QoS can identify and tag all network traffic packets through the application of Windows Group Policy objects. These tags are then used with port-based access control lists on network equipment to ensure that Teams traffic is reserved a specific amount of bandwidth rather than it having to compete with other network traffic types during everyday local area network operation.

Plan for Phone System

Microsoft 365 Teams Phone System provides private branch exchange (PBX) functionality through software. Phone System users can select a name in their address book and place Teams calls to that person. Phone System can be used with mobile devices, PC audio, or an IP phone designed to work with Teams. Calls between users in your organization occur across Teams' infrastructure. You can connect Phone System to the public switched telephone network (PSTN) so that it is possible for calls to people external to your organization to connect to traditional mobile phone and fixed-line devices.

You can connect Phone System to the PSTN using two different methods:

- **Microsoft Calling Plan**   The connection to the PSTN network occurs using Microsoft's cloud infrastructure.
- **Existing telephony**   You can connect your organization's existing telephony infrastructure to Teams' Phone System using direct routing.

Phone System provides the following services:

- **Auto attendants**   You can use these to create a menu system that enables callers to locate the people they want to connect to as well as transfer calls to other organizational users or departments.
- **Call queues**   You can automatically put calls on hold and then route the call to the next available call agent to handle the call. Call queues also provide background music, but the exam probably won't ask you to hum "The girl from Ipanema."
- **Voicemail**   Voicemail is automatically provisioned for users after they are assigned a Phone System license and a phone number.

Plan Microsoft Teams deployment

Teams is enabled by default for all Microsoft 365 organizations. If a user has the appropriate Microsoft 365 license, Teams will be enabled automatically. You can disable Teams on a per-user basis on the user's Product Licenses page, as shown in Figure 4-61.

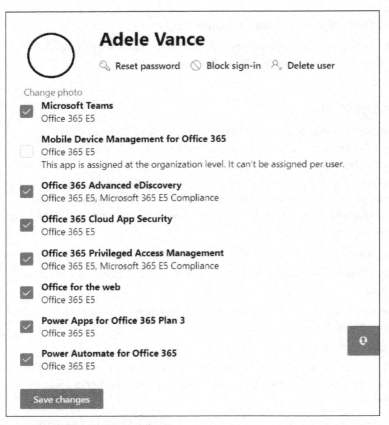

FIGURE 4-61 Microsoft Teams license

MORE INFO **MANAGING TEAMS LICENSING**

You can learn more about managing Teams licensing at *https://docs.microsoft.com/en-us/microsoftteams/user-access*.

Enterprise deployment

When planning your Teams deployment, be aware that the following workloads can be deployed independently of one another and that it isn't necessary to deploy all of Teams all at once:

- Chat, Teams, Apps, and Channels
- Meetings and Conferencing
- Phone System and PSTN

One of the most important elements in planning a Teams deployment is ensuring that your organization's network infrastructure can support how your organization intends to use the product. The Network Planner, available from the Teams Admin Center (see Figure 4-62), can help with this.

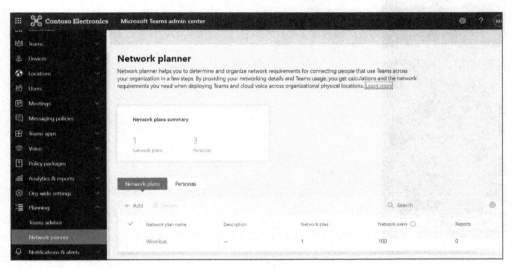

FIGURE 4-62 Network Planner

Teams Advisor

Teams Advisor allows you to assess your Microsoft 365 deployment and will recommend what steps you should take before rolling out Teams for your organization. Teams Advisor will create a Deployment team that includes channels related to each workload you plan to deploy, including these:

- Chat, teams, channels, and apps
- Meetings and conferencing
- Skype for Business upgrade

Each workload in the Deployment team includes a tenant assessment, a planner detailing the rollout tasks related to each workload, a forms user survey, and a Teams Advisor bot. You can launch Teams Advisor from the Planning node in the Teams Admin Center. (See Figure 4-63.)

FIGURE 4-63 Teams Advisor

MORE INFO   **ENTERPRISE SETUP**

You can learn more about setting up Teams for an enterprise at *https://docs.microsoft.com/en-us/microsoftteams/deploy-enterprise-overview.*

Skype for Business migration strategy

You can move users from an on-premises deployment to the cloud by using either the Skype for Business admin control panel or the `Move-CsUser` PowerShell cmdlet. Both tools are used in the on-premises environment. It's also possible to use these tools to move users from Skype for Business Online to an on-premises host when Skype for Business Online is in a hybrid configuration. You can move a user from Skype for Business Online directly to Teams only if Skype for Business Server 2019 or Skype for Business Server 2015 with cumulative update 8 or later is deployed in the on-premises environment.

When migrating users from an on-premises environment to the cloud, the user performing the migration must have the CSServerAdministrator role in the on-premises Skype for Business Server deployment and must have either the Microsoft 365 global administrator role or both the Microsoft 365 Skype for Business administrator and the Microsoft 365 user administrator roles.

Plan Microsoft Teams organizational settings

Teams functionality, including functionality for channels, is enabled on a tenant-wide basis, rather than on a per-team or per-channel basis. This is done by configuring the following policies:

- **Teams policies**   Specify whether private channels can be created.
- **Update policies**   Specify whether preview features are enabled at the tenancy level.
- **Meeting policies**   Control which features are available to meeting participants for meetings scheduled by users in your organization.
- **Meeting settings**   Configure whether anonymous users can join Teams meetings, customize meeting invitations, configure QoS settings, and configure network port ranges for real-time traffic.
- **Live event policies**   Specify whether live events can be scheduled, who can join live events, who can record a live event, and whether live events are transcribed.
- **Live event settings**   Configure a support URL and a third-party video distribution provider for live events.
- **Messaging policies**   Configure policies related to Teams messaging.
- **Teams app permissions policies**   Specify whether apps can be installed by users. Separate permission policies exist for Microsoft apps, third-party apps, and custom apps.
- **Voice calling policies**   Configure policies for voice calls made through Teams.
- **Voice emergency policies**   Configure how Teams can be used for emergency calls.
- **Voice routing policies**   Configure a voice route using PSTN usage records.

Meeting policies

Meeting policies allow you to manage Teams features available to meeting participants. You can configure policies at the per-organizer, per-user, or a combination of per-organizer and per-user levels. You can configure the following policies:

- **Allow meet now in channels**   Allows a user to start an unplanned meeting.
- **Allow the Outlook add-in**   Allows the New Teams Meeting add-in for Outlook.
- **Allow channel meeting scheduling**   Allows creation of meetings on team channel calendars.
- **Allow scheduling private meetings**   Allows users to schedule private meetings.
- **Allow meet now in private meetings**   Allows users to start ad hoc private meetings.
- **Allow transcription**   Enables or disables live transcription.

- **Allow cloud recording**   Enables or disables meeting recording through Teams.
- **Mode for IP audio**   Enables or disables audio in meetings and group calls.
- **Mode for IP video**   Enables or disables video in meetings and group calls.
- **Allow IP video**   Allows you to permit video for some users and block it for others.
- **Media bit rate**   Allows you to manage bandwidth for audio, video, and video-based app sharing.
- **Screen sharing mode**   Allows you to permit or disallow desktop or window sharing.
- **Allow participant to give or request control**   Allows you to give control of a shared desktop or window to other meeting participants.
- **Allow an external participant to give or request control**   Allows you to give control of a shared desktop or window to external participants.
- **Allow PowerPoint sharing**   Enables or disables PowerPoint sharing.
- **Allow whiteboard**   Enables or disables whiteboard sharing.
- **Allow shared notes**   Enables or disables shared notes that can be edited by meeting participants.
- **Let anonymous people start a meeting.**   Allows an anonymous user to start a scheduled meeting without having to wait in the lobby for an organizational user to start the meeting.
- **Automatically admit people**   Allows you to admit people directly into the meeting without making them wait in the meeting lobby.
- **Allow dial-in users to bypass the lobby**   Allows dial-in users to enter the meeting without waiting in the lobby.
- **Allow team members to bypass the lobby**   Allows team members to enter the meeting without requiring them to be admitted by the meeting organizer.
- **Enable live captions**   Allows the meeting audio to be live transcribed and displayed during the meeting.
- **Designated presenter role mode**   Allows limitations as to which users can present, with potential presenters specified by the meeting organizer.
- **Allow chat in meetings**   Enables or disables the chat window during meetings.
- **Video filters mode**   Specifies whether users can set custom backgrounds or if participants can make ongoing assessments of their colleagues' home office decoration skills.

MORE INFO   **MEETING POLICIES**

You can learn more about meeting policies at *https://docs.microsoft.com/microsoftteams/meeting-policies-in-teams*.

Messaging policies

Messaging policies dictate the types of content and control that you allow in Teams. For example, you may want to allow the use of GIFs, stickers, and memes from the internet. If you do enable these settings, you might want to pin a post describing what constitutes acceptable content for your organization, because allowing the posting of some internet memes is likely to trigger a visit from the denizens of the human resources department. You can configure the following settings, as shown in Figure 4-64:

- **Owners can delete sent messages** Allows channel owners to delete all messages in the channel. Disabled by default.
- **Delete sent messages** Allows users to delete their own messages. Enabled by default.
- **Edit sent messages** Allows users to modify their messages to channels in Teams. Enabled by default.
- **Read receipts** Determines whether a message that has been viewed displays information on that status.
- **Chat** Allows users to engage in private chats. Enabled by default.
- **Use Giphy in conversations** Allows users to add animated images to conversations.
- **Giphy content rating** Allows you to set a content rating to determine how risqué animated images can be. The content rating can be set to No Restriction, Moderate, and Strict. It is enabled by default, with the Moderate content rating.
- **Use memes in conversations** Allows users to create and add memes to conversations. Enabled by default.
- **Use stickers in conversations** Allows users to add stickers to conversations. Enabled by default.
- **Allow URL previews** Allows users to preview URLs instead of just showing the URL text.
- **Translate messages** Allows messages to be translated between supported languages.
- **Allow immersive reader for viewing messages** Allows the use of complex formatting within messages.
- **Send urgent messages using Priority notification** Allows users to designate messages as priority messages. Priority messages are tagged with a special notification icon.
- **Create voice messages** Allows for the creation of audio messages.
- **On mobile devices, display favorite channels above recent chats** Configures the display of channels on the Teams mobile device client.
- **Remove users from group chats** Allows any member of a chat to remove other members of the chat.

- **Suggested replies** Allows the display of suggested replies, such as *Great, Thanks, Empowering!, Let's circle back and double click on this later,* and *This meeting could have been an email.*
- **Chat permission role** Allows the use of supervised chat.
- **Enable Giphy so users can add gifs to conversations** Allows gifs from the Giphy services to be added to conversations.
- **Enable memes that users can edit and add to conversations** Allows meme templates to be used to generate memes for conversations but doesn't ensure your cat can has cheezeburger.
- **Allow users to chat privately** Allows users to initiate private chats. Enabled by default.

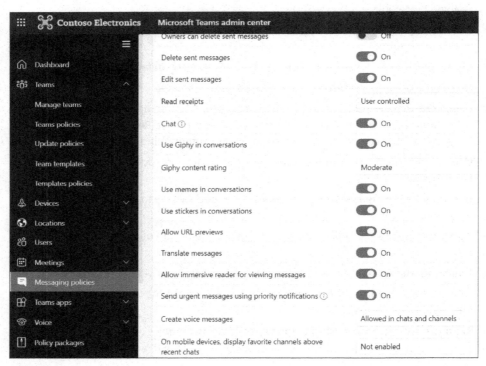

FIGURE 4-64 Messaging settings

> **MORE INFO** **MESSAGING POLICIES**
>
> You can learn more about messaging policies at *https://docs.microsoft.com/microsoftteams/ messaging-policies-in-teams.*

Voice-calling policies

Voice-calling policies allow you to manage which calling and call-forwarding features can be used by users in your organization. You can configure the following policies:

- **Make private calls** Determines whether calls can be made to PSTN numbers outside your organization using Teams.

- **Call forwarding and simultaneous ringing to people in your organization** Determines whether incoming calls will ring multiple people at once or whether they are forwarded.

- **Call forwarding and simultaneous ringing to external phone numbers** Determines whether incoming calls can be forwarded to external numbers or will simultaneously ring the Teams client and the external number.

- **Voicemail is available for routing inbound calls** Determines whether voicemail is available.

- **Inbound calls can be routed to call groups** Allows calls to be forwarded to multiple Teams recipients.

- **Allow delegation for inbound and outbound calls** Allows inbound calls to be routed to delegates or for delegates to make outbound calls on behalf of users when they have been delegated permission.

- **Prevent toll bypass and send calls through the PSTN** Routes calls through the PSTN rather than across the network.

- **Busy on busy is available while in a call** Specifies how calls are handled if a user is already in a call, in a conference, or has a call placed on hold.

- **Allow web PSTN calling** Allows calls to PSTN numbers when using the Teams web client.

- **Allow music on hold** Allows you to enable or disable hold music, but doesn't allow you to improve the quality of hold music.

> ***MORE INFO* VOICE-CALLING POLICIES**
>
> You can learn more about voice-calling policies at *https://docs.microsoft.com/microsoftteams/teams-calling-policy.*

Plan for guest and external access

Guest access allows you to provide people outside your organization with access to Teams, documents in channels, resources, chats, and applications. Guests can be added from partner organizations that have their own Azure Active Directory account in a tenancy separate from the one associated with your organization's Microsoft 365 deployment. It is also possible to add guests to Teams where users have Hotmail.com, Outlook.com, or gmail.com accounts.

A guest can be added to a Microsoft 365 Team through the following general method:

1. A team owner or someone with Microsoft 365 administrative privileges adds a guest to a team, specifying the guest's Microsoft 365 email account address or third-party email address.

2. The guest receives a welcome email. Guests who have a work or school account associated with an Azure Active Directory instance can accept the invitation and authenticate directly. Users with third-party email addresses will be sent a one-time passcode to validate their identity.

> **MORE INFO** **GUEST ACCESS IN MICROSOFT TEAMS**
>
> You can learn more about guest access in Microsoft Teams at *https://docs.microsoft.com/en-us/microsoftteams/guest-access*.

Plan for Microsoft Teams hybrid connectivity and coexistence

Connectors allow organizations to siphon content from services outside Microsoft Teams directly into Teams channels. For example, connectors allow Teams users to receive information directly into the chat stream from services, including Twitter, Trello, GitHub, and Visual Studio Team Services.

Any member of a specific team can connect that team to a cloud service using a connector. This allows all members of that team to be notified of activities from that service. Removing a user from the team removes any connectors added to the team by that user.

Users can add a connector to a team using the Microsoft Teams Desktop or web client. To add a connector, perform the following steps:

1. Enter the Teams channel to which you want to add the connector.

2. Next to the channel name, select the ellipses (**...**) icon. Then select **Connectors**.

3. From the list of connectors (see Figure 4-65), select the connector you want to add. Then select **Configure**.

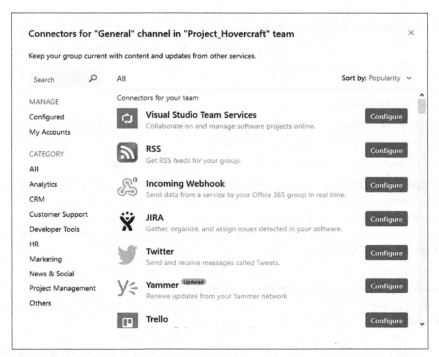

FIGURE 4-65   Available connectors

Depending on the connector, you'll need to provide information that allows data to be streamed from the connecting service into Teams. Figure 4-66 shows the details of the Twitter connector, which requires a sign-in to an existing Twitter account.

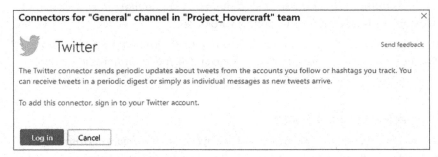

FIGURE 4-66   Twitter connector

4. After the connector is configured, data will automatically be streamed into the channel for which the connector is configured.

Organizations can develop custom connectors to integrate with line-of-business applications using the included Incoming Webhook connector. This connector creates an endpoint for a channel and can extract data from applications using HTTP post methods.

Hybrid Skype for Business

When configuring Skype for Business in a hybrid configuration with Skype for Business Online, you will need to ensure that the following steps are taken:

- Skype for Business Online must be enabled in the Microsoft 365 tenancy.
- On-premises servers must all run Skype for Business Server 2019, Skype for Business Server 2015, or Lync Server 2013. A deployment that has a mixture of servers is also supported as long as that mixture is limited to two different versions of Skype for Business Server or Lync Server. You cannot configure a hybrid deployment if all three servers are present in the on-premises environment.
- You must federate the on-premises environment with Microsoft 365. Although federation is more complicated than the default Azure AD Connect identity synchronization option, you can use Azure AD Connect to configure federation. Doing so will require the deployment of Active Directory Federation Services servers in your on-premises environment, although Azure AD Connect makes this process easier.
- You must configure the on-premises environment to share SIP address space with Skype for Business Online. This will allow Skype for Business Online to host user accounts for the same set of SIP domains as the on-premises environment. It will also allow messages to be routed within the hybrid environment.
- You must enable the share SIP address space for Skype for Business Online. Configuring this shared address space is the second element in ensuring that messages can be routed between the on-premises and cloud environments.

Microsoft also recommends that you configure OAuth between Exchange on-premises and Skype for Business Online if you have both Exchange and Skype for Business in a hybrid configuration.

Skype for Business hybrid connectivity

In a hybrid configuration, all Skype for Business external DNS records must point to on-premises servers. There are specific DNS resolution requirements for the following records:

- A DNS SRV record for _sipfederationtls._tcp.<sipdomain.com> must resolve to the Access Edge external IP addresses. This record must be resolvable by Edge servers in the hybrid configuration.

- A DNS A record or records for Edge Web Conferencing Service must resolve to the Web Conferencing Edge external IP addresses. This record or records must be able to be resolved by any user's computers on the organization's internal network.

Your organization's firewall needs to be configured to accept incoming traffic from the following Office 365 domain names:

- *.lync.com
- *.teams.microsoft.com
- *.broadcast.skype.com
- *.skypeforbusinesss.com
- *.sfbassets.com
- *.skype.com

MORE INFO **SKYPE FOR BUSINESS HYBRID CONNECTIVITY**

You can learn more about Skype for Business hybrid connectivity at *https://docs.microsoft. com/en-us/skypeforbusiness/hybrid/configure-hybrid-connectivity.*

Teams cmdlets

You can use the following PowerShell cmdlets to manage Microsoft Teams:

- `Add-TeamUser`   Add a user or owner to a team.
- `Connect-MicrosoftTeams`   Connect an authenticated account so that it can use the Microsoft Teams cmdlets.
- `Disconnect-MicrosoftTeams`   Disconnect an account from a session where it can use Microsoft Teams cmdlets.
- `Get-Team`   View all of the teams that a specific account belongs to.
- `Get-TeamChannel`   View all of the channels associated with a team.
- `Get-TeamFunSettings`   View the settings for posting GIFs and memes to a team.
- `Get-TeamGuestSettings`   Views a team's guest settings.
- `Get-TeamHelp`   View all Teams-related cmdlets.
- `Get-TeamMemberSettings`   View member settings for a team.
- `Get-TeamMessagingSettings`   View messaging settings for a team.
- `Get-TeamUser`   View the users of a team.
- `New-Team`   Create a new team.
- `New-TeamChannel`   Create a new channel within a team.
- `Remove-Team`   Remove an existing team.
- `Remove-TeamChannel`   Remove a channel from a team.
- `Remove-TeamUser`   Remove a user from a team.

- `Set-Team` Configure the properties of a team.
- `Set-TeamChannel` Configure the properties of a team channel.
- `Set-TeamFunSettings` Configure the settings for posting GIFs and memes to a team.
- `Set-TeamGuestSettings` Configure team guest settings.
- `Set-TeamMemberSettings` Configure team member settings.
- `Set-TeamMessagingSettings` Configure messaging settings for a team.
- `Set-TeamPicture` Configure the picture associated with the team.

> **MORE INFO** **TEAMS POWERSHELL CMDLETS**
>
> You can learn more about Teams PowerShell cmdlets at *https://docs.microsoft.com/en-us/ powershell/module/teams/?view=teams-ps*.

EXAM TIP

Remember how to configure Teams licensing so that only a subset of the users in your organization have access. Remember the general steps required to allow only members of a specific group to create teams.

Skill 4.5: Plan Microsoft Power Platform integration

This skill section deals with Microsoft Power Platform integration with a Microsoft 365 deployment. In this section, you'll learn how to leverage the Microsoft Power Platform Center of Excellence (CoE) starter kit, plan for Power Platform workload deployments, plan resource deployments, plan for hybrid connectivity, manage environments, and manage the resources within those environments.

> **This section covers the following topics:**
> - Implement Microsoft Power Platform Center of Excellence (CoE) starter kit
> - Plan for Power Platform workload deployments
> - Plan resource deployment
> - Plan for connectivity (and data flow)
> - Manage environments
> - Manage resources

Implement Microsoft Power Platform Center of Excellence (CoE) starter kit

A Center of Excellence (CoE) is a set of guidelines that provides an organization with a way of coordinating a Power Platform deployment to ensure that governance and control is maintained as new features and functionality are rolled out on a constant basis. Microsoft provides a starter kit that can be used to identify an appropriate set of standards and governance that align with an organization's business goals rather than individual departmental metrics.

The foundation of the CoE starter kit is a Common Data Service data model and Power Automate flows that collect information about resources across the Power Platform environment. The CoE starter kit also includes a selection of Power apps and Power BI analytics that allow you to view and interact with the data collected by these tools. The final element of the CoE starter kit is a set of suggested patterns, practices, and templates that can form the basis of implementing Power Platform best practices.

> **MORE INFO**   **POWER PLATFORM CENTER OF EXCELLENCE**
>
> You can learn more about the Microsoft Power Platform Center of Excellence starter kit at *https://docs.microsoft.com/en-us/power-platform/guidance/coe/starter-kit*.

Plan for Power Platform workload deployments

When planning for a Power Platform workload deployment, you should account for the following elements:

- Power Platform environments are tied to a specific geographic region. If the data that your environment will host has governance requirements tied to where it is located, you must ensure that the environment is deployed in the appropriate location.

- Environments can be configured for specific audiences. Determine whether the environment is going to be used for development or production workloads. Also determine which users in your organization require access to the resources hosted in the environment and which users do not require this access.

- Consider data loss prevention policies to ensure that data hosted within the environment, such as confidential personal information, isn't inadvertently exposed.

- Determine whether the environment requires a Common Data Service instance. An environment can have one or zero instances.

- Resources in one environment cannot access resources in another environment. Ensure that Power Platform resources are collocated appropriately.

- Identify an appropriate application and data lifecycle management strategy. Ensure that environments are documented in such a way that it's clear when the resources they host are no longer required and can be deleted.

- Ensure that administrative privileges are assigned appropriately. Where possible, assign administrative privileges as close to each resource as possible. A user who only needs the ability to perform administrative tasks in a specific environment shouldn't be provided with the ability to create new environments.

> ***MORE INFO*** **POWER PLATFORM WORKLOAD DEPLOYMENT**
>
> **You can learn more about Power Platform workload deployment at *https://docs.microsoft. com/en-us/power-platform/admin/admin-powerapps-enterprise-deployment*.**

Create flows

A flow allows you to create automated workflows between applications and services. You can use flows to synchronize files, collect data, and collect notifications. You create flows with Microsoft Flow.

To use Microsoft Flow, you must have a Microsoft Flow account. You can sign up for an account at *https://flow.microsoft.com*. Users with Office 365 accounts automatically have Microsoft Flow accounts and simply need to activate those accounts at the Microsoft Flow website. An account can have up to 50 flows associated with it.

You can create a flow from a template or from scratch. To create a flow from scratch, perform the following tasks:

1. Sign in to the website at *https://flow.microsoft.com*.

2. Select **My flows** on the navigation bar. (See Figure 4-67.)

FIGURE 4-67 Flow navigation bar

3. On the **My flows** bar (see Figure 4-68), select **Create from Blank**. You also have the option to create a flow from a pre-generated template or to import an existing flow.

FIGURE 4-68 My flows

In the next step, you'll choose a trigger that will start the flow. Figure 4-69 shows a number of popular triggers. Alternatively, you can search for other triggers. In this example, we'll create a flow that provides an email notification when a tweet is sent using a specified keyword. It requires access to an existing Twitter account.

FIGURE 4-69 Popular triggers

4. Select the **When a new tweet is posted** trigger.

5. When prompted, sign in to your Twitter account to create a connection.

   You will need to authorize Microsoft PowerApps and Microsoft Flow for this Twitter account to continue.

6. In the search text box (see Figure 4-70), type the text you want to be emailed about.

FIGURE 4-70 New tweet posted trigger

7. Select **New step**. Then select **Add an action** (see Figure 4-71) to specify what action you want to take when the trigger occurs.

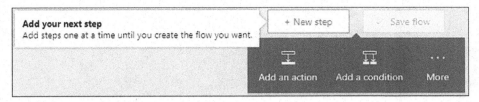

FIGURE 4-71 Add an action

8. Under **Choose an action** (see Figure 4-72), select **Office 365 Outlook – Send an email**.

FIGURE 4-72 Office 365 Outlook connectors and actions

9. Under **Send an email** (see Figure 4–73), provide the email address to which the notification should be sent, the subject that will be used, and the body of the text. Optionally, use the **Add dynamic content** option to select dynamic content, such as the name of the person who wrote the tweet and the text of the tweet.

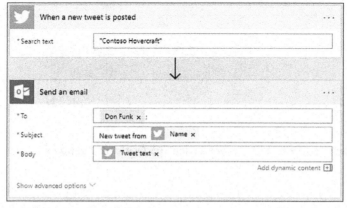

FIGURE 4-73 Send an email action

10. Select **Create flow** to create the flow.

MORE INFO **CREATE FLOWS**

You can learn more about creating flows at *https://docs.microsoft.com/en-us/flow/get-started-logic-flow*.

Create flow actions

You can add multiple actions and advanced actions for the same trigger on a flow. For example, you might have a flow that not only sends an email when someone tweets about "Contoso Hovercraft," but also creates a file in OneDrive for Business that contains information about the tweet that was sent in the email.

To add actions to an existing flow, perform the following steps:

1. When signed in to *https://flow.microsoft.com*, select **My flows** in the navigation bar.

2. In the list of flows that you've created (see Figure 4-74), select the **edit** (pencil) icon next to the flow to which you want to add an action.

FIGURE 4-74 List of flows

3. Select **New step**. Then select **Add an action**.

4. Select **OneDrive for Business**. Then select **OneDrive for Business – Create file**. (See Figure 4-75.)

5. Under **Create file** (see Figure 4-76), provide the path for the OneDrive for Business folder. Optionally, use dynamic content to add information to the flow, such as a user name and the tweet text.

FIGURE 4-75 OneDrive for Business actions

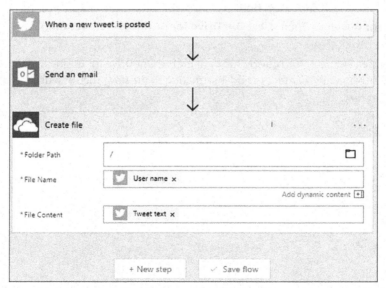

FIGURE 4-76 Create File options for OneDrive for Business

6. Select **Save flow** to save the additional action to the flow. Then select **Done**.

MORE INFO   **ADDING ACTIONS TO A FLOW**

You can learn more about adding actions to a flow at *https://docs.microsoft.com/en-us/flow/multi-step-logic-flow*.

Create PowerApps

PowerApps is a Microsoft 365 service that allows users to create business apps that will run in a browser or on a mobile device such as a phone or tablet. PowerApps is designed to allow users with minimal coding experience to generate an app that uses a data source such as SharePoint, Excel, SQL Server, Salesforce, Dynamics 365, or other common data services.

Users can generate PowerApps automatically simply by specifying the data source that the app will use. Microsoft provides a large number of templates that can be used as the basis of PowerApps. You can create PowerApps using PowerApps Studio for Windows on a computer that has the Windows 10 or Windows 11 operating system. A version of PowerApps Studio for Web that runs in standards-compliant browsers is available that can be used to author PowerApps.

Candidates for the MS-100 exam aren't expected to create a Power App during the exam, but they should be aware of when PowerApps would be a useful tool to solve a particular problem. In this case, you need an app that will run in a browser or on a mobile device that uses a specific data source such as SharePoint, Excel, SQL Server, Salesforce, Dynamics 365, or other common data sources.

MORE INFO   **POWERAPPS**

You can learn more about PowerApps at *https://docs.microsoft.com/en-us/powerapps/getting-started*.

Plan resource deployment

A Power Platform environment is a location that allows you to store, manage, and share organizational data, apps, chatbots, and flows. Power Platform environments also function as containers to partition apps that have different functions, security requirements, or target audiences.

How you provision environments depends on the types of Power Platform applications you are creating. For example:

- You can create separate test and production environments for apps and chatbots.
- You can create separate environments for specific departments that host department-specific data.
- You can create separate environments for different organizational branch offices to meet different national compliance requirements.

When planning a resource deployment, consider the following:

- Each Power Platform environment is linked to a single Azure Active Directory tenant.
- Resources within a specific Power Platform environment can only be accessed by users with accounts associated with that tenancy.
- Environments are bound to specific geographic regions. All resources created in that environment will be hosted in the Microsoft data centers located in those regions.
- Apps created in an environment can only connect to data sources located in that same environment.
- You can move resources between environments. If you move an app to a new environment, it will only be able to connect to resources in the new environment and will be unable to connect to resources in the original environment.

Microsoft recommends that you consider the following when creating a new environment:

- You cannot install Dynamics 365 apps in an environment if you did not select Enable Dynamics 365 apps when provisioning a database during environment creation.
- If you do not need Dynamics 365 apps or you don't need to use Dataverse, you should create the environment without the Dataverse database.

To create an environment with a database, perform the following steps:

1. Navigate to *https://admin.powerplatform.microsoft.com* and sign in with an account that has global administrator, Dynamics 365 administrator, or Microsoft Power Platform administrator privileges.

2. In the **Navigation** pane, select **Environments**. Then select **New**.

3. On the **New environment** page (see Figure 4-77), provide the following information:

   - **Name**   Type a unique name for the environment.
   - **Type**   Select the **Production**, **Trial**, or **Sandbox** option. Production and sandbox environments require a minimum of 1 GB of database storage capacity available. A maximum of three trial-based Power Platform environments can be deployed per Microsoft 365 subscription.
   - **Region**   This is the location where the environment will be stored. The region associated with an environment cannot be changed without contacting Microsoft support, but resources within an environment can be moved to other environments. Some countries have legislative requirements that require their citizens' data to be stored within specific geographic areas.
   - **Purpose**   Type a description of the environment. Make this meaningful enough that someone coming into your job after you've escaped to a beach in Bali can understand the purpose of the environment without contacting you.
   - **Create a database for this environment?**   Choose whether to create a database for the environment. You can add a database after you create the environment.

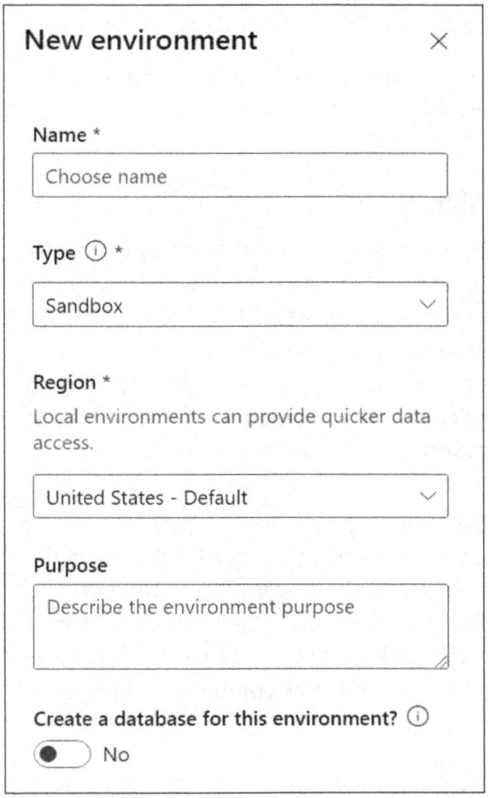

FIGURE 4-77 The New Environment page

4. If you've chosen to add a database, you'll be presented with the **Add database** page. Provide the following information. Then select **Save**.

- **Language** This determines the language collation used for the Dataverse database.

- **URL** This is a unique organizational URL for the database. You cannot have multiple Dataverse databases hosted in the same data center with the same URL.

- **Enable Dynamics 365 Apps** Specify whether Dynamics 365 apps are supported. You can't change this option after the database is deployed.

- **Deploy Sample Apps and Data** This provides you with sample data in the Dataverse database. You cannot enable Dynamics 365 apps and deploy sample apps and data.

- **Security Group** This allows you to restrict access to the environment based on Azure Active Directory security group membership. If a security group is not chosen, all Azure AD users associated with the tenancy will have access to the environment.

Plan for connectivity (and data flow)

The Power Platform on-premises gateway uses Azure Service Bus relay technology to enable hybrid connectivity. You can use the on-premises gateway to integrate on-premises resources with Power Apps and Power Automate services running in Microsoft's cloud. The Power Platform on-premises gateway requires that you deploy a gateway server on a computer running on the same local area network as the resources it will provide hybrid connectivity for. The Power Platform on-premises data gateway can be deployed on a computer running Windows 10, Windows 11, Windows Server 2012 R2, Windows Server 2016, Windows Server 2019, or Windows Server 2022.

After deploying the gateway, you'll need to provide credentials to each data source on-premises that Power Apps and Power Automate needs to access. The computer that hosts the on-premises gateway will need to be able to communicate with Microsoft's services in the cloud on TCP ports 443, 5671, 5672, and 9350–9354. When you install the on-premises gateway, you'll configure a recovery key. You'll need to use this key if you want to move the gateway to another computer or you need to restore the gateway to the same computer in the event of an unforeseen failure.

Manage environments

After a Power Platform environment is deployed, you can perform several management tasks, including placing the environment in Administration mode, configuring the refresh cadence, switching between production and sandbox, and backing up and restoring the environment.

Administration mode

Placing an environment in Administration mode limits access to users assigned the system administrator or system customizer security role. To place an environment in Administration mode, perform the following steps:

1. In the **Power Platform admin center**, select **Environments**.
2. On the **Environments** page, select the environment for which you want to change the Administration mode.
3. Select **Edit**.
4. Under **Administration Mode**, toggle the **Disabled** setting to **Enabled**.

Once Administration mode is set, you can also configure the Background Operations setting. This setting allows you to disable all asynchronous operations, including workflows and synchronization with Exchange.

> **MORE INFO**   **ADMINISTRATION MODE**
>
> You can learn more about Administration mode at *https://docs.microsoft.com/en-us/power-platform/admin/admin-mode*.

Refresh cadence

The environment refresh cadence allows you to specify how often an environment receives updates and features. The options are Frequent and Moderate. When you select **Frequent**, updates and new features are provided multiple times a month. If you select **Moderate**, updates and features are provided at least once a month.

To configure the refresh cadence for an existing environment, perform the following steps:

1. From the **Environments** section of the **Power Platform admin center**, select the environment for which you want to configure the refresh cadence.
2. On the **Details** page, select **Edit**.
3. On the **Edit details** page (see Figure 4-78), open the **Refresh cadence** drop-down list, choose **Frequent** or **Moderate**, and select **Save**.

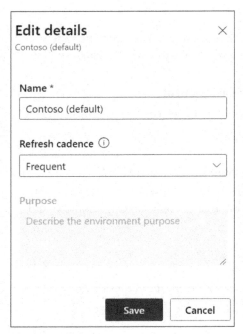

FIGURE 4-78 Refresh cadence

Switch between production and sandbox

Many organizations use a sandbox environment to allow a limited set of users to test and customize Power Platform resources. However, you can easily change a Power Platform environment from a sandbox environment to a production environment. When you change the environment type to production, all users in the organization can access the resources in that environment. You can also switch an environment from production to sandbox if you determine that you need to limit access to perform more customization of Power Platform resources.

To change environment type, perform the following steps:

1. In the **Power Platform admin center**, select the environment that you want to change.
2. In the toolbar above the environment, select **Convert to Production** or **Convert to Sandbox**.
3. You will be informed that the conversion process will pause the environment for several hours. Select **Continue** to complete the conversion process.

Back up and restore an environment

System backups occur automatically for all production and sandbox environments. Automatic backups of production environments are retained for 28 days if the environment is configured for Dynamics 365 applications and for seven days if Dynamics 365 applications has not been deployed. System backups of sandbox environments are retained for seven days.

Manual backup retention occurs using the same rules as system backup retention. Manual backups do not count against storage limits.

To manually create a backup, perform the following steps:

1. In the **Power Platform admin center**, select the environment you want to back up.
2. In the toolbar, select **Backups**, and choose **Create**.
3. Provide a name for the manual backup. Then select **Create**.

Backups must be restored to the same region where the backup was created. A restored backup will overwrite the current environment. You can restore to a separate environment in the same region and do not have to restore to the original environment. To restore a backup, perform the following steps:

1. In the **Power Platform admin center**, select the environment you want to restore.
2. In the toolbar, select the **Backups**, and choose **Restore or manage**.
3. Select the **System** tab.
4. In the **Select a backup to restore** section, select which backup to restore based on the time when the backup was taken.
5. Specify which environment will be overwritten by the restore operation.
6. Confirm that you want to allow the environment to be overwritten to complete the restore operation.

> **MORE INFO**   **BACKUP AND RESTORE ENVIRONMENTS**
>
> You can learn more about backing up and restoring environments at *https://docs.microsoft.com/en-us/power-platform/admin/backup-restore-environments*.

Manage resources

You can use the Resources node of the Power Platform admin center to manage add-on capacity, Dynamics 365 apps, Power Apps, and portals.

> **MORE INFO**   **MANAGE POWERAPPS RESOURCES**
>
> You can learn more about managing PowerApps resources at *https://docs.microsoft.com/en-us/power-platform/admin/view-manage-resources*.

Manage add-on capacity

You can use the Capacity section of the Resources menu of the Power Platform admin center to manage capacity add-ons for business application products. To manage add-on capacity, perform the following steps:

1. In the **Power Platform admin center**, select **Capacity** under the **Resources** node.
2. On the **Capacity** page, select **Add-ons**.

3. On the toolbar, select **Manage**.

4. On the **Manage add-ons** page (see Figure 4-79), select the environment, allocate the add-ons that you want to assign to that environment, and select **Save** to assign those add-ons.

FIGURE 4-79 The Manage Add-ons page

MORE INFO **MANAGE ADD-ON CAPACITY**

You can learn more about managing add-on capacity at *https://docs.microsoft.com/en-us/ power-platform/admin/capacity-add-on*.

Manage Power Apps

You can use the Power Platform Admin Center to manage Power Apps that have been created in your organization. Using the Power Platform Admin Center, you can add or change the users with which an app is shared. You can also delete apps that are currently not in use.

To manage Power Apps, perform the following steps:

1. In the **Power Platform admin center**, select the environment with Power Apps that you want to manage.

2. On the environment's properties page, select **Power Apps** under **Resources**, as shown in Figure 4-80.

FIGURE 4-80 Power Apps under Resources

3. On the list of apps, select the Power App that you want to manage.

4. On the toolbar, select **Share** to configure which users can access the Power App. Alternatively, select **Delete** to remove the app.

> **MORE INFO**   **MANAGE POWER APPS**
>
> You can learn more about managing Power Apps at *https://docs.microsoft.com/en-us/ power-platform/admin/admin-manage-apps*.

Manage Dynamics 365 apps

You can use the Power Platform Admin Center to manage Dynamics 365 apps that run on Microsoft Dataverse. You can manage Dynamics 365 Sales, Dynamics 365 Customer Service, Dynamics 365 Field Service, Dynamics 365 Marketing, and any other apps purchased through Microsoft AppSource. You can view the list of installed or available Dynamics 365 apps on the Dynamics 365 apps page of the Power Platform Admin Center, as shown in Figure 4-81.

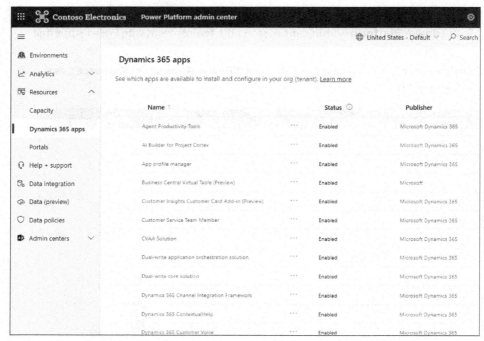

FIGURE 4-81 List of Dynamics 365 apps

Apps in this list can have the following status:

- **Enabled** Apps with this status are already installed in the environment.
- **Configured** These are apps that have been configured to an environment and can be reconfigured to a different environment.
- **Not configured** These are apps that have not yet been configured to an environment.

To install a Dynamics 365 app for a specific environment, perform the following steps:

1. In the **Power Platform admin center**, select **Dynamics 365** apps under **Resources** and select the app that you want to install.
2. Select the ellipsis (**...**). Then select **Install**.
3. On the **Install** page, select the environment in which you want to install the Dynamics 365 app. Then select **Install**.

> *MORE INFO* **MANAGE DYNAMICS 365 APPS**
>
> You can learn more about managing Dynamics 365 apps at *https://docs.microsoft.com/en-us/power-platform/admin/admin-manage-apps*.

Manage portals

Portals are artifacts that you build with Power Apps that provide a website that external and internal users can leverage to interact with data stored in Microsoft Dataverse. You can use the Power Platform Admin Center to manage the following types of portals:

- **Production**   These portals are based on a capacity-based license.
- **Trial**   These portals use a capacity-based license where the license expires after a specific number of days.
- **Production (add-on)**   This is a production portal that uses an add-on license.
- **Trial (add-on)**   This is a trial portal that uses an add-on license.

Portals listed in the Power Platform Admin Center can have the following status:

- **Configured**   The portal is configured for an environment.
- **Suspended**   The trial period for the portal has expired. Expired portals will be deleted within seven days unless converted to a production portal.
- **Not configured**   The portal is ready to be configured for an environment.

> **MORE INFO**   **MANAGE PORTALS**
>
> You can learn more about managing portals at *https://docs.microsoft.com/en-us/powerapps/ maker/portals/admin/power-platform-admin-center*.

Thought experiment

In this thought experiment, demonstrate your skills and knowledge of the topics covered in this chapter. You can find answers to this thought experiment in the next section.

There are an increasing number of iPad and Android tablet users at Contoso who want to use these mobile devices to perform work tasks. Several Android tablet users have already installed apps from the Google Play Store but are unable to access documents stored in Share-Point Online. Some iPad users have heard that Office apps are available but don't know where to start when it comes to obtaining them. For your desktop computers, you are interested in centrally deploying Microsoft 365 Apps for enterprise using click-to-run files.

Don Funk is a user at Contoso. Don has just purchased a new consumer laptop for use at home and wants to set up Outlook and Skype for Business. Don signs in to his domain-joined work computer using the contoso\don.funk user name. Don signs in to Office 365 using the don.funk@contoso.com user name. Single sign-on is configured with Office 365.

With this information in mind, answer the following questions:

1. What instruction should you give to iPad users about locating Office apps?
2. What instruction should you give to Android tablet users who have already installed apps from the Google Play Store?

3. Which tool should you use to obtain the Microsoft 365 Apps for enterprise click-to-run files from the Microsoft servers on the internet?

4. Which file should you edit to retrieve a specific version of the Microsoft 365 Apps for enterprise click-to-run files?

Thought experiment answers

This section contains the solution to the thought experiment. Each answer explains why the answer choice is correct.

1. You should tell the iPad users to sign in to the Microsoft 365 portal. This will allow them to view the available Office 365-related apps for iPad. It will also provide them with direct links to those apps in the app store.

2. You should instruct them to sign in to their Microsoft 365 accounts in each app so that they can gain access to documents stored in enterprise locations.

3. You should use the Office Deployment Tool, also known as the Office Deployment Tool for click-to-run, to obtain the Microsoft 365 Apps for enterprise click-to-run files from the internet.

4. You must edit the appropriate configuration.xml file to specify a specific version of the Microsoft 365 Apps for enterprise files.

Chapter summary

- Exchange hybrid deployment requires Exchange 2007 or later on-premises.
- The version of Exchange that you have deployed determines the type of hybrid deployment that is available. When selecting a hybrid deployment option, you should choose the most modern version available to your organization.
- The SharePoint primary web application on the on-premises SharePoint farm must use a certificate from a trusted public third-party CA.
- You use a remote move (also known as a batch) migration when you have an existing Exchange hybrid deployment.
- In a staged migration, you migrate mailboxes from your on-premises Exchange deployment to Microsoft 365 in groups, or *batches*.
- In a cutover migration, all mailboxes in an on-premises Exchange deployment are migrated to Microsoft 365 in a single migration batch.
- Network upload allows you to import PST files into Microsoft 365.
- Most organizations migrating from an on-premises SharePoint Server deployment to SharePoint Online will use the SharePoint Migration Tool.

- An activated copy of Microsoft 365 Apps for enterprise must be able to communicate with Microsoft servers on the internet every 30 days. If this communication does not occur, Microsoft 365 Apps for enterprise will enter reduced functionality mode.

- The Office Deployment Tool is a command-line utility used if you want to centralize the deployment of Office 365 click-to-run files from a location on your local area network.

- You can use the Office Deployment Tool to download the Office 365 click-to-run files and language pack files from Microsoft servers on the internet.

- You use the Office Deployment Tool in download mode to retrieve files from the Microsoft servers on the internet.

- You use the Office Deployment Tool in configure mode to install Office 365 using an installation source on the local area network.

- The configuration.xml file is used with the Office Deployment Tool in both download and configure modes. In download mode, it allows you to specify which files are downloaded. In configure mode, it allows you to specify how Office click-to-run applications and language packs are installed and how updates are applied.

Index

A

U-V

W

X-Y-Z

Plug into learning at

MicrosoftPressStore.com

The Microsoft Press Store by Pearson offers:

- Free U.S. shipping

- Buy an eBook, get three formats – Includes PDF, EPUB, and MOBI to use with your computer, tablet, and mobile devices

- Print & eBook Best Value Packs

- eBook Deal of the Week – Save up to 50% on featured title

- Newsletter – Be the first to hear about new releases, announcements, special offers, and more

- Register your book – Find companion files, errata, and product updates, plus receive a special coupon* to save on your next purchase

 Pearson